Hearts and Bones: Bone Raw Material Exploitation in Tierra del Fuego

Vivian Scheinsohn

BAR International Series 2094
2010

Published in 2016 by
BAR Publishing, Oxford

BAR International Series 2094

Hearts and Bones: Bone Raw Material Exploitation in Tierra del Fuego

ISBN 978 1 4073 0570 7

COVER IMAGE *Button Island near Woollya, Drawing by Conrad Martens published in FitzRoy, R. 1839.* Narrative of the surveying voyages of His Majesty's Ships Adventure and Beagle between the years 1826 and 1836, describing their examination of the southern shores of South America, and the Beagle's circumnavigation of the globe. Proceedings of the second expedition, 1831-36, under the command of Captain Robert Fitz-Roy, R.N. *London: Henry Colburn.*

Translated by Alasdair B Lean

BAR Publishing is the trading name of British Archaeological Reports (Oxford) Ltd. British Archaeological Reports was first incorporated in 1974 to publish the BAR Series, International and British. In 1992 Hadrian Books Ltd became part of the BAR group. This volume was originally published by Archaeopress in conjunction with British Archaeological Reports (Oxford) Ltd / Hadrian Books Ltd, the Series principal publisher, in 2010. This present volume is published by BAR Publishing, 2016.

Printed in England

BAR titles are available from:

BAR Publishing
122 Banbury Rd, Oxford, OX2 7BP, UK
EMAIL info@barpublishing.com
PHONE +44 (0)1865 310431
FAX +44 (0)1865 316916
www.barpublishing.com

For Jorge, Ana and Ale, with love.

INDEX

PREFACE

Between my finger and my thumb
The squat pen rests.
I'll dig with it.

Seamus Heaney, "Digging"

This work, to be published for the first time in book form, is the reflection of my doctoral thesis, the manuscript of which was presented at Buenos Aires University in 1997. In other words, it is over ten years later that it is appearing as a book. Much of what I held at that time, however, has remained unaltered with the passing years, and certain aspects have even been reinforced. The part that underwent most aging is that related to background, specially Fueguian, archaeological context as new research has been carried out since then. Still, on the one hand, they have not been render this work outdated; on the other, I have not wished to update it in any way that does not respect the context in which the research was carried out. Just as Borges pointed out in *Pierre Menard, autor del Quijote*, this work can only be understood within the context of its elaboration. In any other context it would be a different one, even without altering a single word.

And a final observation. Although it has never been published, the following research has enjoyed a certain amount of circulation in manuscript form among Argentine and Chilean colleagues. Now, on presenting it in English, it is possible a larger public may be added to these early readers. I understand that, despite its application context is restricted to the Isla Grande de Tierra del Fuego, the theoretical framework, model, and methodology followed, as I then suggested, might be useful and applicable in other parts of the world.

I hope that whoever reads it may enjoy this work as much as I did in producing it.

This is a story of life and death at the end of the world. This is a story of hearts and bones.

Vivian Scheinsohn,

Buenos Aires, November 2009

ACKNOWLEDGMENTS

In the course of this work many have been the persons and institutions that collaborated with me, to the extent that to draw up an exhaustive list is difficult. Among the institutions it is essential to mention the Consejo Nacional de Investigaciones Científicas y Técnicas (CONICET), which supported a great deal of the work carried out herein by means of successive fellowships. Yet it would have been impossible to complete the work without the backing of the Fundación Antorchas which, during a specially difficult period for me, both personally and economically, provided me with a grant to complete my doctoral studies in my country.

Also fundamental was the support received from the then Museo Territorial (now Museo del Fin del Mundo) in Ushuaia, both from the staff, among whom I must mention Víctor ("Tim") H. Cuello and Emilio Massi, as from its director, Oscar Zanola. It was possible to study the sample from the Chilean Rock Shelter I site thanks to a *Study Collection Grant* I received from the American Museum of Natural History. My thanks go to the personnel of the Laboratory of South American Archaeology of that institution, particularly its then director, the late Craig Morris, and to the anthropology register collection manager Barbara Conklin. It was possible to study the ethnographic collection included in this work thanks to the invaluable collaboration of the staff of the Ethnographical section deposit at La Plata Museum, and that of its director, Héctor Lahitte.

I must likewise mention those researchers that allowed me to study bone tools they obtained in their excavations: Luis Borrero, Victoria Horwitz, Luis Orquera, Ernesto Piana, and Hernán Vidal.

Many Argentine colleagues offered me their time with great generosity. I have received important suggestions and criticisms of previous manuscripts from Cristina Bellelli and Luis Borrero, who generously devoted part of their scant time to the task. Victoria Horwitz also helped me clarify my ideas on the planification of the research involved. Norma Ratto provided me with data on Fueguian timbers when these were as yet unpublished, which I greatly appreciate. I would also like to express my gratitude for the statistical advice received from Hugo Yacobaccio. Some of the illustrations appearing in the work were authored and yielded by Diana Alonso. Others were drawn by Ana Fondebrider. Unless indicateed all other figures and photos are of my own. Jordi Estévez, Assumpció Vila, Luis Orquera, and Ernesto Piana offered me the possibility of contacting Spanish colleagues through a stage financed by their project in 1988. Among those whose acquaintance I was able to make I must thank Emiliano Aguirre, Ignacio Barandarián, Carlos Diez, Rafael Mora, and Gerd Weniger. In France, I enjoyed the support of Henriette Camps-Fabrer, who invited me to participate in the meetings of the Commission of Nomenclature. I am also grateful to Danielle Stordeur, with whom I did a stage at the Institut de Préhistoire Orientale (CNRS) in 1991, for all her dedication, support, and agreeableness. I thank Marylène Patou for her comments, discussion and the possibility of assisting to the *Eight Bone Modification Conference* and contact its american organizers. Among these I specially wish to mention Susanne Miller and L. Adrien Hannus for the backing they provided to enable me to participate at the *Eight Bone Modification Conference* held in Hot Springs. The conversations I held there with Sandra Olsen, Genevieve LeMoine, Eitan Tchernov, and Bruce Bradley were most helpful.

In like manner I have received valuable assistance from researchers wholly unrelated to archaeology. The development of the mechanical tests would have been impossible without the help, first of all of Gerardo Herbst and Tulio Palacios, and subsequently José Luís Ferretti and his team.

For the photographic record of some of the pieces I have received significant assistance and advice from Víctor ("Tim") H. Cuello of the then Museo Territorial, Alfredo Pavón, and Silvana Turner (EAAF). Luis Chiappe aided me in the identification of bird-bone remains. Under his guidance Alejandra Di Baja, Matilde Lanza, and Laura Tramaglino also collaborated in this task. Jorge Fondebrider made numerous and desperate corrections of style in this text. Finally, my thesis director, Carlos Aschero, as well as my co-director, José Luís Lanata, put up with my pestering till the end. I extend my gratitude to them.

And of course I must thank my parents, Esther Len and David Scheinsohn, who stoically endured the fact of having an archaeologist daughter.

CHAPTER 1

INTRODUCTION

"(...) *we can't return we can only look behind from where we came* (...)"
Joni Mitchell, "The Circle Game"

"*One can hardly change the past, give it a sumptious new hue, a slightly different tone (...) The past, specially a somewhat remote past, is a very, very pliable material.*"
J.L. Borges

Bones and Humans

Humans have made use of diverse raw materials to make tools. Some were used just as they were found, without any modification (e.g. antlers used as digging tools). Others underwent different processes that adapted their properties to the tasks they were to perform. In other words, a tool was designed.

Design is here understood as a set of metrical, physical, and morphological attributes selected from pre-existent elements or artificially obtained ones[1]. In this sense the present definition is related to that other one that considers design as the adaptation of certain media to a preconceived goal. (*Webster's Encyclopedic Unabridged Dictionary of the English Language*, 1989).

Design is constrained by natural factors (such as the mechanical properties of the raw materials, their availability, and their natural shape) and artificial or cultural factors (such as the function of the tool or the technology available to the craftsman). In their evolutionary history humans have managed to minimize natural factors by developing artificial raw materials (e.g. plastics). But at the very beginning natural factors were important and determined which raw materials were used and how.

Bone was one of the first materials used by hominids (cf. Shipman 1989) and still is —even in our industrialized society— though on an artisanal level. After stone, it is bone that has accompanied our species the longest. Due to its problems of preservation, however, it has not received the attention it deserves.

This has also happened on the Isla Grande de Tierra del Fuego (Figure 1.1), where a considerable percentage of the recorded tools found in archaeological sites was made from bone.

Figure 1.1 - Map of Tierra del Fuego

The intention of this work is to explain how bone was used as a raw material on this island. In order to do this three main lines of research were devised:

1) The determination of the mechanical properties of bones used for tools on the Isla Grande de Tierra del Fuego.

2) The proposal and evaluation of a model derived from a Darwinian Evolutionary Theory.

3) Metric and morphological analysis of Fueguian bone tools.

The temporal scale chosen for this work is from the earliest arrival of humans on the island— archaeologically recorded as some 10.000 years ago (Massone 1983 and 1987)— to the 19th century. The spatial scale is limited to the Argentine side of the island, (with one exception, see below).

This study

The following limits were applied for this study:

1) Bone tools[2] from Isla Grande de Tierra del Fuego were analysed. Every artifact, not considered as a finished tool —base-forms, preforms, debris in general (splinters, chips), or ornaments and furniture— was excluded. The reason for this is to eliminate ambiguities introduced by the analysis of fragments and the need, related to the theoretical framework, to study only such elements that are directly related to the survival of the group[3];

2) Formatized, as well as little- or non-modified, bone tools were studied. In this last case (given the difficulty of identifying them as tools, see below) only those identifiable as such to the naked eye were included;

3) Only whole tools or those 2/3 of their total estimated size were included, so as to avoid malinterpretations related to the presence of tiny fragments of tools whose total shape is unknown;

4) The whole bone tool sample (with the only exception of Rock Shelter 1[4], studied by J. Bird), comes from systematically excavated archaeological sites on the Argentine side of Isla Grande. Reasons of economy, time, and accessibility precluded the study of Chilean sites, but it can be argued that the Argentine sample is representative of the island since, according to archaeological bibliography of the region, there exist no great variations between the two sides of the border.

5) This work is centered on the bone raw material concept and not on the more traditional "bone industry" concept deeply rooted among Old World Prehistory researchers[5]. From the *Dictionnaire de la Préhistoire* industry is defined as an "(...) *Ensamble des techniques et des activités par lesquelles un groupe humain transforme la matière première pour en tirer des objets fabriqués. Par métonymie, collection des objets résultants de ces activités* (...)" (Leroi-Gourahn, 1988:512). According to this source, the stereotypical character of human industry allows it to be used to differentiate ethnic groups. This kind of definition is associated with a normative idea of archaeology. Such terminology will not be used in this work as I am not agree with the theoretical framework in which it was generated. The concept of bone raw material instead allows the researcher to focus not on the products seen as mental templates, but on the raw material as the starting point of technological production. In this work bone raw materials are spoken of in the plural as it is considered that —even though bone can be spoken of as a single material, different from stone or wood— there are differences in the properties of the various bones (i.e. humerus or femur) of the same animal or in the same bone but from animals of different species.

Bone Tools Production

Among the diverse groups of hunter-gatherers, the degree and quality of bone working depends on local conditions. Several factors either natural or cultural, can be considered with regard to the manufacture of bone objects.

Natural factors are:

1) the mechanical properties of bone available in a certain area which, balanced against a set of cultural needs, will determine whether those materials will be used or not.

2) Environmental factors as:

a) faunal richness: bone use rests on natural producers of bone, namely vertebrate animals. The variety of species potentially available will influence the decision of whether this material is to be used or not;

b) raw materials availability: bone will be exploited if there is no other material with similar properties or, if there is, bone will be easier to work or more available;

c) climate: given a systemic context (*sensu* Schiffer 1972) and a comparison of diverse raw materials, certain climates will favour the preservation of bone over other perishable materials (such as wood), which will lead to its being preferred;

Postdepositional processes determining whether the researcher will recover or not existing materials must be taken into account. Among them should be mentioned taphonomical agents acting in the area, the time span between deposition and recovery, the kind of matrix of the deposits, etc.

Cultural factors are:

1) the economic system (hunter-gatherer, pastoral, agricultural, etc.), which defines technological availability and needs;

2) the technological organization (*sensu* Nelson 1991)[6] of a given population and its capacity of tool design.

Design modifies the geometric and structural properties of a raw material in terms of the task to be performed, which necessitates exploring the available raw materials and adapting the design to them.

Contents

As a way of approaching this work, and in order to be able to discuss the model which will be proposed in Chapter 6, a history of Bone tool research with special focus. in Europe, where the main trend in such studies was developed, will be presented in Chapter 2. Their results inform us about the use of that raw material in Palaeolithic Europe. The following chapters will be devoted to specifying and analyzing the way in which these factors appear in Tierra del Fuego. Firstly (chapter 3), the mechanical properties of bone material will be referred to. In chapter 4 the environmental and geological setting of Isla Grande will be presented. In chapter 5 a synthesis of all that is known about the Fuegian populations from an archaeological point of view will be presented. In the same chapter brief reference will be made to the island's regional taphonomy, as this question is closely related to archaeological problems. Chapter 6 will expose the theoretical framework used for this work, Evolutionary Theory in its classical version, Punctuated Equilibria Theory and concepts of both, such as that of species, as well as attempts to apply them to archaeology. Finally a bone raw material model will be discussed. Methods and materials employed will be presented in chapter 7. Chapter 8 gives results of the determination of mechanical properties of Tierra del Fuego bones. Chapter 9 will expose the results of tool morphological analysis. In chapter 10 those results will be discussed. Finally in chapter 11 conclusions and further paths for exploration will be offered.

---

[1] The definition given here is broader than that of Nelson, who defines Design as "(...) conceptual variables of utility that condition the forms of tools and the composition of toolkits." (1991:66) For Nelson, the variables of design are: reliability, maintainability, transportability, flexibility, and versatility. In this work, design is considered to be determined by the properties of the material and the modifications it undergoes by artificial means. The purpose of these modifications is to maximize or minimize the said properties.

[2] A tool is "(...) an implement, especially one held in the hand, for performing or facilitating mechanical operations (...)" (*Webster's Encyclopedic Unabridged Dictionary of the English Language* 1989). The *Dictionnaire de la Prehistoire* defines tools as "(...) objets par lesquels l'homme intervient sur la matière en prolongeant sa main afin de la spécialiser en fonction d'objectifs técniques à réaliser" (Leroi-Gourhan 1988:788).

[3] Some researchers may hold that objects of art or ornaments, insofar as they have symbolical or social connotations, are related to the survival of the individual or group. However this may be, in the case of Tierra del Fuego there are as yet no available models by which to evaluate the relation between those objects and the survival of the group and how it has functioned.

[4] The Rock Shelter 1 site is located on Navarino Island (Chile) on the coast of the Beagle channel. The materials taken from this site are deposited in the *American Museum of Natural History*, New York, and it was possible to study them thanks to a *Study Collection Grant* extended by that institution.

[5] In the specific bibliography on the subject, bone industry is understood as a set of instruments made of bone; but there is a certain degree of confusion, as the term has been used to define three different categories of concepts:

1) expeditive bone artifacts, also known in Spanish as "industria del hueso poco elaborada"

2) "(...) objects whose shape shows a degree of technical finish that has largely or wholly transformed the natural shape of the bone" (Cabrera 1985:158), in other words, tools;

3) "(...) objects whose analysis is based on the decoration expressed on them (...) and are a kind of artistic object" (Cabrera 1985:158).

[6] Defined as the set of strategies to make, use, transport, and discard instruments and the materials necessary for their manufacture and maintenance (Nelson 1991).

CHAPTER 2

BONE TOOLS: RESEARCH HISTORY

From the Beginning of the 20th Century to the 1960s

The earliest work referred exclusively to bone tools arose when the first paradigm of scientific archaeology, evolutionism, had been established. Yet the evolutionary theory developed in archaeology was not the Darwinian biological evolution but that of Social evolution later known as social Darwinism. Laid down by Herbert Spencer and other authors, the doctrine of social evolution was at that time considered the most adequate for the interpretation of archaeological remains (Daniel 1977).

At the same time as the idea of consecutive eras —established by Gabriel de Mortillet at the beginning of the 20th century— began to be questioned, the works of Capitan (1906), Büchler (1907), Martin (1907 and 1910), and Chauvet (1910) were published. Those works dealt exclusively with bone tools. These short works postulate the existence of certain manufacturing techniques (Capitan 1906) or a first classification (Chauvet 1910).

Henri Martin (1906, 1907a and b, and 1910) was the first to hold that bone was one of the raw materials employed by hominids. He worked with Mousterian levels of bone material from the La Quina deposit, where he found an abundant and varied collection of pieces with diverse marks. Martin considered from the very beginning the necessity of isolating marks related to meat consumption from others related to the use of bone as a tool. Though based mainly on speculation, his work was pioneering those developed during the 1970's on that subject.

In 1912 Abbé Breuil elaborated a classificatory scheme for the SW France Upper Palaeolithic. He thus initiated a normative trend that sought to define cultural entities by means of particular types of tools established as "guide fossil". At the Chinese Zhoukoudian site (Breuil 1939) he also carried out a study similar to that of Martin, and continued by Pei (1938).

The model put forward by Breuil and Peyrony (who, in 1933, splinted Breuil's Aurignacian in Aurignacian and Perigordian) is the basis of the Phylogenetic Paradigm (Straus 1987). This Paradigm interpreted the variability between archaeological collections in terms of technological progress and ethnic or cultural differences. This model was not applied only in France but in all Western Europe, where it exerted a definitive influence on the prehistoric archaeology of the region throughout the 20th century (Straus 1987).

By 1940 a considerable number of works on the supposed Mousterian bone industry existed. The polish of those tools was later attributed to the action of natural taphonomical agents (Koby 1942, Jéquier 1975).

In the mid-50s the study of the bone industry acquired new momentum thanks to Raymond Dart's work. He proposed the existence of an "osteodontocheratic" industry associated with the australopithecines of Makapangast (Dart 1957). Though it is now known many of these supposed artifacts were produced by natural causes, Dart's work brought about a renewed interest in the question.

From the 1960's till the Present

The study of bone tools in this period is influenced by two factors:

—the predominance in Europe of the Phylogenetic Paradigm (Straus 1987), as a result of Breuil and Bordes' work;

—the development of taphonomy and the study of bone modifications, based on the tenets of New Archaeology.

"La Méthode Bordes" and the Phylogenetic Paradigm in Europe

In the early 60's, François Bordes elaborated his method (1961), a continuation of Breuil's proposals. Binford & Sabloff (1983) consider Bordes to have based his thinking on an "ethnic vision" of culture. It started out from the premise that it was possible to show the continuity among materials left in different places by a single "people" or race. His method consists essentially in the establishment of a list of types or categories. The basic unit of observation is the assemblage, defined on the basis of the principle of association. That is, the assemblage comprises all the tools found in a single unit of deposition within a site. The assemblages are described by the tabulation of the items in the type list. This tabulation generates a quantitative pattern that is presented in the form of cumulative graphs. Thus, according to Bordes, a culture was represented in terms of similar relative frequencies found among diverse assemblages in different sites. Bordes understood the variability of assemblages as the result of different cultures living together in the same region. The cultures, which did not change, replaced each other, within a single region, following complex historical patterns. Bordes advocated a lack of temporal continuity, whereby the industries were described as "alternating" (Binford & Sabloff 1983).

Palaeoethnology, under the leadership of André Leroi-Gourhan, began to take shape alongside Bordes' proposition. Strongly influenced by structuralism, Leroi-Gourhan (1943, 1945, 1964-65 and Leroi-Gourhan et al. 1966) disregarded the time variable, while proposing an ethnographic study of the activities that presumably had taken place in the archaeological sites, also on the basis of the association of artifacts on a single level.

Sonneville Bordes (1960) applied "la méthode Bordes" to Upper Palaeolithic tools just as her husband, François Bordes, did in the case of Lower and Middle Palaeolithic. Perhaps due to the abundance of the bone tools of this period, Sonneville Bordes' work represents the application of "la méthode" to bone tools.

New Archaeology, headed by Lewis Binford, has taken issue with Bordes' position as "(...) these conventions for interpretation do not admit the possibility that aspects of a single cultural system could appear as different assemblages at different places.(...) If 'la méthode Bordes' is followed rigorously, it absolutely prevents us from ever seeing any organizational facts about past systems beyond those which may be manifest within a single occupation or a single level at a site." (Binford and Sabloff 1983: 405). In fact this is the criticism Binford and Binford (1966) point out when they suggest that the variability of Mousterian assemblages might be due to site functionality instead of ethnic differences —as Bordes had interpreted—.

Binford places Bordes within what he calls the "normative school of culture." The normative point of view considers culture to be a mental construction consisting in ideas. In Binford's terms, "(...) a normative theorist is one who sees as his field of study the ideational basis for varying ways of human life— culture. Information is obtained by studying cultural products or the objectifications of normative ideas about the proper ways of life executed by now extinct peoples. The archaeologist's task then lies in abstracting from cultural products the normative concepts extant in the minds of men now dead" (Binford 1972:196). It is in opposition to this view that New Archaeology arose.

Actualistic Studies, Taphonomy, and Bone Modifications in Archaeology

Whereas in the field of archaeology Dart's work had led some researchers to the task of discriminating products of human activity from the pseudo-artifacts owed to natural causes, palaeontology began to study the natural factors modifying and causing the burial of fossils (Efremov 1940, Gifford 1981). These studies led to a new discipline, taphonomy, which can be defined as the study of the history of fossils from the death of an organism until its recovery by the researcher. In Behrensmeyer and Kidwell's words, taphonomy is "(...) the study of processes of preservation and how they affect information in the fossil record" (1985:105).

Traditional archaeology presumed that cultural systems produced the archaeological record and that this record could easily be differentiated from non-cultural events (Bonnichsen 1989). That is, it took for granted that all elements present in a site defined as archaeological were the product of human activity. It was only when taphonomy was acknowledged as a discipline within archaeology —a circumstance that occurred in the late 70's— that it began to be understood that "(...) the earth's subsystems produce a very complex and intertwined matrix of records, cultural and non-cultural" (Bonnichsen 1989:2). This concept brought about a revolution in the interpretation of bone assemblages.

The recognition of taphonomy as a discipline of interest for archaeologists is related to the theoretical proposals of New Archaeology and, specifically, to Lewis Binford's call to give meaning to the archaeological record (Binford 1978, 1981a and 1988). From the 1980's onwards, the number of works generated around taphonomic factors is countless, and the study of bone marks began to acquire significant importance. The idea supporting the majority of these works is the possibility of defining criteria that allow the identification of agents that produce marks and, among them, specifically human agents. In this respect it is worth mentioning the works of Andrews and Cook (1985), Behrensmeyer y Hill (1980), Behrensmeyer et al. (1986), Binford (1981a), Bromage (1984), Bunn (1981), Bouchoud (1974b), Clayton Wilson (1982), Fiorillo (1984, 1987 and 1989), Hill (1976 and 1989), Johnson & Shipman (1986), Miller (1970 and 1975), Morel (1989), Morlan (1984), Olsen & Shipman (1988), Patou (1994), Potts & Shipman (1981), Reixach (1986), Shipman (1981 and 1989) Shipman & Rose (1984) Sutcliffe (1973), Toth & Woods (1989), and Walker & Long (1977) among others.

The Study of Bone Tools

The recognition of human action on bone remains and its effects —accomplished thanks to studies related to taphonomical analysis— produced a considerable increase in works related to bone tools. In this way, from the mid-70's to the end of the following decade, it is possible to recognize at least four lines of work:

1) A line related to the development of the study of marks on bone, which can be divided into:

a) works dealing with almost unmodified bones known as the "industria del hueso poco elaborado" (in Spain), "industrie de l'os peu elaborée" (in France) or "expeditive tools", intimately connected with the identification of human agents among which, in chronological order, may be mentioned E. Bonifay (1974), M-C. Bonifay (1974), Bordes (1974), Stordeur (1974), Cabrera & Bernaldo de Quirós (1977), Sonneville-Bordes (1977), Freeman (1978), Corchón (1980 and 1981), González Doña (1981), Cabrera (1984), Lyman (1984b), Shipman et al. (1984), Bonifay (1985), Delpech & Diez (1985), Barandarián (1987), Vincent (MSa, b and 1988), Johnson (1989), and Stordeur (s.f.). There also exist works that attempt to identify human activity through fracture patterns of bones found in archaeological sites. Some of them are interesting on account of certain bone artifacts or fractured used bones dated at Lower Palaeolithic. Among others must be mentioned those of Aguirre (1973, 1985 and 1986), Aguirre & Hoyos (1977), Biberson & Aguirre (1965), Bonifay (1974), Bunn (1989), Diez (1986), Patou (1985), Rincón & Aguirre (1974), Saddek-Kooros (1972), and Standford et al. (1981).

b) a series of works intended manufacturing technique identification: despite the fact that Semenov (1964) defines an important field of study for stone and bone tools, in the case of bone tools, proposals for functional analysis of micro-wear patterns study have had hardly any continuators. It was only in the mid-70's that works with that orientation began. Among them must be differentiated:

- those that seek to identify manufacturing techniques on a macroscopic level. For instance, the works of Clark (1953), Clark & Thompson (1953), Allain et al. (1974), Newcomer (1974a and 1977), Otte (1974a and b), Poplin (1974a), Berke (1977a and b), Bouchoud (1977), Camps-Fabrer & D'Anna (1977), Bouvier (1979), Murray (1979), Yesner & Bonnichsen (1979), Bonnichsen & Will (1980), Olsen (1980), Pickering (1980), Stordeur (1980a and b), Olsen (1984), Rigaud (1984) and Piel-Desruisseaux (1986);

- those centred on manufacturing traces on a microscopic level, as those of Bouchoud (1974), Olsen (1979), Campana (1980), D'Errico et al. (1982-1983 and 1984 a, b and c), Stordeur (1983), D'Errico & Giacobini (1985), Peltier (1986), Campana (1987), Campana (1989), and LeMoine (1991).

c) works that study patterns of micro-wear traces on bone tools being formatized or not. They can be differentiated into those that work on a macroscopic level (Julien 1978-1980 and 1985, Bouchoud 1977, and Desse 1975, among others) and those that do so on a microscopic level (Campana 1987 and 1989, LeMoine 1989, Olsen 1980, 1988 and 1989, Peltier 1986, Peltier & Plisson 1989, Runnings et al. 1989, Stordeur 1983, Stordeur & Anderson-Gerfaud 1985). It must be pointed out that, despite the influence that taphonomical studies has had on these works New Archaeology criteria did not have any effect on them. Many respond to a normative vision such as Bordes'.

2) another line is related to the study of formatized bone tools, in which the action of human agents is beyond question, and classification is the methodological tool. In this case a normative vision is generally observed, and the Bordes method or another derived form it is followed. Nevertheless there are some works by archaeologists enlisted in New Archaeology in this group. Given the quantity of works on the subject, it is convenient to distinguish those centered on:

a) morphological types: they analyze the type of a given object, defined according to morphological criteria, and which may give rise to chronological proposals. There are works dealing with weapon heads and dart points (Alaux 1971, Bouvier 1974, Deffarges et al. 1977, Delporte & Mons 1977, Delporte et al. 1988, Hahn 1974, Howell & Freeman 1983, Kozlowski & Kozlowski 1977, Larsson & Larsson 1977, Leroi-Gourhan 1983, Leroy-Prost 1974 and 1978, Movius 1973, Otte 1977, Pape 1980); harpoon heads (Barandarián 1977, Bouge 1950, Deffarges et al. 1974a, Julien 1977, Julien 1982, Laurent 1974, Mons 1979, Quiroz Larrea 1988, Ramseyer 1988, Stordeur 1986, Thompson 1954, Weniger 1987); bone hafts (Julien et al. 1987, Martin 1935, Stordeur 1987); needles (Stordeur 1977a); atlatl hooks (Garrod 1955); awls (Mons 1980, Stordeur-Yedid 1976) or other types (Deffarges et al 1974b, Mons & Stordeur 1977, Stordeur 1974). These works generally respond to a normative and/or Bordesian view;

b) sites or regions: they present a picture of the situation of bone tools for a site, location, or region. The following may be mentioned: Barandarián (1978 and 1985), Billamboz (1977), Bonnichsen (1979), Camps-Fabrer (1976), Delporte (1958), Delporte & Mons (1977), Julien (1977), Legoupil (1978 and 1980), Leroy-Prost (1975), Lyman (1991), Newcomer (1974b), Olsen (1979 and 1980), Rodanés Vicente (1987), Rueda i Torres (1983 and 1985), Stordeur (1978b, 1979, 1981, 1982, 1984, 1985a and 1988), Thompson (1954), and Vincent (1986 and 1989), among others. From a theoretical viewpoint the focus can be Bordesian (e.g. Delporte 1958) or belonging to New Archaeology (e.g. Bonnichsen 1979);

c) classification and/or typology: as a consequence of the importance acquired in this period by the discussion about classification, in terms of the development of the Bordesian method, and the possibilities computers are beginning to offer, there has arisen a series of works centered on bone tool classification. These works— whose authors are generally European, French in particular— in the best of cases seek types or classes allowing for stylistic and/or technical identifications (the drawbacks of which we have already gone into). Many of them do not explain their guiding objectives. In general these are logical constructions without much practical utility. The situation created at the end of the 1970s, regarding tool classification, has been well described by Adams: "Where once we had successful but rather inarticulate field practitioners trying to find words to describe what they were doing, we now have sophisticated theoreticians trying to find ways to do what they are saying; that is, to find practical applications for their computer-generated classifications" (1988: 41). Among these works (which include systems of classification, guidelines, definitions, and conventions) we can mention those of Albrecht (1972), Albrecht et al. (1972), Barandarián (1967a and b 1969-70), Cabrera Valdés (1985), Camps-Fabrer (1966, 1967, 1968, 1971, 1976 and 1977a), Camps-Fabrer & Bourrelly (1972 and 1974), Camps-Fabrer et al. (1974), Camps-Fabrer & Stordeur (1979), Christidou (MS.), Clement & Leroy-Prost (1977), Commission de Nomenclature (1977), Conkey (undated and 1977) Dewez (1974), Fritz (1977), Leroy-Prost (1971), Otte (1974a and 1977), Prost (1972), Ruiz Nieto et al. (1983), Stordeur (1978 and MS.), and Voruz (1978 and 1983-1984). The works that had most influence on European archaeologists are those of Barandarián, Camps-Fabrer, and Stordeur, for which reason these will be analyzed in some detail.

Barandarián's typological list (1967a) consists in a taxonomic grouping of objects that start out from five families subdivided in groups, and these in turn into primary and secondary types. Secondary types are those that "(...) while participating in the essential characters of the corresponding primary, they possess a peculiar entity (due to the section of the piece, its relative size, some accessories on the shape of the bases) such as to allow, in certain cases, the definition of a sub-period or a local facies" (Barandarián 1967: 285, translated from Spanish). Camps-Fabrer, Bourrelly & Nivelle (1974)'s analytical code proposes recording every character of every object of an excavation, which raises plenty of doubts regarding its feasibility. Camps-Fabrer suggests describing objects according to rigorous and non-subjective morphological criteria. For this purpose she resorts to notions of simple geometry. Like Barandarián, setting out from the types, she attempts to establish regional and chronological typologies. Stordeur (1977) proposed an automatic classification on the basis of four orders of criteria that define four grids of classification:

- the technical: which includes the raw material and the degree of transformation;
- the morphological: based on the inscription of the objects in geometrical shapes;
- the metrical: which takes into account the pieces' dimensions; and
- the technological: which considers the shape of the distal or active end. In this way types decrease in importance as compared with the works of Barandarián and Camps-Fabrer.

3) Works that take the bone raw materials as their unit of analysis, and which appear at the end of the period. Some of them can clearly be associated with the New Archaeology. They are centered on the determination of bone raw materials or the study of a tool assemblage starting out from the raw material category, something similar to what the present work will propose. Among them may be mentioned Bouchoud (1974), Poplin (1974b), Guthrie (1983), Mac Gregor & Currey (1983), Mac Gregor (1985), Russen (1983), and Sidera (1989). These considerations are also to be found in the synthetic work of Johnson's (1985).

4) Finally we must mention works guided by a postprocessual paradigm, e.g. Dobres' (1995) work.

Also in the mid-70's researchers began to feel the need to get together, share experiences, and generate conventions. Camps-Fabrer was the first to organize a meeting for bone-industry scholars. The First International Colloquium on Prehistoric Bone Industry took place in France in 1974.

There the Comission Internationale de Nomenclature sur l'Industrie de l'Os Préhistorique was set up, created within the UISPP (Union Internationale des Sciences Préhistoriques et Protohistoriques). In 1976 this commission decided to publish booklets with a series of typological index cards on the prehistoric bone industry, for which it called on diverse European specialists (v. Delporte et al. 1988 on dart heads). Within the commission the Groupe de Travail N°1: Outillage peu élaboré en os et en bois de cervidés was set up. This group was created and directed by Emiliano Aguirre and it held its first meeting in Madrid in 1979. From that moment on, a further eight meetings were held (the Second and Third in France, 1982 and 1984; the Fourth in Belgium, 1986; the Fifth in West Germany, 1987; the Sixth in Sardinia, 1988; the Seventh in France, 1990; and the Eighth in USA, 1993). In addition to this workgroup, without doubt the most active, there existed within the framework of the Commission the Groupe de Travail N° 3: Industrie de l'os Néolithique et de l'Age des Métaux and the workgroup ETTOS (initials of Expérimentation, Traces, Technologie, Os) for the study of the technique and functionality of bone tools.

The First International Conference on Bone Modification, which took place in USA in 1984 must also be mentioned, whose works were published in one volume (R. Bonnichsen & M. Sorg 1989). A new concept arose then, that of bone modifications. As mentioned, bone modifications are brought about by both the action of human agents and that of natural ones. At this conference fields that until then had been separate, such as taphonomy and bone technology, were brought together. The advantages offered by this new perspective are beyond doubt: the analysis of site-formations and the way in which these affected bone tools is essential to the consideration of the technological factors that lead to the utilization of certain tools.

Summary

Without doubt the major volume of works by European authors can be placed within a normative paradigm such as that held by Bordes. The development of bone tools in the European Upper Palaeolithic —which could be regarded as the "Cambrian explosion" of bone tools— gave rise to a greater attention being paid to them by European authors. Therefore, European theoretical frameworks were applied for this kind of formatized industry. Instead, works that can be placed within the New Archaeology and deal with bone tools are generally focused on expeditive tools and on marks present on bones. This circumstance may be related to the specific set of problems North American archaeologists must deal with at Paleoindian sites.

Our goals do not justify the use of any of the classificatory systems put forth from a Bordesian/ normative perspective. In keeping with Hill & Evans (1972), it is here held that there are no neutral classifications. Every classification attempts to impose a certain order in terms of a certain theoretical framework or explicit goal. It is not the intention of this work to make use of "guide fossils" to establish chronologies or delimit ethnic groups, cultures, or industries.

However, many of the criteria developed on the basis of the reviewed works are useful. From here on, with regard to the nomenclature employed in tool morphological description the criteria established by Stordeur (1977) and Voruz (1983-84) will be followed. Regarding orientational norms, we will follow Camps-Fabrer (1977b and 1984) and the Commission de Nomenclature (1977).

The works of Stordeur (1977) and Voruz (1983-84) are also important for considerations on the metrical and morphological structure of tools.

It must be noted that in Argentine archaeological literature, apart for the mention of the presence of artifacts in this or that site or the isolated discovery of one of them (e.g. Outes 1916) no specific interest for bone tools appears until the pioneering works of Jorge Fernández in Chenque Haichol site (Fernández 1988-1990) and Casiraghi (1984a, 1984b, 1985 and 1987). This last researcher has carried out an important classificatory job, attempting to establish reduction stages in the bone material (1984a). Casiraghi has worked mostly on Fueguian materials being the direct antecedent for this work; and she offer interesting contributions that did not even exist in the international debate at that time (Casiraghi 1987). To the extent that many of the criteria followed by this author are based on those of Camps-Fabrer and Stordeur, they will be taken into account here.

Finally, as was mentioned, there exist some precedents regarding the use of raw material as a unit of analysis. Despite the fact that the viewpoint does not necessarily coincide —as none of those works sets out from a Darwinian evolutionary framework— this collection of works lends a useful backing, since they served to focus emphasis on the mechanical properties of bone raw materials. However, a series of works that considered these properties for stone raw materials, for instance, the pioneering work of Speth (1972), and those of Ratto (1988, 1991 a and b, 1993 and 1994) in Argentina were also important.

Old World Palaeolithic Bone Raw Material Exploitation

Besides the dominance of stone, in the hominids' archaeological record (possibly owing to the preservational problems of other raw materials) there is evidence of the use of bone since very early times.

Lower Palaeolithic

For a long time it was a subject of debate whether a bone industry could be claimed for this period. After the failure of Dart's (1957, v.s.) "osteodontocheratic industry", many researchers dared not posit that bone raw materials were exploited during the Lower Palaeolithic. Nowadays anthropical action on the bones from that period can be documented faithfully. During the Lower Palaeolithic bone was employed as a raw material in two ways:

a) in the form of utilized bones: they were fractured, and put to use with no great modifications. Among the best-documented cases can be mentioned the 1,700,000-year-old bones used in Melka Kunturé (quoted in Stordeur 1985b) and those reported by Brain (1989) at Sterkfontein and Swartkrans, in South Africa;

b) bones worked by percussion: the bone is treated as if it was an animal "lithic" raw material, and is percuted directly. The most ancient bone tools belonging to Olduvai layers I and II, dated at 2,000,000 AP are among these (Shipman 1989). According to Shipman "(...) The unusually high frequency of flaking on these bones suggests that the hominids transferred their familiar stone-working techniques to the problems of working bones— and deliberately selected those bones with thick cortical walls upon which those techniques worked best" (1989:330). In this group Aguirre (1981) includes bone artifacts from Torralba and Ambrona in which only the active part of the tool has been worked. In this case, as at Olduvai, bones from large-sized animals (proboscideans) were used.

Shipman (1989) acknowledges that, for this time tools made of bone are scanty in relation to the total size of the sample, and considers three possible reasons: a) that other possible bone tools have not been identified; b) the danger involved in obtaining bones of a suitable size for percussion as large animal carcasses tend to attract predators for a long time, creating risks for the hominids; and c) the scanty frequency of these tools bespeaks their use in few tasks. She considers that stone was more efficient than bone in the tasks carried out by hominids so that, if stone raw materials were available, bone should not be used (Shipman 1989)

Middle Palaeolithic

No significant changes are detected with regard to the previous period (Camps-Fabrer 1976 and Stordeur 1985b). Some tools show morphologies that anticipate bone awls and darts, as for instance in the French sites of the Grotte Ermitage, Néron and Abri Chaudourne (quoted in Camps-Fabrer 1976), but these types of tools only appear in the Upper Palaeolithic. Certain techniques, peculiar to bone-working, are recognized, such as sawing, scraping, boring, and abrading, yet these were not applied to bone raw materials, but in an isolated fashion (Stordeur 1985b). According to Stordeur (1985b) bone tools will acquire well-defined morphologies only towards the end of the Mousterian. Apparently Neanderthals could not distinguish the knapping qualities of bone from stone.

During Middle Palaeolithic times —as suggested by Shipman (1989) for the African Lower Palaeolithic—, there might have been a scarcity of stone raw materials in certain places, for which reason bone was used. Bone could be procured to the extent that game was obtained for consumption (even scavenged or hunted), and the hominids depended on this factor for their subsistence. Thus, bone is not employed for its own qualities, but as a poor quality "lithic" material. This would then be a moment of experimenting with a new raw material, the properties of which are not entirely known. This experimenting would then have led to the elaboration of a suitable technology for bone. Other cases of knapped bones for this period are offered in González Doña (1984) at El Castillo (Spain); Freeman (1978) at the Cueva Morín (Spain); Trommnau (1983) at Rhede (Germany); and Vincent (1985, 1986 and 1988 in France).

Yellen et al. (1995) reported evidence of a well-developed bone industry in three archaeological sites in Katanda (Upper Semliki River, Rift Valley, Zaire). Among the artifacts that were found there were recorded multibarbed heads, barbless points, and a dagger-like object of unknown function. All of them were fashioned from large mammals rib fragments or bone splinters. Radiocarbon datings obtained for these sites correspond to 90,000 AP (Brooks et al. 1995). Bone technology— with an unexpected development for African Middle Stone Age sites— might indicate that at that time there existed an important and complex specialization, also made evident by the presence of fish remains. This argumentation was used by the authors to justify an African origin of modern humans.

Traditionally it had been posited that only in the Upper Palaeolithic did hominids acquire sufficient knowledge of bone raw materials as to design complex tools like harpoon heads (cf. Stordeur 1985b and Camps-Fabrer 1976). The existence of such ancient harpoons presents a serious challenge to this model. However, given its isolated character, it could be supposed that it is a local development related to a specific situation. New research and the discovery of further bone materials will allow an evaluation of whether this presumption is correct or the traditional models need revision.

Upper Palaeolithic

According to Dennell (1987), Lower and Middle Palaeolithic technologies were focused on the use of four basic techniques: percussion, whittling with knives, scraping, and cutting. As from 30,000 AP the number of techniques grew enormously on incorporating pressure-chipping, boring, torsion, and polishing, among others. The repertoire of techniques was not amplified again until 8000 AP, with the incorporation of ceramics and metal tempering. Dennell (1987) believes that at that time the number of components in artifacts and the number of stages in their manufacture were also increased.

With regards to bone, the rise of new techniques explains the blossoming of a veritable bone industry: longitudinal and transversal sawing (which make possible the extraction of preforms), the polishing of splinters obtained by percussion, groove and splinter technique (cf. Clark & Thompson 1953) which makes it possible to obtain predetermined preforms, scraping with a burin edge or flank (for the final formatization of a piece), boring, abrasion, etc. (Camps-Fabrer 1976, Stordeur 1985b).

In the Aurignacian, bone objects acquire definite and precise outlines, taking shapes that were impossible to obtain with stone materials. Pointed tools such as awls appear, and diversify; long, flat objects called lissoirs (burnishers, presumably used to work skins) or chasse-lame (intermediaries for flint knapping); batons percés, and spear or dart points (Camps-Fabrer 1976, Stordeur 1985b).

According to Stordeur at this moment "(...) il en a découvert les qualités plastiques propres mais en même temps il semble qu'il ait mis momentanément de côté une vieille tradition qui impliquait elle aussi une réelle connaissance de la matière osseuse: le choix de l'os pour sa forme naturelle, utilisable telle quelle. En façonnant des objets à partir de languettes de forme géometrique simple, l'artisan ramène en effet l'os au statut de matière première amorphe. (...)" (1985b:50). In saying this, Stordeur does not seem to perceive that, as will be seen further on (v. bone structure), no matter how much a bone fragment is formatized, it does not lose the material's properties. In any case it can be claimed that, at that moment, artisans seek to obtain preforms with a highly predictable morphology.

During the Magdalenian, bone crafting took on a new momentum (Camps-Fabrer 1976, Stordeur 1985b). The techniques used during the Aurignacian were improved, and others appeared that could be considered artistic, such as bone sculpting, and decorative, such as engraving. At this time spear points acquired different shaft form. Needles with eyes, harpoons, and spearthrower hook also appeared. In like manner compound utensils began to be used: bone bodies or supports held in side grooves geometrical microlithic blades, stuck with mastic, being the active part of the piece and easily replaceable. In this way were made harpoons (Northern Europe), knives and sickles (Middle East).

After the Upper Palaeolithic, during the Mesolithic and Neolithic bone continued in use but less intensely (Camps-Fabrer 1976). Morphologies became less diversified and frequent (Camps-Fabrer 1976, Stordeur 1985b). In the Near-Eastern Natufian bone raw materials are employed as components of compound tools. From the Natufian up to the Neolithic, bone industry was directed to domestic and agricultural activities, while in Europe bone tools continue to be connected with fishing and hunting, though rarer (Stordeur 1985). The Neolithic is characterized by the presence of axe handles. In Classical Antiquity the use of bone is documented in comb-making (Mac Gregor & Currey 1983 and Mac Gregor 1985) and diverse kinds of figurines. Its use, in a limited way, continues till the Middle Ages (Mac Gregor 1985) and more recent historical times (Stordeur 1980c). By this time an important tendency towards its use for decorative purposes becomes apparent. From the Louvre Cour Carré excavation, layers dated in 16th century, showed bone under the form of dice, objects for women's coiffeurs (combs of different sorts), toothbrushes, and for knife handles or sheaths. In many present-day populations of hunters-gatherers one can find bone materials used for tool manufacture. In terms of the quantity of bone used the Eskimos take pride of place (Stordeur 1980b and 1986). Yet even in our industrialized Western society, though hardly detectable, its use continues in the guise of artisanal objects (Stordeur 1980c).

Summary

As a resumé, a model describing the history of the exploitation of bone materials can be posited, which comprises two stages. The first is that of experimentation: this makes possible the recognition of the material one is working with through the direct use of bones, which are employed with no prior formatization. For this purpose its natural shape is taken advantage of. Bone is also worked as if it were a stone raw material, by knapping. Both correspond to the Lower and Middle Palaeolithic. Later, when the material's characteristics become more familiar, techniques suited to those particularities arises. This emerged during the Upper Palaeolithic. As will be seen further on, a model of these characteristics agrees with the theoretical framework that will be used for this work.

CHAPTER 3

MECHANICAL PROPERTIES OF BONE

Introduction

This chapter will look into bone as a material, and its mechanical properties. Its most important characteristics will be explained and basic notions of bone biomechanics will be summarized in order to understand why it is important to determine the mechanical properties of bones employed as raw material in Tierra del Fuego. Regarding these, they will be presented in Chapter 8.

Bone as a Material. Its Structure

Bone at the Molecular Level

Mammal bone can be considered as a "(...) highly complex, multiphased, heterogeneous, composite material that is viscoelastic and anisotropic having contrasting mechanical properties that respond differently to an external stimulus but in combination are stronger than either substance alone" (Johnson 1985:165-166). It is a composite material consisting of a fibrous protein, collagen, stiffened by an extremely dense filling and surrounding of calcium phosphate crystals. Collagen is a structural protein that comprises about 85 to 90% of the protein in bone. (Currey 1984, Ferretti Ms.)

The inorganic fraction of bone accounts for 70% of the tissue, and is made up of tricalcium phosphate (85%), calcium carbonate (10%), magnesium phosphate (2%) and salts (sodium, silicon, etc.) in smaller quantities.

These substances form hydroxyapatite crystals that surround the collagen fibres (Figure 3.1a). They are needle-shaped and are lined up and integrated into the collagen fibres (Currey 1984, Ferretti Ms.)

Bone microstructure depends on osteoblasts, bone-building cells, which produce a collagenous matrix, osteoid, in which mineral is deposited. The mechanical capacity of bone material depends on osteoblasts and these, in turn, depend on four factors:

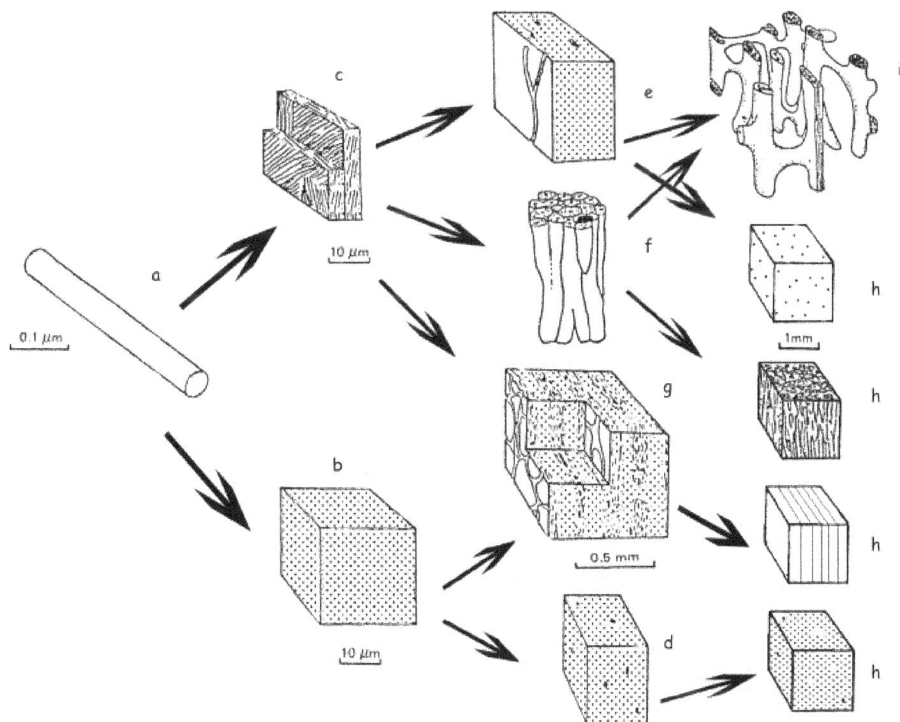

Figure 3.1 – Mammal bone structure at different organizational levels (drawn by Ana Fondebrider based on Mac Gregor 1985)

a. Collagen fibre
b. Woven Bone with random collagen fibres
c. Lamellar bone with fibres disposed in the same way inside each lamella
d. Woven bone in a bigger structural level
e. Primary Lamellar bone
f. Haversian bone
g. Fibrollamelar bone
h. compact bone
i. cancellous bone

1) genetical;

2) mechanical loads of matrix microelements;

3) food deficiencies that may alter the presence of critical elements (such as proteins, calcium, phosphorus, etc) or affect endocrine factors and alter the secretion of osteoactive substances and hormones involved in the phosphorus-calcium metabolism (Ferretti Ms.)

Osteocytes, derived from osteoblasts, are the cells in the body of the bone. The larger the animal the lower the density of osteocytes (Currey 1984).

Woven, Lamellar, and Parallel-Fibred Bone

According to Currey (1984), above the collagen fibre level, three different types of bone can be distinguished (Figure 3.1): woven (1b), lamellar (1c) and parallel-fibred. Woven bone is formed in the foetus and in the callus produced during fracture repair. In this kind of bone collagen is oriented almost randomly. Lamellar bone is more precisely arranged. The collagen fibrils and their associated mineral are arranged in sheets (lamellae). They are disposed along the shorter axis and deposited more slowly. The orientation of the fibrils changes from one lamella to another. Parallel-fibred bone is structurally intermediate between lamellar and woven bone, and found only in certain bones and situations (cf. Currey 1984).

Fibrolamellar and Haversian Bone

In mammals there are, on a higher structural level, four types of bone (Figure 3.1): woven (1d), lamellar (1e), Haversian (1f), and fibrolamellar (1g).

Haversian systems are created when lamellar bone placed around a blood-vessel is eroded by osteoclasts (bone-destroying cells). The action of osteoclasts leaves a cavity (around 100 microns in diameter). The cavity walls become smooth and bone, in concentric laminae, is deposited on the inner walls. The final appearance is akin to a leek, with clearly distinguishable cylindrical layers and with a central cavity containing one or more blood-vessels.

Fibrolamellar bone is found in large mammals whose bones must grow in diameter very rapidly. It consists in a scaffolding of parallel fibres that is quickly deposited and later filled in by lamellar bone. Frequently the lamellar disposition makes room for one in which each blood vessel anastomoses and each is surrounded by more or less concentric layers of lamellar bone, which produces a resemblance to a Haversian system. However, this kind of disposition is generated in primary osteons whereas Haversian systems form in secondary ones, that is, those that replace previously existing bone.

Primary and Secondary Bone

In bone it is necessary to differentiate three processes: growth, modelling, and remodelling (cf. Ferretti Ms.) Bone growth is connected with the development of ossification points in the foetus.The bone resulting from this process is determined by inherited patterns and the species' philogenetic history. Bone modelling is a different process that retains the shape and architecture of the bone. It includes the formation of secondary bone and endosteum reabsorption that makes room for the bone's central cavity. This is how the shape of the growing bone is modelled during the juvenile stage. Bone remodelling occurs as a product of osteoblasts (conjunctive cells in calcifying tissues) and osteoclasts that function on the level of the Haversian systems. Remodelling maintains the bone's functional perfomance throughout the adult stage.

The normal modelling and remodelling cycle of bones constitutes an adequate mechanism to maintain bone mechanical capacity as it grows older. The result of this process in humans is an optimization of structural properties immediately after adolescence, while decreasing in senescence (v. Ferretti Ms.)

Primary bone (resulting from bone growth) is replaced by secondary bone (resulting from modelling) by means of the erosion of the surface and the deposition of a new layer of bone or by the formation of Haversian systems.

Compact and Cancellous Bone

Compact bone is composed of lamellar and Haversian bone. It includes numerous elements (Bonnichsen & Will 1980, Barone 1966, Bouchoud 1974, Currey 1984, and Ferretti Ms):

1) osteons: cylindrical and ramified structures with thick walls composed of concentric layers of hydroxyapatite incorporated into the collagen fibrils (Barone 1966). The osteons surround the Haversian canals and are oriented according to the bone's longitudinal axis. They are disposed in such a way that the diaphysis' mechanical resistance will be greatest in the sense in which greatest forces are exerted;

2) Haversian systems: in each osteon can be seen a narrow central canal —Haversian canal— which is traversed by blood vessels and nerves. Around this canal, the bone lamellae are disposed concentrically;

3) Volkmann canals: small oblique canals that join Haversian canals of neighbouring osteons;

4) bone cells (osteocites), which derive from the osteoblasts. They are fusiform cells placed between the lamellae or inside them;

5) small cavities or lacunae that connect with one another and with neighbouring blood vessels by means of canals called canaliculi. Each lacuna contains osteocites.

Cancellous bone consists of a network of plates and rods conforming a trabecula. This tissue occupies the extremes of long bones. It has a porous appearance. On an ultrastructural level it is formed by short, highly dilated, and irregular osteons. Haversian canals are rough, twisting cavities that are more or less communicated. Bone lamellae surrounding those cavities join up with those of neighbouring systems to form trabeculae. Bone marrow is more abundant in cancellous than in compact tissue, and therefore blood interchanges are more frequent here.

Bone architecture

Taken as a whole —that is, as an organ—bones can be:

a) long: They are usually thick-walled, hollow tubes, expanded at the ends and having cancellous bone under these expanded ends (Currey 2002). The diaphysis of a long bone has a marrow cavity along the bone's axis, surrounded by a thick compact bone cylinder made up of three different layers: 1) the periosteum. on the outside; 2) the fundamental internal system and endosteum, made up of concentric lamellae elaborated by the marrow cavity (which behaves as a gigantic Havers canal), and 3) the intermediate system, made up of osteons (placed parallel to, and longitudinally to the bone axis), and the debris of lamellae and osteons destroyed by secondary ossification (Barone 1966).

b) flat or short: they have a thin surface layer of compact bone and are filled with cancellous bone. There is no marrow cavity but the marrow is present in the cancellous tissue. Bone marrow is a blood-vessel-rich conjunctive tissue. It occupies all bone cavities, the marrow cavity, the Havers canals, cancellous bone, etc. (Barone 1966, Currey 1984).

Bone Biomechanics

These characteristics determine a set of mechanical properties that are peculiar to bone and define it as a material. Those bone characteristics are studied by a discipline called bone biomechanics (Ferretti Ms.).

Mechanics is the physical science that deals with the effects of forces on objects. When these are living bodies, then we speak of biomechanics (Evans 1961 quoted by Bonnichsen 1979). Two application fields of biomechanics can be recognized (Ferretti Ms.):

a) dynamic: it studies the characteristics of the locomotor system with regard to the performance of movements;

b) static: it deals with the analysis of structural properties of the locomotor system, regarding the bones as rigid columns, in relation to the application of forces or loads that, in general, cause some sort of deformation. This last field is of particular interest for physiologists, traumatologists, and endocrinologists. In the pharmacological field this type of studies relates to the investigation of the effects of different osteoactive agents on bone's capacity for deformation or its resistance to fracture (Ferretti Ms.).

Biomechanical studies have three main objectives (Ferretti Ms.):

1) to analyze the mechanisms of bone fracture in relation to its mechanical properties (the study of bone as an organ or structure);

2) to determine the quality of the material composing the bone and the efficiency of its spatial distribution (the study of bone as tissue or material);

3) to understand the mechanisms involved in the optimization of bone resistance, whether at a tissue level or that of the bone as a whole (the study of bone as a biological system).

Here some concepts related to static bone biomechanics (henceforth "biomechanics") will be studied and the mechanical properties of bone will be characterized.

Mechanical Tests

Mechanical properties are evaluated by means of tests. Five types of test are known (Figure 3.2) :

- compression (a): a shortening of the sample is produced, by pressing its ends or its faces;
- tension (b): the sample is stretched by applying traction to its ends;
- torsion (c): part of the piece is twisted with respect to the remaining portion;
- shear (d): a displacement of a section of the sample is produced along a certain plane, while the rest remains still;
- bending (e): a bow-shaped deformation is produced. This test can take three forms:
  1) cantilever (ei): one extreme of the piece is fixed while the force acts on the other (like a diving-board);
  2) on three points (eii): the piece rests on its extremes and a force is applied at a single central point;
  3) four points (eiii): the piece rests on its extremes and a force is applied by two elements between them;

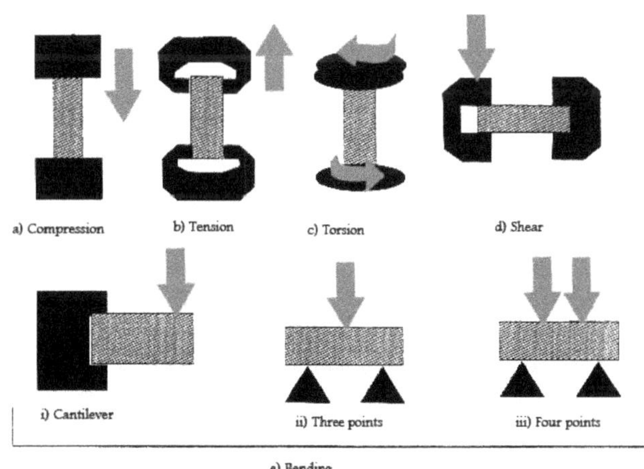

Figure 3.2 – Mechanical Tests

a. compression b. tension
c. torsion d. shear
e. bending: ei) cantilever
eii) three points
eiii) four points

Mechanic Characteristics of Bone

Fracture

The patterns of bone fracture are determined at a microstructural (osteons) and a macrostructural level (shape of the bone and the presence of sigmoid torsion).

On a microstructural level, according to Johnson (1985), the mechanical unit of compact bone is the osteon. The mechanical response is controlled by the interaction between the collagen fibres and the hydroxyapatite crystals. Osteons tend to reduce the tensile resistance and the elastic modulus, whilst lamellae tend to increase their resistance and rigidity (Johnson 1985).

Fractures initiate as microfractures that take place at the cellular level and amplify to a larger scale. When the bone is struck, a fault is produced, outside the surface of contact with the impacting object, in the area adjacent to the blow, which is the place of greatest tension (Bonnichsen 1979). Hollows in the bone (i.e. canals) concentrate the force and initiate the microfracture.

The fracture breaks the unions between particles, and these travel along as kinetic energy is released. This is dissipated as elastic waves. A complex interaction of elastic waves then occurs (Bonnichsen 1979).

Gifford (1981) holds that the shape of the fracture in the bone is determined by its morphology and internal structure. The spiral fracture—typical of certain long bones—depends more on the structure of the bone's transversal section than on the agent producing the fracture.

Miotti & Salemme (1988) come to the same conclusion, relating the presence of a spiral fracture to sigmoid torsion: "(...) In cases in which the epiphyses of bones are twisted with respect to the diaphysis, which is called sigmoid torsion, the position of Havers canal systems also adopts that twist. (...) Therefore, in bones with sigmoid torsion the fracture will tend to be in a spiral, be it the result of intentional action or not, whereas in long bones that structurally do not possess such a rotation of the epiphysis, the resulting fracture will tend to be straight, parallel or longitudinal with respect to the bone's main axis" (Miotti & Salemme 1988: 44, my translation).

Rigidity, Elasticity, and Plasticity

On an organ level, bone resistance can be determined as if it consisted of a column of homogeneous material. In this case, following Koch (1917 quoted in Burr 1980), the resistance of the column depends on:

a) the material it is made of,

b) the area and shape of the transversal section of the column,

c) the proportion of the column diameter relative to its total length.

Whatever static force is applied to a sample some kind of deformation is produced (Figure 3.3). That deformation consists in a change in the dimensions of the sample. The deformation in a bone produces produces an intrinsic deformation of the material which is called strain. Such a deformation produces a suffering in the bone structure known as stress. Stress is best thought of as the intensity of a force acting across a particular plane (Currey 2002). Certain critical stress values correspond to the tissue's limit of resistance to fracture. If these values are exceeded, tiny microfractures are produced (see Currey 1984, Ferretti Ms, Herbst et al. 1994, Scheinsohn & Ferretti 1995).

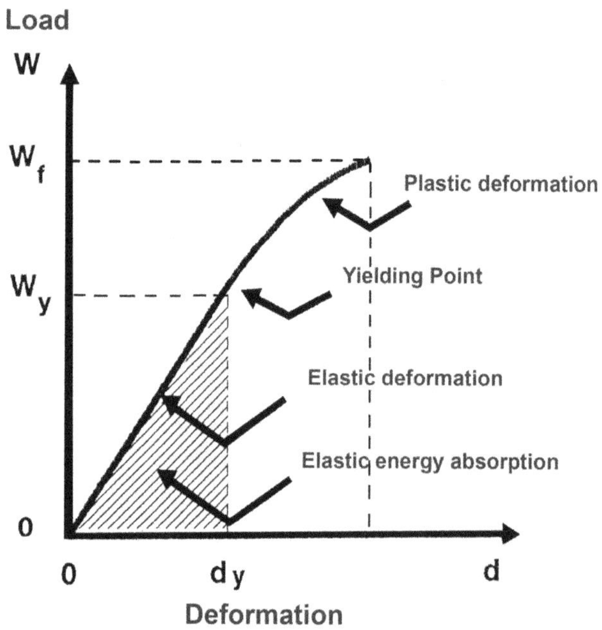

Figure 3.3 – Stress/strain curve

Elastic deformation (Figure 3.3) occurs in such a way that, should the force applied to an object be removed, it recovers its original shape. In other words, it is reversible. When microfractures occur, it is considered that the deformation is plastic (Figure 3.3), that is, partially or totally irreversible (Bonfield & Li 1966, Currey 1984, Ferretti Ms, Herbst et al. 1994, Scheinsohn & Ferretti 1995).

The relationship between the force or load and the deformation applied to a material can be expressed as a curve, called stress-strain curve, which is peculiar to that material (Figure 3.3). The region of elastic deformation is the straight part of the curve, in which an increase of the load produces a proportional increase in the deformation. If the force is released, the deformation returns to zero. If the force rises beyond the yielding point, elastic behaviour ceases: the deformation no longer returns to zero on suspending the force and the material remains permanently deformed. This is the plastic zone of the curve. Beyond this point the curve becomes progressively flatter until the material breaks. The load/ deformation (or stress/ strain) curve is used to determine the structural and material properties of a given material. Those properties, alongside the geometric ones, define the mechanical behaviour of a material.

Anisotropy and Mechanical Heterogeneity

An anisotropic material is one that presents a different response according to the direction of the load. In bone anisotropy arises as a product of the spatial disposition of the elements that determine each of the levels of structural complexity of bone tissue (Frost 1986 quoted by Ferretti Ms.). As said it is considered that mineral crystals possess a greater resistance to compression and greater rigidity while collagen shows greater resistance to traction. This results in that the bone modulus of elasticity is an intermediate value between these two components.

The apatite crystals, ranged along the collagen fibrils, minimize the probability that a fracture will travel from crystal to crystal. As Currey points out, "(...) for any particular direction of stress, a two-phase material will be stronger, weight for weight, if its fibres are arranged along the line of action of the stress than if they are arranged randomly" (1964:8 in Bonnichsen 1979).

Anisotropy has the advantage that a greater resistance can be achieved in the direction normally subject to maximum loads or forces than those attained by a similar volume of isotropic material (v. Bonfield & Li 1967).

Mechanical Properties

A mechanical test on bone can determine three groups of significant properties (Ferretti Ms. and Scheinsohn & Ferretti 1995):

a) Structural properties: they are the mechanical properties of the whole bone or sample determined on an organ level. They depend on the geometry and mechanical quality of the material, and define the resistance to deformation.

b) Geometric properties: they estimate the quantity or spatial distribution of the bone material in the whole bone or sample.

c) Material properties: they express the intrinsic properties of the bone tissue. When bone is spoken of as a material, reference is made to this type of properties. The mechanical properties of the material are determined by expressing any one of the correlative structural properties in terms of any of the described geometrical properties.

Structural Properties

Load (W)/deflection (d) curves, showing both the elastic (linear) and plastic components separated by the yield point (graphic departure from linearity), allow the determination of the following structural properties (Ferretti Ms. and Scheinsohn & Ferretti 1995):

- Stiffness (Wy/dy) or load-to-deformation ratio at any point of the elastic part of the curve. It corresponds to the slope of the straight part of the graph (Figure 3.3);

- Load-bearing capacity (Ultimate load or ultimate strength) (Wf): determined by the load at the point of fracture;

- Elastic energy absorption (EAC): area under the curve up to the yielding point (Figure 3.3). It is interpreted as the energy absorbed by the bone as it is elastically deformed.

Material Properties

These are variables that do not depend on the shape or size of the piece. The most common are (Ferretti Ms. and Scheinsohn & Ferretti 1995):

- Limit elastic stress (or tenacity at the end of elastic deformation S) expresses the amount of load a surface, perpendicularly oriented to the load, can stand without ceasing to behave elastically. It is a more descriptive variable of bone quality than stiffness and allows for comparisons between species.

- Deformation or strain (s): is the amount of deformation produced in the material with respect to an initial reference measurement.

- Young's elastic modulus (E): an estimation of bone tissue stiffness regardless of its geometry, given by the relation E= S/s.

- Elastic absorption of energy to volume ratio (EAC/vol): it expresses the same property as EAC but referred to bone mass.

It is known that small variations in the mineral content of bone bring about large variations in the main mechanical variables like E and S (see Ferretti Ms.) As hydroxyapatite is the component with the highest Young's elastic modulus, resistance to compression and tension is higher in areas of great mineralization. An increase in mineralization is correlated (in a non-linear manner) with an increase in the Young's elastic modulus, but any relation between mineralization and resistance exists only up to a certain critical level. At this point, the bone's reduced capacity for elastic deformation diminishes its resistance. In turn, a great increase in the mineral density brings about a reduction in the absorption of energy. Increased mineralization also produces a reduction in the trabecula's capacity to resist bending (Burr 1980).

Geometrical Properties

Those most often used in the bibliography are (Currey 1984, Ferretti Ms., and Scheinsohn & Ferretti 1995):

- volume of the piece;
- thickness of the wall (wall to gap ratio, Figure 3.4);
- moment of inertia of the fracture section (Ix): this allows the evaluation of particularities of the shape and/or irregularities according to the direction in which the load is applied. It is considered an architectural efficiency indicator of the distribution of the material in space. The spatial placement of all the structural elements at a higher level than the cellular have a non-arbitrary orientation. That orientation is determined by force lines that represent the preferred load direction (Ferretti Ms.) The different mechanical requirements a bone must respond to during its existence determine and localize the modelling and remodelling processes. The geometry of the diaphysis section of a long bone responds to these phenomena by means of periostic apposition and endostic resorption, which increases the size of the marrow cavity.

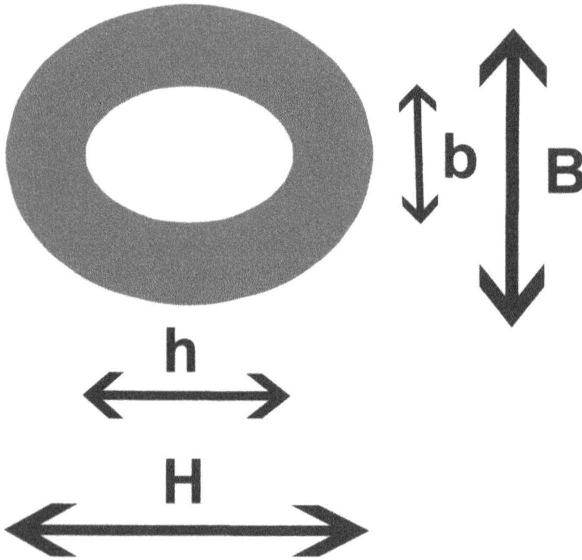

Figure 3.4 – Mammal long bone cross-section area

This process determines:

1) the thickness of the bone walls according to whether the regions are subjected to some local force;

2) the local turnover, that is, the difference between construction and destruction of a bone which is proportional to the intensity and historical frequency of the mechanical requirements.

The resulting redistribution may have no effect on the section area but it will bring about a progressive increase of the moment of inertia (Ferretti Ms.)

Conclusion

On designing a tool it is necessary to bear in mind raw material properties. Bone is chosen for certain tools due to its characteristics as a material. In other words, on choosing a bone to make a tool, certain properties of that bone are being selected. The determination of these properties will make it possible to consider whether the differences found among raw materials available justify their differential exploitation and will allow to test expectations regarding the mode of action of that tool. In the bibliography on biomechanical bone determinations no data exist for taxa available in Tierra del Fuego. Given the importance of these data it was necessary to generate them. For this purpose a suitable methodology was designed which is presented in Chapter 8, together with the determinations that were carried out. Thus the results obtained via mechanical tests, added to those got by morphological analysis, will allow conclusions regarding the different types of tools found in the region.

CHAPTER 4

THE NATURAL SETTING: ISLA GRANDE DE TIERRA DEL FUEGO

General Remarks

The Isla Grande de Tierra del Fuego is part of the Fueguian archipelago, at the extreme south of the Americas between 52° 25' and 56° South latitude and 63° 47' and 74° 45' West longitude. It is the largest island in this archipelago, comprising some 48,000 sq. km (some 14,600 sq. mi.) In terms of size it is 28th largest island in the world (Boninsegna et al. 1989). Its outline is roughly that of an equilateral triangle, limited on the south by the Beagle Channel, on the east by the Atlantic Ocean, and on the north by the Magellan Strait. The eastern side of the island belongs to the Argentine Republic, while the western side belongs to the Republic of Chile. The border between the two countries is set at 68° 36' W longitude (see Figure 1.1).

Together with the south of Patagonia, it shows the following general characteristics (Bondel 1988):

1) it is the only existing land-mass of the southern hemisphere beyond 46° South and, consequently, the only one that interrupts atmospheric and oceanic circulation in the hemisphere;

2) as a result of the preceding, it is characterized by strong winds, generally from the West (called Westerlies, prevailing winds in the middle latitudes between 35 and 65° lat.);

3) high luminosity, with short days and long nights in winter, and the reverse in summer;

4) the average winter temperature is low, (between 3 and 4 degrees Centigrade below freezing (some 27 and 25° F), and there is no pronounced or hot summer;

5) seasonal ice and frozen ground.

Geological History and the Palaeoenvironment

The geological structure of the Isla Grande is a product of Andean tectonics and the activity of the South Pacific crustal plate (Moore 1983). Most of the island was below sea-level throughout the Tertiary until, during the Pliocene, it began to emerge. The plains of the north and east of the Isla Grande were formed by Tertiary sediments deposited in marine and terrestrial conditions upon which gravels, sands, and clays were deposited during the retreat of the Plio-Pleistocene glaciers (Moore 1983). The formation of those glaciers strongly modified the landscape. There exist abundant signs of their presence in the central mountain range and adjacent regions. Several glaciations have been recognized at the northern end of the island, and at least two in the Beagle Channel. The last is equivalent to those of Llanquihue in the Chilean Lake District and the North American late Wisconsin glaciation. The Last Glacial Maximum in Tierra del Fuego took place between 18,000 and 20,000 years ago, and the retreat of the ices may have begun before 14,700 BP (Rabassa et al 1990).

Following the Last Glacial Maximum a general retreat of the ices took place, although there is evidence of new advances of the ice. The Tardiglacial —defined as the moment between the retreat of ices after Last Glacial Maximum and the Holocene (Rabassa et al 1990)— was characterized by fluctuating climatic conditions, with two cold climatic events. Of these, the latter has been correlated with the Younger Dryas in Europe (Rabassa et al. 1990, Heusser & Rabassa 1987).

During the Holocene there were also new glaciers advances, the last of these called Little Ice Age (Rabassa et al. 1990). At this time volcanic activity becomes particularly important. The evidence of volcanic manifestations is visible by means of fine ashes layers in steppes and forests sediments. According to Stern (1990), the sources of Tierra del Fuego tephras (fragmental material produced by a volcanic eruption) are diverse volcanic episodes. The eruption of the Volcan Reclus would have originated Auer's Tephra I around 10,330 BP, while that of Mount Burney would have generated Tephra III (2500-3000 BP). Data from the section of a peat moor indicate that considerable volcanic eruptions took place around 10,000 BP, 9400 BP, 8900 BP, 6600 BP, between 5500 and 3500 BP, 4500 and 2200 BP (Rabassa et al. 1990).

After ice retreat, around 9400 BP, the Beagle Channel was probably occupied by a glacial lake (Rabassa et al 1986). The level of the lake was 30 metres or even higher above the present level. The Beagle Channel opened up to the sea around 8000 BP, thanks to the rise of the sea level and subsequent moraines erosion (Rabassa et al. 1986). At that same time the Magellan Strait would have already opened up (Porter et al. 1984 in Borrero 1993a). Around 7600 BP marine environment was totally established at the whole length of the channel and probably all around the Isla Grande. On the Atlantic coast, from the Middle Holocene on, rapidly eroding sea cliffs and complex intertidal systems evolved.

According to palynological records, at the time of the ice retreat, Beagle Channel surroundings would have been covered with tundra-type vegetation, dominated by grasses and shrubs, which indicates a cold, dry climate (Heusser 1989a and b). During the early Holocene the climate in the

Beagle Channel was warmer and drier than the present, with steppe-forest ecotone characteristics. In Middle Holocene the relatively cold, humid, cloudy conditions that prevailed after 5000 BP established. These favoured the development of continuous forests —which replaced the open, non-continuous ones— and the accumulation of sphagnum-moss peat according to the polinical profiles from Puerto Haberton and Lapataia (Rabassa et al. 1990).

Also during the Mid Holocene, another geological process took place: the rising of the shores. In general this phenomenon is ascribed to isostasy or tectonic movement (Rabassa et al. 1990).

Topography

Cordillera de los Andes is the axis that organizes the Isla Grande. They run in a West-Easterly direction and are formed by four ranges: a) the marginal one (Sierra Beauvoir, to the north of lake Fagnano); b) the central one (Valdivieso, Alvear, Lucas Bridges, Lucio López, and Noguera sierras); c) the Darwin chain, which includes the greatest heights on the island; and d) a fourth chain, which emerges south of the Beagle Channel on Hoste and Navarino islands.

Bondel (1988) divides the island into two sectors:

a) the North or extra-Andean zone of plains and terraces, which corresponds to the continuation of the Patagonian Plateau (Figure 4.1). It is an undulating plain whose height oscillates between sea-level and 200 m (650 ft). It is cut by two important rivers, the Río del Oro —in the Chilean sector—, which ends in Bahía San Felipe, and the Río Grande, which flows into the Atlantic Ocean. The general aspect is given by fluvioglacial and fluvial terraced levels worn down by erosion, with wide extensions of gently sloping interfluves. The terraces end up at the sea in cliffs that give way to a broad abrasion platform. Between San Sebastián (Argentina) and Inútil (Chile) bays there is a depression, excavated by glaciers. Also another remarkable depression is located, South of the former occupied by the Admiralty Sound (Seno del Almirantazgo) the Azopardo river, and lake Fagnano. To the south of this depression is found the Fueguian Andes.

b) the South, or Andean area, geologically the more ancient part of the island, which was strongly shaped by glacier action. The valleys have a dominant West-East orientation and are presently taken up by the sea, lakes, or peat-bogs (Figure 4.2). They evidence many glacial geoforms such as lateral, deep, and terminal moraines. In general the landscape shows a rugged relief, glacial morphology, and a periglacial environment.

Climate

The Isla Grande climate is temperate-cold, subhumid in the North and oceanic in the mountain forests (Bondel 1988). The oceanic character and the westerlies winds place the climate in a uniform summerless regime. There is little variation between the average extreme values, although in a general framework of homogeneity, the interior of the island experiences greater winter rigours for not receiving a direct maritime influence. (Bondel 1988).

Figure 4.1 – Steppe landscape near Río Cullen (North Isla Grande)

Figure 4.2 – Beagle Channel. At the front Navarino Island (Chile), at the back Ushuaia city (Argentina)

The Andes' condensing effect generates differentiated climatic conditions on either side of the mountain-range. The mountain range affects the circulation of the winds. Whereas in the North they circulate without interference, in the South, the Andean range conditions the circulation. Rainfall is also associated with a rainshadow effect from Andes. It increases from north to south and east to west.

Vegetation and Fauna

Isla Grande is the world's southernmost forested region and the closest to the Antarctic (Boninsegna et al 1989).

It is part of three phytogeographic domains: the Andean-Patagonian Domain, the Subantarctic Domain, and the Magellanic-Oceanic Domain (Cabrera & Willink 1973).

The present vegetation at the Andes range corresponds to the Subantarctic Deciduous Forest from sea level to 700 m a.s.l. Above this altitude, the High Andean Desert develops. The presence of moss and peat bogs is frequent.

Terrestrial fauna is not very varied (only 10 species of autochthonal terrestrial mammals, Schuerholz n.d.) Birds are the most varied group of the Fueguian fauna. According to Prosser Goodall (1979), there exist 197 bird species representing 45 families. Schuerholz (n.d.) considers 171 species representing 43 families, while Humprey et al (1970) consider 168 species.

Cabrera & Willink (1973) divide the biogeographical regions in domains and provinces based on vegetation, with plants and animals occupying the same territories. Then the distribution of the fauna fit with the phytogeographic detailed provinces.

From these animals indigenous groups exploited pinnipeds heavily, mainly *Arctocephalus Australis* (Southern fur seal Figure 4.3) and *Otaria flavescens* (Southern sea lion). Orquera and Piana also argued that its exploitation is explained by the high body volume and caloric value of their edible parts. Guanacos (*Lama guanicoe*, a South American camelid Figure 4.4) could have been an alternative, but they have fewer fat and their capture possibly should be ratted as more costly (Orquera and Piana 1999). Having an appropriate technology (which included canoes and detachable harpoons), pinnipeds should be less costly in terms of capture and transportation (Orquera and Piana 1999, Orquera 2005). Consumption of molluscs, mainly mussels and limpets, had produced shell middens (Orquera and Piana 2000, Orquera 1987, Orquera and Piana 1983) but their caloric contributions were poor. As Orquera and Piana (1999) posited the caloric equivalent for one *Arctocephalus australis* should be approximately 50.000 mussels.

Postdepositional Processes

With regard to the natural factors that determine the presence of exploited bone raw materials, in Chapter 2 postdepositional processes were mentioned. These affect the preservation, in the archaeological record, of bone

Figure 4.3 – Southern fur seal (Arctocephalus Australis)

Figure 4.4 – Guanaco (Lama Guanicoe). Photo by Sebastián Muñoz

tools as well as that of bones in general. What are the possibilities of preservation in the case of the Isla Grande? In order to answer this question we must here look into some data relative to the regional taphonomy.

By regional taphonomy is understood the study carried out on a certain space so as to recognize those environments or microenvironments in which exist greatest possibilities for deposition, burial, and preservation of bones (Borrero 1988). In other words, what is sought is to have an idea of the range and magnitude of potential taphonomic processes in a certain region (Lanata 1991).

Following Lanata (1991), the following natural processes that might affect bones on the Isla Grande can be enumerated:

a) *Animal Agents*:
— trampling: the tread of certain animals (e.g. guanacos) produces the migration of modern bones to older layers. The saturation of archaeological sites in some regions and the conditions of winter stress in guanaco populations increase the possibilities of a modern animal falling down dead over an archaeological site and, due to the constant circulation of guanacos along the same pathways, their bones could be buried into it (Borrero 1988). The movements of modern livestock are also an important trampling factor;

— action of rodents and rabbits: the main rodent in the North of the island is the *Ctenomys* sp. (Lanata 1991). The action of rabbits, introduced to the island in XIX century with European colonization, is also important. Both animals dig burrows that alter the arrangement of archaeological materials; in addition they usually leave marks on bones, including the ones made into bone tools, as I could see in a harpoon head from Tunel I shell midden;

— action of carnivores: the action of grey fox (*Pseudolopex griseus*) and red fox (*P. culpaeus*, local species) on bones was recorded by Borrero (1988), Lanata (1991), Muñoz (1996) and Borrero & Martín (1996), among others. Red fox hunts small prey (lambs, rabbits, birds) and scavenge abandoned carcasses. In general the information deriving from archaeological sites and taphonomic studies suggests that this carnivore exerts a low destructive power (Muñoz 1996), often leaving its tooth-marks on bones;

— action of birds: birds of prey attack rodents, newborn pinnipeds and other birds; they were also reported to consume guanaco carcasses (Lanata 1991). Larger birds, such as the condor, might drag and carry elements (Lanata 1991);

— action of beavers: beavers were introduced with XIX century European colonization for fur hunting purposes. Their introduction provoked almost an environmental cataclysm. In archaeological terms as a result of dam-building, beavers could produce the sinking of archaeological sites. This sites could end up uncovered, as Lanata (1991) reports, and present characteristics that can be attributed to having been submerged (colouring of the bones);

b) *Geomorphological Processes*:
— the movement of sediments: relates to the presence of loose or sandy sediments, rain, and slopes. These movements can transport or cover archaeological material (Lanata 1991);

— the movement of dunes, a highly likely process in coastal areas; according to Lanata (1991) these would be long-term processes;

c) *Wind Processes*:
— wind action is one of the most important climatic characteristics on the Isla Grande. The average speed of winds is 20 km/h in the North, and 15 km/h in the Beagle Channel, though there are maximum gusts of 200 km/h and 100 km/h respectively (Bondel 1988). The wind can bring about the transport of materials and alter the configuration of the sites, although this of course depends on the presence of forests and mountains that might moderate its effects in the South (Lanata 1991);

d) *Water Processes*:
— rainfall: the rain regime is fairly variable with regard to localities, and shows notable annual variations (Bondel 1988). In areas with sandy sediments the rain can produce the removal or burial of materials. In forested areas, though drainage is faster, there could be soaking below the surface;

— rivers: they show a marked seasonal variation. In thaw season their volume increases significantly, carrying along fairly large elements. Very often there are crumblings on slopes, which suggests that sites close to riverbanks could be affected. The fact that the river mouths, specially in the Fueguian southeast, are very dynamic areas, may have caused the disappearance of nearby sites;

— ravines: these are water-courses that drain rainwater or thawed ice accumulated in lagoons and peat-bogs. Given the slope and the volume, they are able to drag larger elements;

— dampness: in areas of forests constant humidity helps in the preservation of materials once they have deposited on sediments. Instead, on grasslands, that very humidity, combined with greater exposure to the sun, may produce differential effects;

— snow: in this region one may expect a series of phenomena related to the presence of snow, such as the effects of thawing, freezing of soils, etc. although these have not been studied in detail;

e) *Plant Perturbations*:
— falling trees: in senile forests falling trees are common. These can produce the uncovering of archaeological sites (by the removal of sediments from the roots) or hide a site.

— roots: in addition to the effect mentioned above, roots can also produce movements of archaeological materials in their matrix (Lanata 1991);

f) *Organic and Mineral Decay*: Lanata (1991) proposes the following ranking of elements according to their greater possibilities of preservation:

1) stone artifacts
2) bone artifacts
3) burnt wood
4) mineral pigments
5) wood
6) other burnt or scorched plant remains
7) plant and animal fibres
8) organic pigments.

The expectation of finds in fueguian archaeological sites is limited to the first four items (Lanata 1991).

Conclusion

The environmental characteristics of Isla Grande of Tierra del Fuego make it a very special region. Firstly, it is an island. This condition determines easily recognizable limits, which behave like ecological barriers (Borrero 1991). Its latitudinal position determines certain climatic characteristics and relates it to other regions located at high latitudes in other parts of the globe. Archaeological comparison with those regions is an interesting possibility, as Borrero (1991) suggested.

The cold oceanic climate of Tierra del Fuego makes its seasonal variations not very marked. Its topography is rugged in the South, and gently undulating in the North. Internal differentiation coincides with the one that can be sketched in phytogeographical terms. Human populations permanently occupied the Andean-Patagonian Domain (Patagonian Province)—in the Northern part, with a steppe-like vegetation and patches of forest, known as the Fueguian Park (Bondel 1985 y 1988)— and the Subantarctic Domain (Subantarctic Province) —in the South, with its evergreen and deciduous forests. Environmental differences suggest human adaptation to those regions would have been also different. Indeed, ethnographically it is known that in the North there would have been human adaptations centred on the consumption of terrestrial resources (with the guanaco as the main staple), whereas in the South the emphasis was placed on the exploitation of marine resources. This will be analyzed in more detail in Chapter 5.

The brief environmental description of the Island offered here was aimed at considering what natural environmental factors may have enabled the exploitation of bone raw materials by the prehistoric populations in the region. Let us then go over those characteristics in terms of the natural factors mentioned in Chapter 1:

a) availability and faunal richness: the richness of land fauna is not important. Nevertheless the diversity of available fauna is notably increased on considering marine fauna (marine mammals, molluscs, crustaceans, and fish) and birds. The groups that could afford bones suitable for fashioning bone tools are the camelidae (guanaco), cetacea, birds, canidae and pinnipeds. The presence of these taxa allows for a notable variability in the size and mechanical properties of the different bone raw materials;

b) preservation of the materials: it is known that in a climate like the Fueguian certain materials do not last for long. The case of wood is one of the best known. Gusinde (1986), for instance, points out that a new canoe had to be built every year since they did not last longer than that. Thus if one wishes to make tools with certain characteristics (such as greater longitudinal resistance) and for them to be long-lasting, bone is a better option than wood;

c) competitive raw materials: the only available material in Tierra del Fuego that can be considered as a replacement for bone is wood. However, the tree species present in Fueguian forests can be divided into the semi-hard woods (such as lenga, c.f. Tortorelli 1946, Tinto 1978, Ratto Ms.) or soft ones (as guindo, Tinto 1978 and 1997). In other words, for activities in which the tool involved requires rigidity and hardness, it is necessary to make use of another material. Indeed, ethnographically, the use of wood is reported in tasks requiring great flexibility (bows, harpoon heads), large size or mass (harpoon shafts), or a light, straight material (arrow shafts). Even so, in the case of harpoon heads —the only bone instrument made of wood according to ethnographic sources— it was not a tree that were employed but a bush, such as *Maytenus magellanicus* (Hyades & Deniker 1891:14-15, Hyades 1885:539) and *Berberis ilicifolia* (Gusinde 1986:462), although in all cases their use is pointed out as being exceptional;

d) with regards to the postdepositional processes that affect the formation of archaeological record, it is necessary to stress that, as has been seen, these can be of great magnitude. All the same, the ones that specifically affect bones are no more important than those affecting archaeological materials as a whole. According to Lanata's (1991) proposal, bone materials have a high likelihood of being found in Fueguian sites. In fact, when they are deposited in shell beds, their survival probabilities increase, as an alkaline environment prevents the action of humic acids (Piana pers. com.). What this means is that, beyond certain local circumstances that may have affected the presence of bone remains in general, or the greater antiquity of a site —which reduces the probabilities of finding those remains—, it can be assumed that the destructive processes affecting bones on the island have not affected particulary bone survival in the archaeological record, leaving aside the variable state of preservation in which they may present.

In view of what has been stated, Tierra del Fuego should offer good conditions for the development of a system of exploitation of bone raw materials, just as for the archaeological recovery of their products.

As distinct from natural, cultural factors will be considered in the next chapter.

CHAPTER 5

ARCHAEOLOGY AND ETHNOGRAPHY

The History of Archaeological Research in Isla Grande

The first to carry out archaeological investigations in the area of the argentinian Isla Grande was Vignati (1927). But Junius Bird work on Navarino Island and Isla Grande (Chile), during 1933-1938, was the one that set systematic archaeological research in the area and, according to Schobinger (1973: 49), this work also marks the beginning of systematic archaeology in South America.

In Fell site, a cave situated in continental Patagonia, near the Magellan Strait, Bird (1946) defined five periods. This categorization influenced all subsequent research in Patagonia until very recently. Briefly, the phases (named Bird, Fell, or Magellan) can be characterized as follows:
— Phase I: characterized by the presence of "fish-tail." lithic projectile points. Radiocarbon dating obtained by Bird for this period oscillates between 11,000 ± 170 and 10,080 ± 160 BP (Orquera 1987).

— Phase II: characterized by the absence of lithic projectile points, and abundance of bone awls. It was dated at between 9100 ± 150 and 8180 ± 135 BP (Orquera 1987).

— Phase III: It was defined by its triangular lithic projectile points and the presence of "bolas." Dating range from 8180 ±135 to 6560 ± 115 BP (Orquera 1987).

— Phases IV and V include small stemmed triangular lithic projectile points with stone bolas, and scrapers that can be attached to a handle. In phase V the lithic projectile points would be smaller (Bird called them "ona type" projectile points), and bone tools abound. Dates for these phases would go from 6560 ± 115 BP for phase IV to 685 ± 90 BP for phase V (Orquera 1987).

In the 1950s, Sánchez Albornoz (1958) and Menghin (1952 and 1956) carried out prospections in the area and initiated a debate related to the presence of the casa-pozo (pit-house) in the area. In the next decade, the French couple Emperaire and Laming-Emperaire (1961, Emperaire et al. 1963) worked at the Marazzi and Punta Catalina sites, in the Chilean sector of the island, and on the Magellan Strait.

In the 70s Chilean archaeologist Ortiz Troncoso (1973) worked on Navarino Island, while Argentines Orquera, Sala, Piana, and Tapia (1977) did likewise at the Lancha Packewaia site (Argentine coast of the Beagle Channel). Towards the end of this decade and the beginning of the next, archaeological investigations in the Argentine sector of the Isla Grande acquired great weight: Orquera and Piana worked at numerous Beagle Channel sites (see Orquera & Piana 1983, 1985, 1986-1987 and 1987, and Piana 1984, among others); Borrero worked in the North of the island and the southern part of continental Patagonia (see Borrero et al. 1981, Borrero 1985 a and b, 1988, 1989-1990, 1991, 1993, and Borrero & Lanata 1988, among other works); Lanata (1985, 1988, Lanata et al. 1988, Borrero & Lanata 1988, 1993 among others) and Vidal (1984, 1985 a and b, Acedo de Reinoso et al. 1988) worked at the northern and southern coast of Peninsula Mitre (Eastern tip of the Isla Grande), respectively; Mengoni Goñalons (1983, 1986 and 1988b) and Figuerero Torres (1987) have worked on Tierra del Fuego National Park (Isla Grande); Horwitz carried out her investigations on the Isla de los Estados (Horwitz 1990 and 1993).

Also from that point on, researches carried out in the Chilean sector of the island acquired importance, with the work of Massone and his team (Massone 1983, 1987, 1988 and 1989-1990, Jackson 1987, Prieto 1988, among others), the French research group headed by Legoupil (Legoupil 1978, 1980, 1988 and 1989, Léfèvre 1989) and, more recently, those of Ocampo and Rivas (1996).

This work laid down the bases of Isla Grande de Tierra del Fuego archaeology. We will now briefly describe the main lines of archaeological research in this area.

Archaeology of the Isla Grande

The first signs of human occupation in the extreme south of continental Patagonia are based on a number of sites that show indications of human coexistence with extinct pleistocene fauna (Cueva del Medio, Palli Aike, Cueva del Milodon, Cañadon Leona, Cerro Sota, Cueva Fell, etc.) They were dated at around 11,000 BP. Archaeological record for that time shows the remains of large extinct herbivores (milodon, American horse), guanacos and also fishtail and fluted lithic projectile points (as in Cueva del Medio, see Nami 1987).

On the Isla Grande, the oldest discovered sites so far, are both located in Chilean Isla Grande: Tres Arroyos (Massone 1983 and 1987) —whose layer V was dated at 10,280 ± 110, 10,420 ± 110, and 11,880 ± 250 BP— and the Marazzi site (Laming-Emperaire et al. 1972), 9590 ± 210 BP. At the coast, the oldest occupations corresponds to Túnel I site at the Beagle Channel, whose lowest layer was dated at 6980 ± 110 BP (Orquera & Piana 1986-1987).

As for the settlement and occupation of the Isla Grande two models have been put forward,: the one proposed by Orquera and Piana (e.g. 1984-85 and 1987) and Borrero's (1989-1990 and 1994-1995).

Orquera and Piana's Model

Orquera postulates his model on the basis of a general but soft critique of Menghin's outline (Orquera 1987). This author considered the coexistence of two cultural traditions: the Epiprotolithic (composed of the Neuquense, Rio Gallegense, and Magellan or Bird II industries), and Mioepimiolithic (Toldense, Casapedrense, Patagoniense industries). Orquera criticizes the definition of industries, as statistically not very representative, and on account of the chronologies ascribed in each case.

From a gradualist perspective he suggests the existence of degrees of adaptation: "The stages are really sections of gradual and continuous evolution, and in the cultural phases we must continue tracking the process of growing adaptation. Applied to Patagonia this means that the 'superior' hunter phases were at the beginning not so adapted to the environment as at the end, and that the changes did not represent merely historically arranged permutation values. Rather, the toolkit of that cultural tradition reflects evident advances towards greater specialization and standardization," (Orquera 1984-1985:258 translation mine). Thus Orquera posits a first stage with a low degree of specialization ("sub-stage of settlement and getting used to the environment," in his own words, Orquera 1984-1985:259) defined by Fell, Bird, or Magellan phases I and III.

In the specific case of the Isla Grande, Orquera and Piana (Piana 1984, Orquera et al. 1987a and b) hold that the first occupation they detected at the Beagle Channel (Túnel I site) is the reflection of a summer excursion in search of guanacos. This statement is based on the following evidence: 1) the raw lithic material used for stone tools is not local; 2) the lithic projectile points found there are not fitted to marine animals hunt; 3) the season of the occupation was established as summer; and 4) there are scanty bone remains in the layer (Orquera et al. 1987a). They therefore consider it would be a sporadic occupation.

Orquera considers there would probably have been a second stage in Patagonia around 5300-4000 B.C.: "It would be exaggerated to state that an episode of cultural effervescence took place, but something happened in Patagonia that led to the experimentation of more efficient media and formulae in exploiting the environment, which led to diversification." (Orquera 1984-1985:259 translation mine).

He then suggests the existence of three "evolutionary lines":

1) a less innovative one, in the south of continental Patagonia;

2) another in central Patagonia, represented by the Casapedrense industry;

3) another at the western portion of the Magellan Strait and at the Beagle Channel.

Bahía Buena, Punta Santa Ana, Englefield (all of them in Chile) and the Second Component of Túnel I represent the moment of complete adaptation. At all the sites— with the exception of Englefield— pinnipeds predominate. These sites are characterized by the abundance of bone tools (in Túnel I more than 45%, see Orquera 1984-1985). Orquera (1987) considers that a same type of adaptation characterizes these four sites. He can not determine whether it is a matter of an expansion from one region to another or contemporary subtraditions with a common origin, but the correlation that appears between the beginning of the adaptation process and the expansion of the Nothofagus forest leads him to think that the former alternative is more probable (Orquera 1987). Within this same adaptation can be fitted the ancient component of Lancha Packewaia and the third through sixth components from Túnel.

According to Orquera, once those lines were established, their evolution would have been slow. In fact, for the Fueguian case he suggests that "(...) the Tradition of the Magellanic-Fueguian channels and islands, established on a refuge with a great abundance of resources and to a certain extent protected from external pressures (...), advanced but slowly in time without its bearers feeling incited to further refinements" (Orquera 1984-1985:260 translation mine). This author supposes that technological and stylistic peculiarities reflect distinctive adaptational strategies (Orquera 1987: 349).

Borrero's Model

It is also starting from a critique of Menghin that Borrero (1989-1990 and 1994-1995) offers his model. But his critique involves a new paradigm for Patagonian archaeology. Orquera does not break away from Menghin's line of thought, but seems to discuss it in the same terms.

Borrero starts out from a general model of settlement that presupposes three phases for the occupation of a given space:

a) *exploration*: the phase of initial dispersion towards an empty area. It is characterized by:

—utilization of non-optimal localities;
—lack of redundancy is expected in the use of sites;
—fewer sites than those created by later occupations;
—spatial discontinuity;
—occupational alternation with carnivores and rodents;
—low expectations of finding sites (due to low integrity and because they should be covered with sediments);
—a larger home range.

b) *colonization*: the phase of initial consolidation of

human groups in certain parts of the space, with specific home ranges. Its characteristics are:

—repeated use of sites with optimal localization;

—discrete groups of sites due to non-overlapping home-ranges;

—more restricted home ranges than in previous phase;

—high archaeological visibility;

—good resolution.

In addition, an increase in the variability of material culture and rapid processes of change can be expected. Changes must also show seasonal variation respect to the distribution of resources and topography. The basic indicators are: a greater redundancy in the occupation; greater repetition in using certain subsistence strategies to the point of becoming an adaptive strategy and a net difference from previous occupations.

c) *effective occupation*: all desirable space is occupied and density-dependent mechanisms appear (Borrero 1989-1990:134). Its characteristics are:

—high visibility but low resolution due to overlapping of home-ranges;

—small home-ranges.

In the specific case of the Fueguian settlement, Borrero is critic with dispersion models such as those proposed by Menghin (1960) and Chapman (1986). Both suggest a cultural continuity North and South of the strait, and consider the existence of the Fueguian populations as "arrinconadas" (pushed) in the Isla Grande by other stronger populations. Borrero considers that the biogeographical concept of vicariance describes the situation better: "Vicariance is mentioned when a natural barrier (in this case the Magellan Strait) divided an ancestrally occupied area" (Borrero 1989-1990:135 translation mine). The vicariance model affects many *taxa*, not only humans. The appearance of the Magellan Strait produced a rearrangement and enabled a process of independent evolution of the populations that inhabited the island. Human osteological evidence corroborate this idea, as the Fueguian populations are more similar to each other than to those of continental Patagonia (Cocilovo & Guichón 1985-1986, Guichón 1985). With the vicariance model, changes are not necessarily adaptive— as Orquera (1987) maintains—, but the product of partial isolation. This is what is known as non-adaptive divergence, or drift.

Borrero (1994-1995) proposes for the Isla Grande:

a) Early exploration phase: based on Marazzi and Tres Arroyos sites. Both were able to function with, or within, overlapping home ranges with Río Chico Basin sites before the formation of the Magellan Strait (Borrero 1994-1995). Marazzi shows no intensive exploitation of marine resources. Besides, the ancient Pleistocene/ Holocene coast are presently under water, which makes it difficult to know more about this period. Exploration of the coast would probably have been later. In Borrero's view, from around 8000 BP, the opening of the Magellan Strait give rise to the conditions for a differential microevolutionary development on the Isla Grande.

b) Colonization phase: middle levels of Marazzi, Cabeza de León 1, bottom levels of Bloque Errático 1 and top levels of Tres Arroyos. Cabo San Pablo and María Luisa sites represent the colonization of the ecotone with the forest. The Magellanic-Fueguian channel-and-island adaptive cultural Tradition (as defined by Orquera & Piana, v. Orquera 1987, Orquera & Piana 1983) also represents a colonization moment (Borrero 1994-1995).

c) Phase of effective occupation, in which Borrero (1994-1995) distinguishes two strategies:

—stable occupation: adaptations depend on density, but the population distribution does not fluctuate greatly. Populations are placed underneath carrying capacity. A series of continuous occupations, or separated by small and similarly-sized intervals, must be observable in the archaeological record. The sites that represent this type of occupation are Punta María 2, Cabo Domingo, San Genaro, the less visible deposits in San Pablo, María Luisa, and sites in the Southeast tip of the island;

—saturation of the space: massive appearance of mechanisms that depend on human density, including population adjustments, cultural drift, or competition for highly productive territories characterize this moment. The populations are very close to carrying capacity. It is defined by highly competitive situations between populations. It supposes the proliferation of archaeological materials, and on a supra-regional scale, the exchange of essential products for subsistence. In the archaeological record the discrete character of distributions is lost as a result of greater occurrence of archaeological materials.

The sites that represent this phase are located at the north, and owing to the presence of large farms installed there during the XIX century at lake Fagnano and the mouth of the Río Fuego.

Ethnographic Record

The Isla Grande's ethnographic record is abundant (v. T. Bridges 1892 and 1893, L. Bridges 1978, R. Bridges 1953, Corrain & Zucchet 1962, Cooper 1967, Chapman 1986, Gallardo 1910, Gusinde 1982 and 1986, Hyades 1885, Hyades and Deniker 1891, Lista 1887, Lothrop 1928, Lovisato 1883, Skottsberg 1913, Spegazzini 1882, among others). To give a brief description of what is known ethnographically about the island it can be stated that at least four groups of hunter-gatherers were recognized (Figure 5.1). These were divided into canoe and pedestrian hunters. In the first group were the Yamanas (or Yaghans) and the Qawashqar (also called Halakwulup or Alacalufes). In the second, the Selk'nam (also called Onas) and the Haush.

The Yamanas inhabited the southern litoral of Isla Grande,

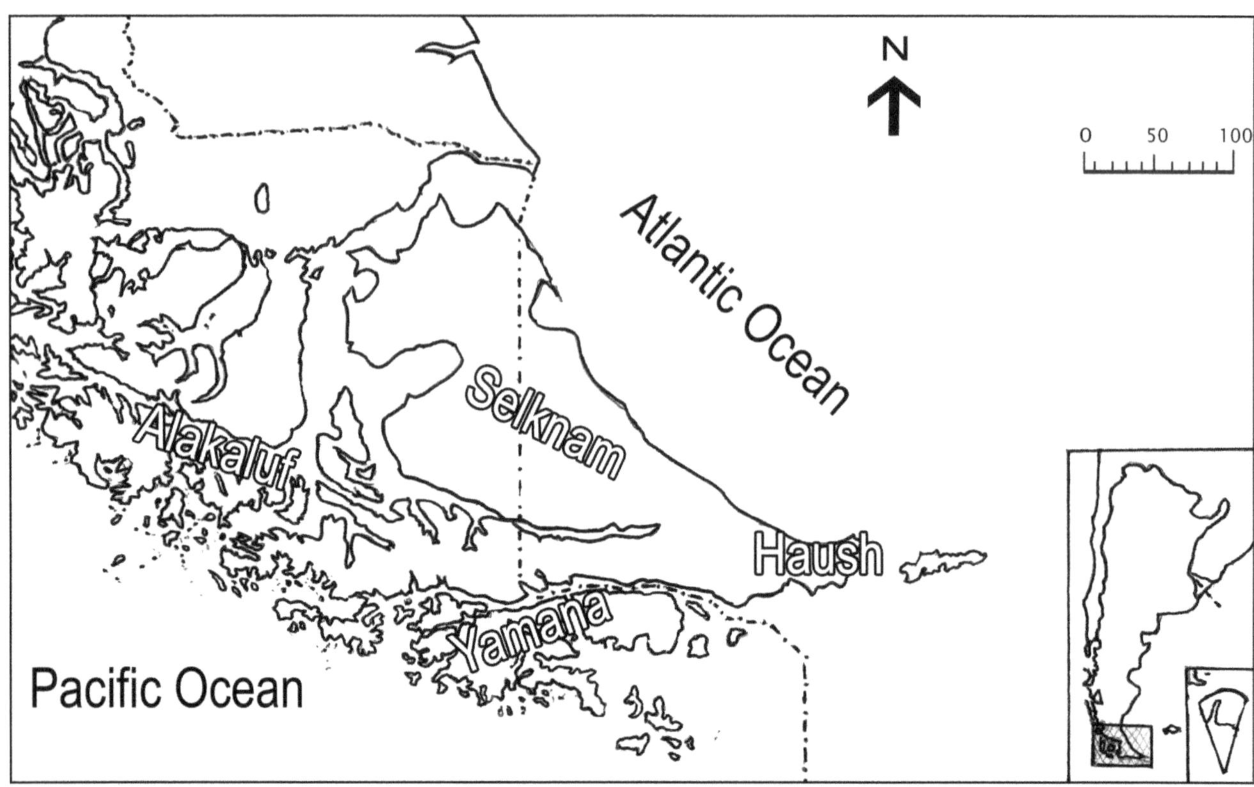

Figure 5.1 – Location of ethnographical known groups from XIXth-XXth century

along the Beagle Channel. In other words, the territory along the southeast coast of Peninsula Brecknock and the Cape Horn islands.

The Alacalufes —whose distribution corresponds to the present Chilean sector of the island— lived on the southern coast of Bahía Inútil (Useless bay) and on the southwestern coast of Chile.

The Selk'nam occupied most of the Isla Grande. From North to South they spread out from the Magellan Strait down to the environs of the Darwin Cordillera; from East to West from the Atlantic coast to the Gente Grande and Inútil bays, including the Seno del Almirantazgo.

The Haush occupied the present Peninsula Mitre, that is, the whole of the territory that extends eastwards from an imaginary line joining Cabo San Pablo (on the Atlantic coast), to Bahía Sloggett (on the Beagle Channel). According to Borrero, everything suggests that the differentiation of the Haush might be owed to the fact that in the Peninsula Mitre there was a greater availability of marine resources and these groups were more isolated (1991).

The main staple of the pedestrian hunters was the guanaco (*Lama guanicoe*). They also hunted small rodents (such as *Ctenomys* sp.) and birds (bustard, cormorants, and ducks). They also exploited some coastal resources such as pinnipeds, fish, and molluscs. Now and again some cetacean would be stranded, whose meat and fat were utilized. The diet might be filled out with fruits, seeds, and mushrooms.

The main staple of canoe hunters was pinnipeds. It was trapped on land as well as in the sea. In the latter case it was hunted with harpoons from canoes. They also consumed guanacos, birds, fish, molluscs, and crustaceans, making intensive use of the coast.

The impact of european instalation was terrible. According to Chapman (1986), in 1880 the island population could be estimated at around 7,500 canoe (between Yamanas and Alacalufes) and from 3,500 to 4,000 pedestrian hunters (Selk'nam and Haush). In total, some 11,000 or 11,500 Indians.

In 1884 missionary Thomas Bridges —owner of the estancia (farm) Harberton— had counted 1,000 Yamanas (273 men, 314 women, and 413 children). In 1886 only 397 remained.

Nowadays, only a few half-breeds exist, distributed between Chile and Argentine.

Conclusions

Regarding the model of settlement, it can be said that both Orquera and Borrero's models can be placed within an evolutionary theoretical framework. Still, the concept of evolution in each of them is different. Orquera's model, more closely related to Menghin's school, is gradualist. His basic starting point is that, if the record were not imperfect, we would perceive a gradual continuity ranging from an imperfect adaptation to a complete one, from which time onwards no further changes take place. For Orquera all change is adaptive. Additionally, he considers all phenomena to appear in phases and stages that have a real empirical status.

Borrero's model rests upon a different viewpoint, as he appeals to the vicariance model. It is upheld by biological models involving the use of space. In his view, changes do not necessarily reflect an adaptation, since drift and vicariance play a fundamental role. Phases are neither continuous nor gradual.

Beyond this debate, archaeological record and ethnographic sources allow the recognition, within a hunter-gatherer economic system, of at least two strategies: one, of hunters committed to the use of land-based resources, and the other, that of hunters that exploit maritime litoral environments. This chapter, then, has made possible the knowledge of cultural factors involved in the production of bone tools. However, before it is possible to pass over to the study of the materials, it is convenient to give a few definitions regarding the theoretical framework that will be employed in this work.

CHAPTER 6

THEORETICAL FRAMEWORK
EVOLUTIONISM IN BIOLOGY AND ARCHAEOLOGY

"New facts collected in old ways under the guidance of old theories rarely lead to any substantial revision of thought. Facts do not 'speak for themselves': they are read in the light of theory. Creative thought in science as much as in the arts, is the motor of changing opinion."

Stephen Jay Gould, *Ever Since Darwin* (1977)

Introduction

As this research was set in an Evolutionary theoretical framework, it is essential, then, to define what evolutionism is, its history, its main concepts, and its relationship with archaeology. In this chapter a summary of these points will be presented. In a second section, a concrete proposal will be offered as to how to approach the study of bone raw materials from this theoretical framework.

The Concept of Evolution

Darwin postulated the idea that all organisms, present, past, and future, descend from a common ancestor that existed, as it is known today, 3,500 million years ago[1]. The process involved in this idea was called evolution. According to Darwin, the processes that caused small changes on the scale of human observation (microevolution) accumulated on a great scale (macroevolution), producing greater changes.

In the 1930s, when the Synthetic Theory of Evolution (ST from now on) arose, knowledge proceeding from genetics was incorporated into evolutionism. Thus, evolution was defined as the change of genetic content and frequencies in a population (Dobzhansky 1951). Yet the concept of macroevolution (that is, of great scale changes) was not modified. It continued to be held that macroevolution arises from the simple accumulation of microevolutionary changes in periods of time beyond human capability of experimentation and observation. The problem is that, from ST perspective, only microevolution can be scientifically studied since, given its scale, it is the only one that allows a functional and experimental approach. Then, sciences dealing with macroevolution —such as palaeontology— were considered unscientific and merely historical (Eldredge 1989).

The ST program weakened due to criticisms which came from diverse fields. In biochemistry, neutralist theories arose, with suggestions that certain substantial quantities of DNA would be non-adaptive at the phenotype level (Orgel & Crick 1980; Doolittle & Sapienza 1980 quoted by Gould & Vrba 1982). In palaeontology, the fact that this discipline was reduced to mere history, with no possibility of becoming science, began to be criticised. It is important to realize that the problem of palaeontology (as of all sciences that deal with long-term, large-scale phenomena) is the impossibility of test certain hypotheses[2] (Eldredge 1989). As this author points out, to change the status of palaeontology was tied to the change of the epistemological framework established by ST, because great scale processes can only be faced by adopting an epistemological instance that seeks recurrent patterns within the categories of biological entities.

Macroevolution was considered by ST as synonymous with higher taxa evolution and its study was centred on the history of the adaptive characteristics of those taxa. The new approaches that arose in palaeontology as from the 70s, as Punctuated Equilibrium Theory (PET from here on) are centred on the taxa *per se*. Species or taxa are considered as real entities or individuals. They are thus limited in time and space: they have a birth, a history, and a death.

The debate between ST and PET is relevant to this work insofar as the concepts of macro and microevolution are central in the application of the evolutionary theory to the archaeological record. Within this theoretical context, it is possible to propose an analogy between anthropology and archaeology on the one hand, and genetics and palaeontology on the other. Anthropology, in general, works on a narrow temporal scale, limiting itself to microsituations. In comparison, archaeology considers phenomena on a much broader temporal scale. Thus their methods and conclusions can not be considered of the same temporal scale. The archaeological record can show "coarse-grained" trends (see Borrero 1993 appendix), whereas anthropology offers a "fine-grained" record. In this view, the situation of anthropology relates to that of genetics, while archaeology can be related to palaeontology.

Evolutionary Theory and the Punctuated Equilibrium Theory

Darwin maintained that evolution was gradual and continuous. Yet he did not find the transitional forms his theory predicted in the fossil record. The fossil record showed gaps and abrupt changes. Darwin attributed this disagreement to the imperfections of the record. Palaeontologists, for a long time, attempted to fit Darwin's predictions in the fossil record, proposing diverse *ad hoc* hypotheses to justify a presumed continuity. Eldredge & Gould (1972) proposed to recognize that disagreement and offered Punctuated Equilibrium Theory (PET) as an explanation.

Both Eldredge and Gould, independently, recognized similar patterns in the fossil record they were studying. Eldredge, while studying the Middle Devonian trilobites of the North American West, found that no net change had taken place in a period of 3 or 4 million years. The change, when it did occur, appeared suddenly. Gould came across a similar pattern while studying pleistocene snails on the Bermuda islands. Both researchers began to call "stasis" the unchanging stage (see Eldredge 1985).

The "stasis-rapid change" pattern can be interpreted in two ways:

1) from a Darwinian viewpoint: in which the pulsative aspect of the record is not true but a product of the fossil record's imperfections;

2) from a saltationist viewpoint: in which evolution proceeds by jumps.

Eldredge and Gould enrolled in a different viewpoint given that saltationism shows a series of divergences in relation to Eldredge and Gould's stance. Among these the most important are:

1) changes are abrupt and on a large scale: they go from one morphological configuration to another without intermediates;

2) mutations are the preferred mechanism to explain changes. Such is the case of Goldschmidt's (1940 quoted. by Eldredge 1985) "hopeful monsters", even though the majority of large-scale mutations are lethal, some may not be so and may produce a healthy though abnormal organism, which would permit great morphological changes;

3) in contrast with PET it does not require the stratigraphic superposition of species considered ancestral and descendent.

This last difference is fundamental in explaining the difference between saltationist models and PET. For PET the "stasis-rapid change" pattern is explained by means of allopatric speciation. Eldredge & Gould (1972) considered that, to explain the fossil record —which is coarse-grained— a kind of process, coarse enough to be detected in that record, is needed. This kind of process is speciation; that is, the separation of a coherent reproductive community into two or more daughter reproductive communities.

Species and Speciation

Biologists recognize that, when considering members of the same sex, those belonging to a species tend to be more similar to each other than to members of another species. In other words, the notion of species has to do with the phenotypic similarity that separates certain organisms from others.

Ernest Mayr, (1942 quoted. by Eldredge 1985), one of the biologists that conceived ST, recognized two modes of speciation: sympatric and allopatric. In the sympatric (or non-geographical) case, pronounced anatomical discontinuities arise when two species that live simultaneously in the same place must distinguish themselves due to competition. Instead, allopatry occurs when two organisms live apart, so discontinuities can be less pronounced as there is no direct competition.

Within the ST framework it is considered that morphological (non-reproductive) differences that separate one species from another arise as a by-product of the development of reproductive discontinuities. This is why, when formulating the definition of "species," stress was placed in reproductive aspects. A species is considered to be "(...) that stage of evolutionary process at which the once actually or potentially interbreeding array of forms becomes segregated in two or more separate arrays, which are physiologically incapable of interbreeding" (Dobzhansky quoted by Eldredge 1985:109). Along the same lines, Mayr defines species as "groups of actually or potentially interbreeding natural populations which are reproductively isolated from other such groups" (Mayr quoted by Eldredge 1985:111). This would be the so-called biological concept of species (BCS).

The BCS dominated in biology for years. In accordance with Darwin, who —given the continuity of evolution— considered species as ephemeral, this concept alluded to species as mere transitional stages. Species were transformed by the simple accumulation of phenotypic change as time goes by.

For the PET, on the contrary, species are historical entities with definite limits and can be regarded as individuals, in other words, as limited by space and time. Speciation theory, such as it appears in the field of ecology, is the explanatory matrix of PET for which reason speciation is crucial in the process of adaptive change.

PET's main objection to BCS is related to cladistics and the difficulty of recognizing a reproductive community in terms of the fossil record (in concordance with the fact that this theory arises within the framework of palaeontology). There is no way of recognizing a reproductive community in the fossil record unless it is held that a group of morphologically similar organisms make up a reproductive community, which is not necessarily true. This is why palaeontologists look for elements of the Specific Mate Recognition System (SMRS see Eldredge 1989), that is, those elements that allow the members of a species to recognize potential mating partners (e.g. antelopes' horns). If these elements persist, palaeontologists will recognize the species in the same way that members of that species recognize each other for mating purposes (v. Eldredge 1989).

According to Eldredge (1989) the SMRS concept is important when considering the process of speciation since a speciation event is actually one of SMRS disruption. From that disruption two separate reproductive communities arise. Large-scale changes (at least in metazoans) are highly improbable in the absence of speciation. Therefore speciation acts as a trigger and not as a result of adaptive change.

Thus, Eldredge (1989:132) defines species as a reproductive community composed by organisms sharing a single system of fertilization; they are distributed discontinuously and their component organisms play analogous economic roles in different local ecosystems. Additionally they are largely redundant packages of genetic information, but that information is related mainly to the economic adaptations of the organisms.

Speciation and Macroevolution

For ST, processes within a species and those that occur on a macroscale are one and the same. Thus evolutionary tendencies reflect the macroscale accumulation of directional natural selection. The adaptationists hold that selection functions as a referee that chooses to maximize reproductive potentials by means of optimization arguments. Macroevolution emerges as the sum of all the small-scale adaptive modifications. Consequently, speciation is a function of adaptive change (Eldredge 1989).

Instead, within the PET framework, change is a function of speciation. For Gould and Eldredge (1974), of the three possible answers to environmental change —adaptive adjustment, extinction, and migration— the most likely is migration. Species track down the same environment as it moves in space. From this, the explanation of stasis is derived. There is more than one good reason not to expect organisms to exhibit evolutionary change even in the face of a serious environmental change. In this way, adaptation becomes a magnet for stability. According to Eldredge, once reproductive isolation has been established, local populations can bring the latent adaptive traits to the fore and rapidly focus them on the particular set of environmental conditions in which they live. This is the trigger to set off a rapid phase of adaptive modification (see Gould & Vrba's 1982 concept of exaptation). For this reason speciation is opportunistic: species persist over long periods, but every so often new species arise in the lineage. If their special habitat persists and they are sufficiently different —in ecological terms— to their near kin as to survive competition, we have a multiplication of not very different species within a given lineage. Macroevolution, then, could be explained by means of species selection[3]. The possibility of species selection within a population of organisms, akin to natural selection, is one of the key propositions of PET.

Evolutionary Theory and Archaeology: Dunnell's Criticism and His Proposition

Within the field of anthropology and archaeology several theoretical schools attempted to follow an evolutionary framework. These schools, blanketed under the general label of evolutionism, include such dissimilar proposals as those of Ameghino (1880), Julian Steward (1955), and Dunnell (1980, 1989). The last has carried out an extensive critique of the different anthropological and archaeological theoretical schools that were labelled as evolutionary. As a general criticism he points out that they were not as faithful to evolutionism as it was formulated in biology. His criticism of Steward's cultural evolutionism, for example, is centred on the following points:

1) Steward was based in contemporary populations' data to explain contemporary populations;

2) cultural evolutionism is tautological: the rules that explain the human record are reformulations of intuitive observations made from that record;

3) cultural evolutionism is vitalist: it attributes causation to the phenomena under study instead of placing it in the theoretical system. Human intentions are the only proximate cause.

4) cultural evolutionism is typological and essentialist: the phenomenal world is constituted by types from which phases and stages are established which are then adjudicated empirical status (Dunnell 1989).

These characteristics are contrary to the theory of evolution as it was defined in the field of biology. Within the attempts Dunnell considers faithful to Darwinism, two strategies are distinguished:

1) that which considers that the sole possible way for the transmission of human phenotypic characters is genetics, a strategy followed by Sociobiology;

2) the one that considers that, by generalizing the principles of biological theory, two ways of transmitting characters can be recognized: the genetic and the cultural. In this last case, it can be said that if culture is a mechanism of transmission then cultural phenomena can be interpreted as those elements of the human phenotype that are generated by this process of transmission. This is a key-point in Dunnell's line of thought as, in his opinion the only important alteration needed by the biological theory of evolution to become a general scientific theory is to increment the number of mechanisms of character transmission.

Dunnell's (1980, 1989) concrete proposal is centred on the direct application of the theory of evolution to the archaeological record. The archaeological record is not, nor does it reflect, human behaviour or populations. In fact it is the lack of behaviour that allows it to be identified as archaeological record. Dunnell posits that the human phenotype possesses two components: the individual (material component) and its behaviour. Both genetic and cultural transmissions are responsible for the phenotype, whether in humans or other animals. Artifacts are the hard part of the phenotypes' behavioural segment. In other words, the objects in the archaeological record are part of human phenotypes of the past: this is so as bird nests and beaver dams are part of those species' phenotypes (v. O'Brien & Holland 1992). Thus, "(...) Artifacts do not 'represent' or 'reflect' something else that is amenable to evolutionary theory; they are part of the human phenotype. Consequently, artifact frequencies are explicable by the same processes as those in biology (...)" (Dunnell 1989:45). Therefore, "(...) the way in which archaeologists have typically acquired and described their data precludes the use of even general evolutionary theory because of the typological metaphysic that underlies traditional practice. Variation, not modal description, is required in an evolutionary view" (Dunnell 1989:49).

Yet it is necessary to bear in mind that artifacts are not units of reproduction. They must be seen in terms of their replicative success (Leonard & Jones 1987) and can be related to the adaptive potential of the humans responsible for their replicative success or failure (O'Brien & Holland 1992). As Borrero well points out (1993), artifacts will increase or decrease in their frequency according to the advantages they afford to their bearers.

Dunnell's proposal opens a door to a scientific application of the evolutionary theory in archaeology. However, it is not enough. I hold that it is necessary to take sides within the debate about the concepts of macro and microevolution.

I believe that part of the failure of the evolutionary schools in anthropology and archaeology—in addition to Dunnell's reservations— is owed to the time-scale differences existing between these disciplines, and the implications these scales should have on an evolutionary theoretical framework. In this sense, as was previously pointed out, the situation of archaeology must be put on the same level as that of palaeontology, since both sciences deal with macro-scale processes though their scales are, of course, not the same.

Theoretical Proposal

In this work it will be considered, following Dunnell (1980 and 1989), that artifacts are part of the human phenotype. Accordingly, a direct reading of the archaeological record will be undertaken. Thus artifacts will be interpreted in the same manner as palaeontologists interpret their fossil populations. But palaeontologists study the phenotypic characters of organisms by grouping them in species (certain morphological differences justify the separation of a collection of organisms from another). This cannot be sustained in the case of the archaeological record: all artifacts included in this work are the product of a single species, *Homo sapiens sapiens*. That is to say, the morphological differences among artifacts do not justify separating their makers into different taxa. The *Homo* evolutionary trend, which involves an increase in brain size and tool production (c.f. Eldredge 1985), brings about a change of scale with regards to the degree of phenotypic differentiation. This, in the case of *Homo sapiens sapiens*, would lead to a concentration of changes in the behavioural phenotype. In this sense, the distinction made by Hull (1980 quoted in Eldredge 1989) between interactors and replicators is useful. Hull considered that "(...) the two sorts of entities that function in selection processes can be defined as follows:

—*replicator*: an entity that passes on its structure directly in replication and

—*interactor*: an entity that directly interacts as a cohesive whole with its environment in such a way that replication is differential" (Hull 1980: 318 quoted. by Eldredge 1989: 139). While most organisms are simultaneously interactors and replicators (in large-scale entities, such as demes), these characteristics can be separated in humans: the interactors would be the artifacts whereas the replicators are the human beings that fashion them and whose reproductive success depends on them. So, as Hull points out, selection can be defined as a process in which the extinction and differential proliferation of the interactors causes the differential perpetuation of the replicators that produced them. From this it follows that good or bad artifact performance is one of the causes of a human population perpetuation or extinction. As Dunnell states (1989), to the extent that artifacts are part of the human phenotype its frequencies can be correlated with the advantages or disadvantages they afford their bearers. In that way it is not a matter of the artifacts being reproduced or that there are genetic mechanisms involved in the process of cultural transmission, but that the frequencies of the artifacts are related to the advantages they offer their users (Borrero 1993).

In addition to Dunnell's proposals, those of the PET will also be followed in this work. Starting out from a Darwinian evolutionary theoretical framework both the fossil record and the archaeological can be conceptualized as coarse-grain records that show long-term, macro-scale trends. Even Dunnell (1980) considers that the stasis-rapid change pattern, explained by the PET, would also apply to the archaeological record. The frequency variations on artifacts can thus be explained in terms of the stasis-rapid change pattern.

On the basis of this theoretical framework and the mentioned assumptions, a model will be formulated to explain bone raw materials exploitation. This model is also based on the considerations put forward in Borrero's (1989-1990) peopling model, although they are not exactly equivalent as Borrero refers to the peopling of a given region, whereas here a model is proposed that will explain the exploitation of a raw material (as it were, the "peopling" of a raw material). Some of the concepts that led to this model were formulated in Scheinsohn (1994-1995) and Horwitz & Scheinsohn (1996).

The Exploitation Model of Bone Raw Materials

The model proposes the lack of knowledge about bone raw materials by the first settlers of a certain region. As this model was formulated on a local basis, what it means is that we assume that the first settlers on the Isla Grande did not know this material. The attempt to apply this model to the regional context will enable this proposition's being accepted or rejected. As was said, even though there exists the exploitation of some bone raw materials in Patagonia, this did not prefigure the development it later acquired on the Isla Grande.

The PET proposal, centred on the stasis-rapid change pattern, transferred to the interpretation of the history of bone raw material exploitation, requires the recognition of at least three phases: experimentation, exploitation and abandonment. These can be defined as follows:

—*Experimentation*: a moment when the properties of the new material are unknown, which requires exploring its possibilities. It is likely— as mentioned in Chapter 2— that bone was not adopted for its own qualities, but as a replacement for some other material (e.g. stone). Thus contact with this raw material allows the exploration of its intrinsic properties, which will have permitted its subsequent exploitation.

The trigger for a stage of this kind can be owed to diverse factors:

1) unavailability of one or several previously exploited raw materials: the unavailability can be permanent or circumstantial. In the case of bone raw materials, possibly they began to be used when stone was not available. This non-availability may have been seasonal, as in the winter, when snow and frozen ground prevent its exploitation. Unless a certain stock of lithic preforms exists, there are certain moments in which it will not have been possible to work that material. However, even at times of rigorous weather, animals are still hunted for food. These offer bones that can serve as a stone substitute, of poor quality but workable. The unavailability of stone resources can also be related to factors of a territorial nature, as in the case of a phase of spatial saturation (see Borrero 1994-1995). An independent line, which would allow this possibility to be tested, consists in proving the existence of maximization (c.f. Franco 1994) in lithic use that a behaviour that might be linked to unavailability;

2) peopling of a new region that offers raw materials not known until then;

3) availability of new raw materials in an already known and explored area: this could be the case in situations of contact, in which one group provides materials unknown to another;

4) technical innovations that enable the use of previously unavailable or unusable materials: e.g. heat treatment that would allow the use of stone that could not be worked previously;

5) novel needs leading to the search for materials with different properties from those of the known ones.

In the case of Isla Grande, experimentation with bone raw materials could better be connected with situations 2 or 5, though a combination with a type 1 situation can not be ruled out, given the region's climatic conditions.

The characteristics of a moment of experimentation are:

1) diversity of basic designs or morphological tool groups (MTI) since basic designs are being explored. It is even to be expected that certain morphologies that exist in other raw materials (stone, for instance) will be found;

2) no standardized basic designs (great variability in morphological or metrical structure);

3) diversity of the bone raw materials employed: bones of different shapes and different species are tested so as to determine their properties;

4) diversity of techniques: there exists no technology suited to the material, so a series of manufacturing processes are looked into that can be applied to the material. The techniques compete with one another.

—*Exploitation*: the moment when a production system (*sensu* Ericson 1984) is put in motion. The general characteristics of this moment are:

1) less diversity of basic designs: experimentation in tool design results in the less efficient being replaced or disappearing and functional designs are retained. This means less diversity or richness than in the previous stage.

2) basic designs standardization (lack of variability in morphological or metric structure): owing to experimentation, the incorporated designs are perfected and standardized;

3) less diversity and standardization of the raw materials employed: certain specific bones will be used to make certain tools;

4) predominance of one or a limited number of selected techniques;

These characteristics should be understood as a general trend, visible on a broad regional and temporal scale.

—*Abandonment*: the raw material is no longer exploited. The causes are numerous. In the particular case of bone, in Tierra del Fuego, it could be assumed that at the moment of contact with European populations, new raw materials incorporation would have led to certain tool morphologies to be made with those new materials. Thus the absence of bone tools could be positively correlated with an increase other materials presence. In addition, certain bone tools groups could have taken new functions, including non-technological ones (see Scheinsohn 1990-1992). In general it can be said that hunter-gatherers adaptive strategies changes could result in certain morphologies becoming useless. Finally, another factor that brings about the abandonment of a raw material is the extinction of the population that exploited it.

Expectations in the Archaeological Record

A series of archaeological expectations for each moment can be derived from the set of mentioned characteristics:

—Experimentation:
a) variability in design and raw materials employed;
c) variability in tool's metric structure (no standardization);
d) coexistence of one or several alternative and competitive techniques;
e) lack of archaeological visibility: in general a moment of experimentation should not produce large quantities of artifacts, which would render them less visible. But if the application of this model starts out from the premise that this stage must be contemporary with the peopling of the Isla Grande (which should be true if the exploitation of bone raw materials in Tierra del Fuego is linked to the exploration of a new territory) this expectation is magnified since the early sites on Isla Grande are few and —given the geological history of the island— most of it must have been under water.

—Exploitation:
a) lack of variability in bone raw materials employed: the use of certain bones has been standardized for certain morphologies, so that some raw materials have been left aside;
b) lack of variability in tool morphological groups;
c) high standardization in tool metrical structure;
d) predominance of one technology;
e) good archaeological visibility.

—Abandonment:
a) there are no bone tools, and this can not be attributed to sample or survival problems.

The next chapters will contrast this model on Isla Grande.

[1] This is the age established for the first known living being, a fossil bacterium.

[2] For instance, how can the hypothesis that 50 million years of evolution in horses are the result of adaptation through natural selection be put to the test? (Eldredge 1989).

[3] It is legitimate here to differentiate the concepts of "species sorting" and "species selection." Species sorting describes the differential death and birth patterns within monophyletic taxons. Instead, species selection is a theory of causation underlying that pattern (Eldredge 1989). But there are other forms of causation besides the selection of species that can generate that pattern. If the causal mechanism appears at a species level it is a real selection of species, but if it appears at a lower level (that of organisms, or the genetic) it would be what Vrba (1980 quoted by Eldredge 1989) considers as the "effect hypothesis".

CHAPTER 7

METHODS AND MATERIALS: FUEGUIAN BONE TOOLS

In this chapter we will define how the previously described model will be evaluated on the basis of a sample of bone tools from Isla Grande de Tierra del Fuego.

Characteristics of the Sample

The sample is made up of bone tools from different archaeological sites. All those sites were excavated systematically, with the exception of a collection belonging to the Facultad de Ciencias Naturales y Museo (Universidad Nacional de La Plata), which was collected in late 19th century by travelers and chroniclers, which purchased or exchanged with fuegians indians. This sample will allow us to compare the evidence coming from an archaeological context and that from an ethnographic context, but for model evaluation is not pertinent, as it is possible to suspect the existence of strong biases introduced by the collectors given the differences it has with those found in archaeological contexts (for details see Scheinsohn 1990-1992).

To be included in this work, fueguian bone tools must comply with the following requisites:

1) be whole or almost so (presence of around 2/3 of the estimated whole of the piece);

2) be identifiable as a tool to the naked eye: those that, on account of their bad state or scant elaboration, were not identifiable as tools, were discarded;

3) have a clear chronological ascription: given the importance of time for contrast the model, only those tools that can be placed within the broad time-span of this study (see below) were analyzed. This forced the leaving aside of many bone tools that had not been found *in situ*, or had no associated radiocarbon dates.

The characteristics of the studied sites are described in Table 7.1. The sites that make up the sample can be located on the Figure 7.1. Due to the requirements enumerated above, the size of samples from each site in this table do not necessarily match with those published by the authors that researched at those sites.

The Fueguian archaeological record is characterized by having the most recent moments of the sequence represented by various briefly occupied sites. In these cases the bone tool samples are small. In contrast, the earlier moments of the sequence are represented by few sites which —like Túnel I— present great temporal depth. As it will be described later, this obliged to treat the sample in a special way.

Analysis of the Tools

Orientation and Segmentation

Right from the time of Gardin's work (1967), the necessity of explaining clearly the criteria to be observed in the analysis of artifacts became evident in archaeology. These criteria must refer to three kinds of rules: of orientation, segmentation, and differentiation (Gardin 1967). In this case, for the morphological description of each bone tool to be analyzed the criteria proposed by Stordeur (1977), Voruz (1984), Camps-Fabrer et al. (1974), and Camps-Fabrer (1977a) were followed. In some cases, given the particular characteristics of the materials under study, terminological modifications were introduced.

The pieces were oriented according to Camps-Fabrer's (1977a) criteria, which are the following (see Figure 7.2):

1) the piece was placed resting on its lower face. The active part or distal end was placed at the furthest distance from the observer, leaving at the proximal end whatever anatomical parts may have been preserved. The object, once placed in this manner, will allow the definition of right and left sides, which correspond to the observer's right and left.

2) by distal end is understood the point, barb, cutting edge, blunted end, or one that shows a convergence of the lateral surfaces. In the case that both ends have a convergence, the distal end is the one that shows most modifications; and should this criterion be insufficient, the end further away from the thickest point of the piece will be considered the distal one. Thus the proximal end is the unworked one, the one that shows remains of percussion, distinctive anatomical features, or the one prepared to receive a haft.

As for the segmentation of the piece, it can be stated that bone artifacts possess a certain volume that allows them to be likened to rectangular parallelepipeds with six sides: the lower or ventral, upper or dorsal, proximal and distal ends, and right and left (Voruz 1983-1984 and 1984). The face that presents remains of spongy tissue, marrow cavity, or less modification is to be considered the lower or ventral face. The opposite one is the upper face and is defined as the more elaborate, more polished, or corresponding to the outside face of the bone. In the case of total similarity of both faces, the determination is left to the observer's judgment.

Likewise, in the upper, lower, left, and right faces three parts were distinguished: mesial, distal, and proximal

Sites	N	Radiocarbon dates (single or máximum and mínimum for the whole site) *	Excaveted surface (m²)	Rich-ness ***	Depositional rate (bone tools in 100 years)	References
Túnel I (TuI)	188	6980± 110 (CSIC 310) 450±60 (Beta 4388)	120	10	0,42	Orquera & Piana (1986-1987); Orquera & Piana (1987); Piana (1984).
Bahía Valentín (BV)	72	200 **	aprox. 25 (many sites)	9	200	Vidal (1985)
Rock-shelter 1 (RS1)	37	970±90	?	10		J. Bird. (unpublished)
Lancha Packewaia (LP)	54	4215±305 (MC 1068) 4900±70 (CSIC 307) 1080±100 (MC 1065) 280 ±85 (CSIC 1064)	64	8	1	Orquera *et al.* (1977)
Túnel VII (TuVII)	43	100±45	68	10	15	Orquera com. pers.
Punta María 2 (PM2)	36	300±100 (AC-43) 250 or younger (GAK - 10316) 720± 50 (LP-237)	35	5	12,33	Borrero (1985) Borrero com. pers.
San Pablo 4 (SP4)	5	modern ****	25	4		Borrero (1985)
Bahía Crossley I (BCI)	13	2730±90 (BETA 25701) 1527±58 (INGEIS 0874, informe 2817)	11	4	1,08	Horwitz (1990)
Shama-kush I (SHI)	4	1220±10	32	3	0,23	Orquera y Piana (1985)
Museo de La Plata (MLP)	60	XIX/XX centuries		7		
Total	512					

* in years BP unless indicated
** Estimation on account of european materials presence.
*** Bone tools morphological groups by site
**** A. Figini (com. pers. to L. Borrero). Age of the sample: between 1750 and 1950 A.D.

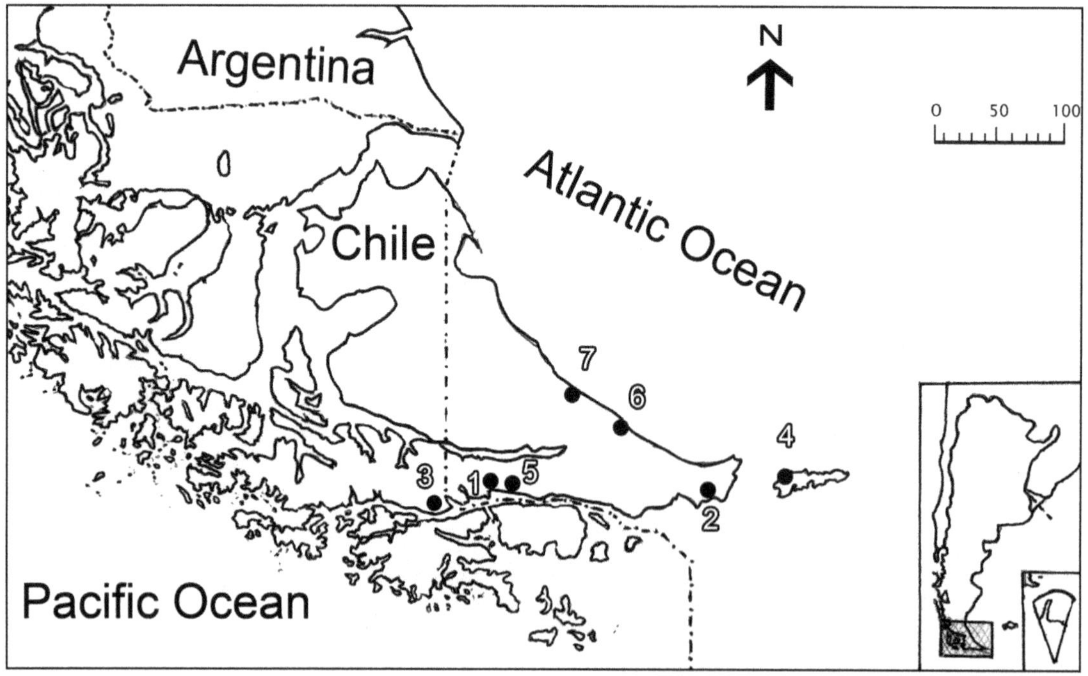

Figure 7.1 – Location of archaeological sites studied in this work
1- Tunel I; 2- BV; 3- RS 1; 4- BCI; 5- SHI; 6- SP4; 7- PM2 and LP

(Camps-Fabrer 1977a). The mesial area or shaft is the area between the ends. The delimitation between the shaft and the distal or proximal part will be carried out in terms of the different technical treatments given to that part or points of inflection (e.g. the end of a polishing, the beginning of a retouched area), anatomical features, or changes in the contour of the piece.

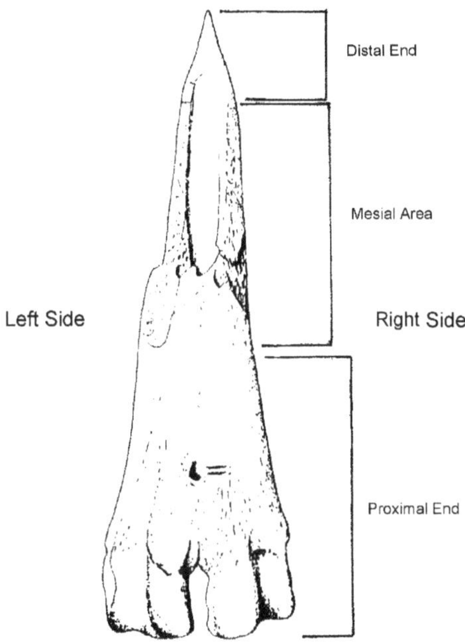

Figure 7.2 – Orientation criteria

Physical, Morphological, and Metric Structure

For each archaeological piece studied a file card was filled. A drawing was also made of each piece, given that this recording work was made between 1990 and 1996 were digital photography was not yet available. On the index-card a series of variables related to the tool's technical, physical, morphological, and metric structure (*sensu* Voruz 1984) were noted down.

For the purposes of the proposed model, the following variables, which correspond to the different structures mentioned, will be analyzed here (see Scheinsohn 1993 and 1990-1992):

a) Physical structure:

—taxonomical category: as such cetacea, camelidae, canidae, pinniped and bird were identified. Nevertheless in the latter taxon a bone piece is sometimes identifiable at a family level. In the case of the camelidae, the only one present in the Tierra del Fuego is the guanaco (*Lama guanicoe*). Both in the case of pinnipeds and that of cetacea it is very difficult to carry out identifications at a lower taxonomic level from incomplete bone pieces.

—bone-blank: in those cases where it is possible, the kind of bone will be identified (i.e. humerus, radius, femur, etc.).

b) Morphological structure:

—shape of the active end: it will be determined if it is a bevel (an edge worked obliquely, formatized on one or two sides, generally by abrasion or burnishing, and which constitutes an active cutting edge *sensu* Aschero 1975), a point (the convergence of the edges of a piece into an end, forming an active apex *sensu* Aschero 1975), barbed point (a point with a barb), or blunt point (a point with a blunted end)

c) Metric structure: the most developed for the purposes of this work. Metric variables are expressed in mm with the exception of angle, which is expressed in degrees and weight, expressed in grams.

The following variables will be taken into account (see Figure 7.3):

—Angle (ANG): of the bevel, point or barbed point. It is not taken in the case of blunt points.

—Maximum length (ML): measured along the longitudinal axis of the piece. It was only considered for the whole pieces.

—Shaft width (SW): it measures the width of the piece on its upper face, at the central part of the shaft.

—Shaft thickness (ST): the distance between the upper and lower faces at the central part of the shaft.

—Active end length (AL): once the active end is defined, both in the case of points and of bevels, following the criteria set out above, its extension is measured longitudinally.

— Shaft Length (SL): resorting to the criteria used to define the shaft, its extension is measured.

—Weight (W): interpretable in terms of the mass it was intended that the piece should have. It is measured only in the case of whole pieces.

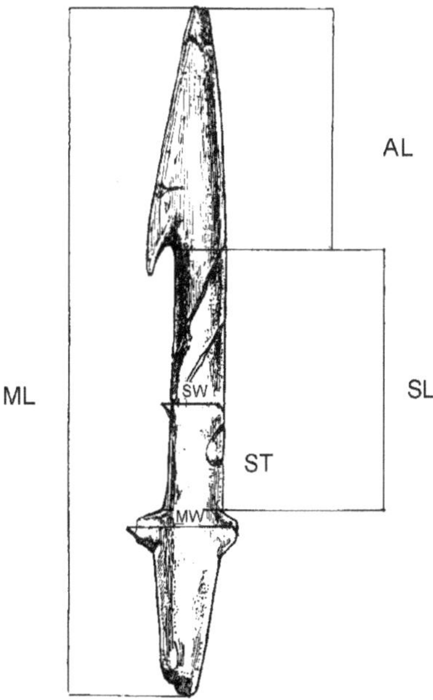

Figure 7.3 – Metrical structure variables

—Indexes:

a) formatization index (FOR, see Voruz 1984 and Camps-Fabrer 1977). It is obtained by means of the formula:

$$\frac{\text{Length of bevel or point}}{\text{Maximum length}} \quad (1)$$

b) resistance index (RES). Obtained with the formula:

$$\frac{\text{Shaft width x shaft thickness}}{\text{Maximum length}} \quad (2)$$

c) elongation index (ELONG, v. Camps-Fabrer 1977). Obtained with the formula:

$$\frac{\text{Maximum length}}{\text{Maximum width}} \quad (3)$$

d) flatness index (FLAT, v. Camps-Fabrer 1977). Obtained with the formula:

$$\frac{\text{Width of shaft}}{\text{Thickness of shaft}} \quad (4)$$

Classification of the sample in morphological groups of tools (MGT)

Bone tools are classified in morphological groups. Two criteria were used in establishing the different groups:

1) the morphology of the active end;

2) the raw material bone— camelid, cetacean, canid, pinniped, bird bones.

These two criteria will allow the evaluation of:

a) the tool's performance, at least in terms of modes of action and functionality hypotheses (see below);

b) the differential mechanical properties of diverse raw materials (see chapter 1 and 3)

c) the relation between a) and b)

Although the morphology of the proximal end is important in terms of the efficiency and action of the tool, it was not included in this classification since the changes appearing in this end do not show the variation exhibited by the distal. However, these variations were taken into account within each class.

Based on those criteria the morphological groups of tools (MGT) were defined, as is presently specified (see Table 7.2 for the combination of criteria):

—Barbed points: known in archaeological literature as harpoon heads, it comprises all those heads that, regardless of the raw material, have a barb at the distal end, or several on one of its sides. They have been classified as:

1) single-barbed heads (SB) made of cetacean bones (v. figure 7.4 g). Two subgroups can be differentiated according to the shape of the barb shield-like base

2) Heads with a single barb made of camelid bones (SBCAM).

3) V-shaped barbed head (VS): made of cetacean bone. They have two barbs set on the same side and in the same space one would occupy, for which reason they look like a single very thick barb divided in two (called "vulpicéfalas" in Piana 1984, see Figure 7.5 d and e);

4) Opposed double-barbed (ODB): they are made of cetacean bone and have a shape similar to European iron spearheads. They have two barbs placed on opposite sides. They are found only in ethnographic collections, and some travelers attribute them to the Alacaluf area (e.g. Lothrop 1928).

5) The same as the previous but in camelid bone (ODBCAM). Likewise, they are only found in the ethnographic collection.

6) Small single-barb heads (SBMICRO), alike to SB but smaller. Given the dimensions, it is inferred they can not have had a technical use;

7) Cetacean bone heads with shield-like tang (PCET TANG). These are single-barb heads that have lost its barb and still have the tang, though with a modified distal end (Figure 7.4 d);

8) Multi-barbed heads in cetacean bone (MB). They are characterized by the presence of two or more barbs placed on one side only (Figure 7.5 a, b and c);

9) Multi-barbed heads in camelid bone (MBCAM). Similar to the preceding.

—Points: they were differentiated as:

10) Cetacean-bone points (PCET): sharpened pieces with variable characteristics (Figure 7.4 f)

11) Bird-bone points (PBIRD): tools with a sharpened distal end, mostly made of cormorant (*Phalacrocorax* sp.) humeri, small procellaridae or anatid tibias. Utilization of different blank-bones would give rise to diverse sub-groups. The proximal end generally retains the epiphysis of the bone (see Figure 7.4 h);

12) Guanaco-bone points (PCAM): tools in which the distal epiphysis of a metapod or another long bone has generally been kept and in which a sharp distal end has been formatized;

13) Pinniped-bone points (PPIN), like the previous;

14) Canid-bone points (PCAN): a single piece with a sharpened end, made of a cubitus;

15) Curved points or "fishhooks" (as it was a small sample and without a clear chronological ascription, this group was not considered in what follows)

—Blunt points:

16) Camelid-bone blunt points (BPCAM). These are tools made of long bones splinters, which may retain part of the epiphysis at the proximal end. The are known as retouchers (Figures 7.4 e);

—Bevels. The bevelled pieces were classified in:

17) Cetacean-bone bevelled pieces (BCET). They are robust tools, generally quadrangular in section, known

in archaeological literature as "spatulas" (Emperaire & Laming Emperaire 1961) or "wedges" (see Figures 7.4 c).

18) Camelid-bone bevelled pieces (BCAM): tools whose bone blank is a guanaco metapod or another long bone, which generally retains an epiphysis at the proximal end. At the distal they have a bevel. They are known as "spatuliform" (Orquera & Piana 1986-1987 - Figure 7.4 a);

19) Pinniped-bone bevels (BPIN). Made of pinniped cubitus or radius. Owing to their bevelled end it might be supposed they were used as chisels, for which reason they were given that name in the archaeological literature of the region (Figures 7.4 b);

20) Bevelled tubes in camelid bone (BTCAM). These are hemidiaphyses or whole diaphyses of long guanaco bones with one end bevelled, but only a few millimetres long. Casiraghi called them "hemidiaphyses with a bevelled end, finished off or polished on one side" (Borrero 1985: Appendix 3 my translation, see Figure 7.6);

The whole of the MGT described for the Isla Grande are not found at any one site. Some are limited temporally and/ or geographically.

Raw Material	Barbed point	Point	Blunt Point	Bevels
Camelid (Guanaco)	SBCAM ODBCAM MBCAM	PCAM	BPCAM	BCAM BTCAM
Cetacean	SB VS ODB SBMICRO MB PCET TANG	PCET		BCET
Avian		PBIRD		
Canid		PCAN		
Pinniped		PPIN		BPIN

Table 7.2. Criteria and morphological groups conformed

Functionality of the morphological groups of tools

As mentioned previously, a key aspect in the design of a tool is its function. One of the necessary ways to define which has been the function of an archaeological tool is the study of wear patterns or microanalysis. However, although works of this kind have been carried out (Nami & Scheinsohn 1997, Scheinsohn & Massi 1996), a full experimental program would require much more time. For

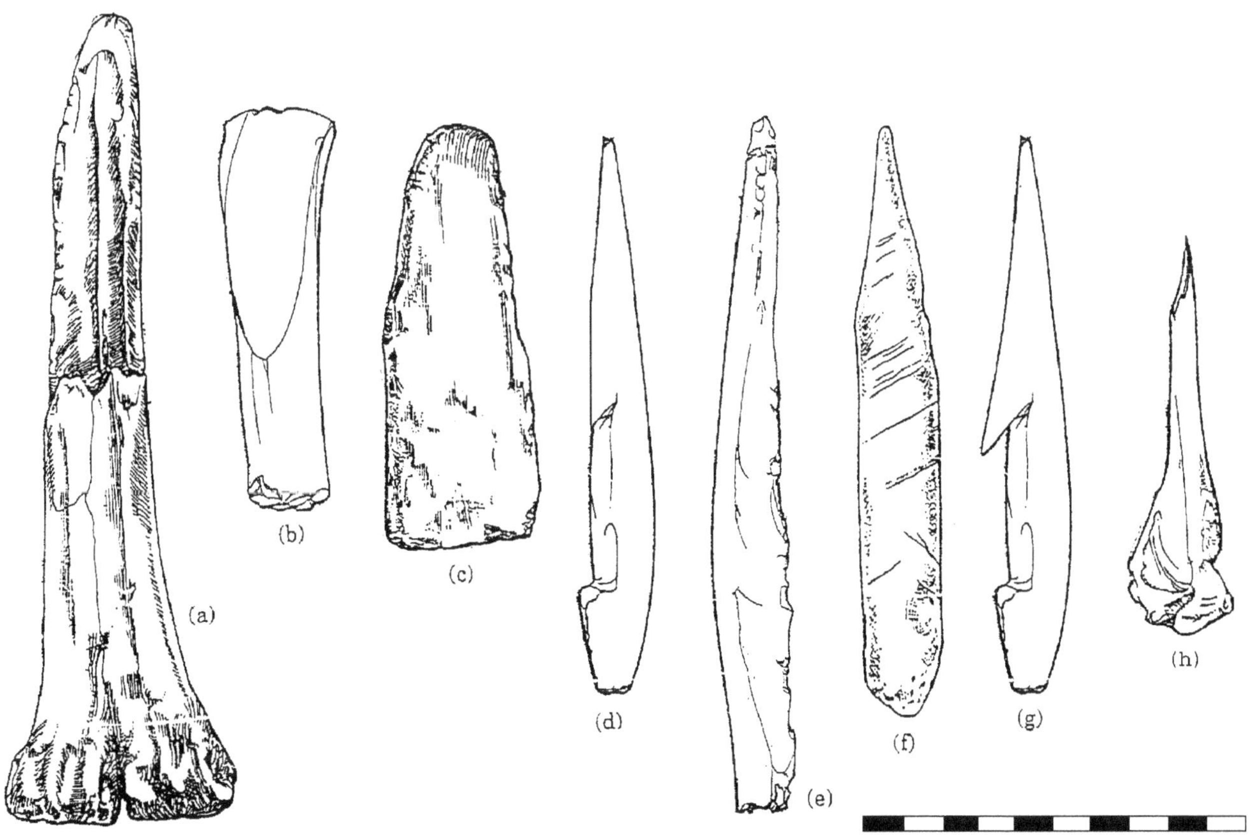

Figure 7.4 – Morphological groups of tools: a) Camelid-bone bevelled pieces (BCAM); b) Pinniped-bone bevels (BPIN); c) Cetacean-bone bevelled pieces (BCET); d) Cetacean bone points with shield-like tang (PCET TANG); e) Camelid-bone blunt points (BPCAM); f) Cetacean-bone points (CETP); g) single-barbed heads (SB); h) Bird-bone points (BIRDP) – Based on a drawing from Diana Alonso.

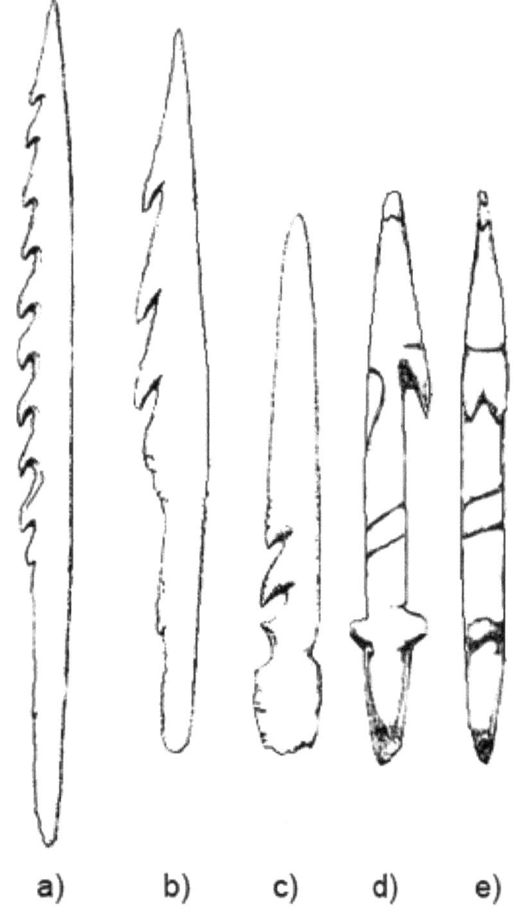

Figure 7.5 – Morphological groups of tools: a), b) and b) Multi-barbed heads in cetacean bone (MB); d) and e) V-shaped barbed head (VS) –Based on a drawing from Diana Alonso

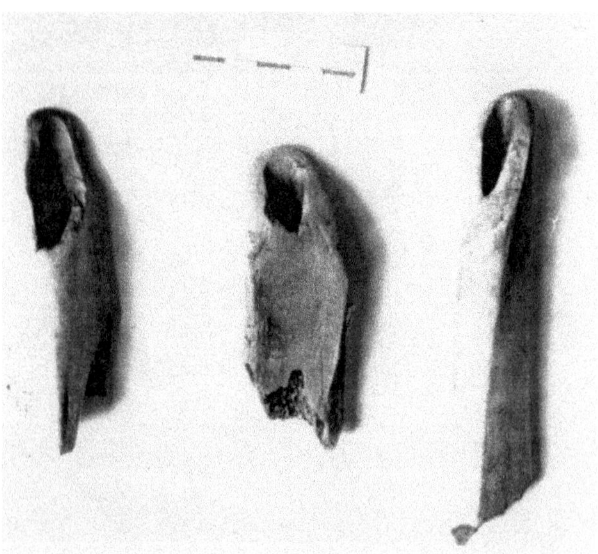

Figure 7.6 – Bevelled tubes in camelid bone (BTCAM)

this reason, in order to evaluate the mechanical properties and design of the tools here involved, the following modes of action were proposed (v. Scheinsohn & Ferretti 1995), based on data obtained from the ethnographic record (Bridges 1892, Bridges 1953, Bridges 1978, Hyades 1885, Hyades & Deniker 1891, Lista 1887, Lothrop 1928, Lovisato 1883) and of an hypothetical character.

The established modes of action are:

1. Rotational penetration;
2. Penetration by impact. Two cases are distinguished:
   a. projectiles: based on velocity and mass. The cases of detachable heads (i) and fixed harpoon heads (ii) were differentiated.
   b. intermediaries: pieces used as intermediary tools;
3. Lever: mode of action linked to the use of tools for the extraction of *Nothofagus* bark;
4. Pressure: the case of retouchers for pressure knapping;
6. Not determined: applied to objects whose mode of action was not determined because there is no ethnographic observations that make reference to tools with this morphology. Their generalized design would make them suitable for a series of wide-range functions.

Table 7.3 presents the modes of action that can be attributed to each MGT in terms of its morphology and the hypotheses of use derived from the ethnographical record.

Analysis of the Samples

One of the expectations of the proposed model suggests that, according to whether the moment is one of experimentation or exploitation, there will be a lesser or greater diversity of tools. For this reason it is necessary to introduce at this point the concept of diversity. The same began to be used by archaeology due to the concern over variability of archaeologists aligned in Darwinian evolutionism (*sensu* Dunnell 1980 and 1989). As Rindos points out: "(...) For the Darwinist, change in diversity is evolution" (1989:22).

Kintigh (1989) considers that the concept of diversity has the following characteristics: 1) it discusses the variation of a nominal variable (i.e. types of artifacts); 2) it is a comparative property of distributions; 3) it has two dimensions: richness (number of different classes present in a sample) and homogeneity (uniformity in the distribution of relative proportions of classes).

If the intention is to analyze the richness of a sample in terms of the quantity of classes, it is first necessary to consider how much of that richness is explained by the size of the sample (Jones et al. 1983). It is known that the diversity of a sample is directly related to the size of the same; that is, the larger a sample is, the greater the diversity to be expected (see Jones & Leonard 1989, Borrero & Lanata 1988). In the particular case presented here it is necessary to bear in mind that samples from the most recent sites are small. Thus one runs the risk of thinking these sites have less diversity and making evolutionary interpretations in that sense, when actually the smaller diversity can be due to the the small size of the sample.

Modes of action	MGT	Functional hypothesis (from ethnographic accounts)
1. Penetration	PCAM	Awl (i.e. Gusinde 1986:478)
	PBIRD	Awl for basket-making (Gusinde 1986)
	PCAN	Awl?. Not specifically mentioned
2. Penetration by impact a.i. detachable harpoon	SB	Detachable harpoon head for sea mammal hunting (i.e. Gusinde 1986:454 y 459)
	VS	Detachable harpoon head
	ODB	Detachable harpoon head (i.e. Hyades 1885:536)
	ODBCAM	Detachable harpoon head.
a ii. Fixed harpoon	MB	Fixed harpoon head (i.e. Hyades 1885:536)
	MBCAM	Fixed harpoon head
	SBCAM	Fixed harpoon head for fishing (Gusinde 1986:226). According to Lothrop (1928) for guanaco hunting
b. intermediaries	BCET	Wood working (i.e.Gusinde 1986:479)
	BPIN	Wood working (Bridges 1892:314)
3. Lever	BCAM	For extracting Nothofagus bark (i.e. Lothrop 1928:65)
4. Pressure	BPCAM	Stone working by pressure (i.e. Lovisato 1883:4)
5. Not determined	BTCAM	Haft?. No references
	PCET TANG	No references
5. Not determined	PPIN	Vignati (1927) mentioned a tool made out of pinniped bone but its use is unknown
	PCET	No references
	SBMICRO	Stirling (1868) mentioned it should accompanied little canoe models (see Piana pers. com. in Scheinsohn 1990-1992) used for exchange with travelers.

Table 7.3 – Morphological groups of tools modes of action

Figure 7.7 shows the relation between the size of a sample and number of classes of bone tools for the different samples under discussion. In this graph a positive correlation (R= 0.6430 and R2= 0.413) can be seen.

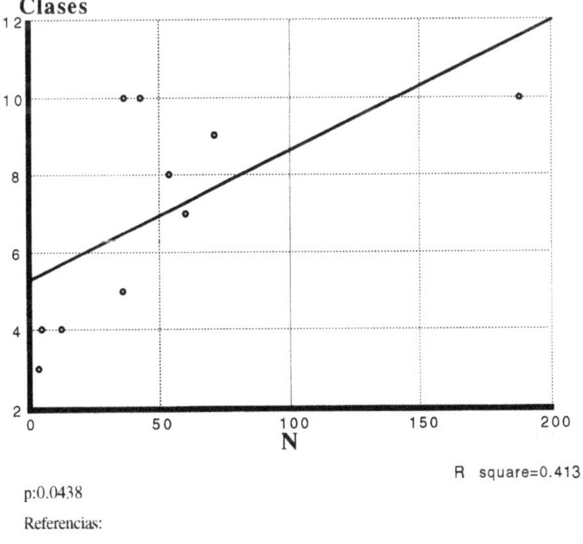

p:0.0438

Referencias:

1: TuI 6: PM2
2: BV 7: SP4
3: RS1 8:BCI
4: LP 9: SHI
5: Tu VII 10:MLP

Figure 7.7 – Regression for simple size (N) and MGT from sites analyzed in this work.

There are other factors that may influence the observed richness; Bobrowsky and Ball (1989) evaluated some of them. Among those factors they mention: a) biased collection: one that tends to favour only certain types or a wide variety of them; b) problems related to the typology employed (if it tends to splitting classes or lumping them together); c) the researcher's mistakes or inexperience. Despite the fact that some of these problems might be tracked down in the samples under study, it must be pointed out that, by using the same classification criterion to study them, factor c) remains, at least, minimized.

Nevertheless, if it is a question of managing a regional scale— as is here the intention— the treatment of the material can not be carried out studying the samples of each site since, then, another sort of problem arises.

The Possibility of Comparison between Sites

Sites have a different degree of temporal depth. Late sites may present a single archaeologically fertile layer, of little thickness and small samples, while others, whose occupation was longer in time, have several fertile layers of great tickness and large samples. This pattern can be related as much with guidelines for the occupation of space at late moments as with problems of archaeological visibility for sporadically occupied ancient sites (see chapter 4).

In addition, the model requires the study of bone tools according to different time segments. The fact that the sets to be analyzed belong to multi-layered sites or those with a single fertile layer and with different chronologies presents a serious problem as regards how to segment the sample. To consider segmentation on the basis of sites would be an error as, how can a site such as Túnel I, which spans 6000 years of occupation, be compared with other sites in which there are only one or two radiocarbon dates with shorter periods of occupation?

As a way of dealing with this problem it was decided to group the different samples from sites in time segments, of the same duration in time, on a regional scale. In this way comparisons were made easily between assemblages of different chronology and sample size. In addition, the samples generated by time segmentation allowed to conform a larger size of sample and thus the bias produced in the richness by size sample was reduced.

Thus multi-layered sites were divided into time segments according to the radiocarbon dating of their layers. Each of these subdivisions was included together with other sites located in the same time span, in one of the predetermined time segments.

Owing to this— as mentioned above— tools that could not be assigned a chronology allowing their inclusion within some time segment were not considered in this analysis. This circumstance affected the representation of a single MGT, that of curved points or fishhooks.

A precondition of the model as much as of the characteristics of the available samples was that the time segments (TS) should be "coarse-grained." In this way four time segments were determined, as they figure in Table 7.4

The small number of radiocarbon dates per site (with the exception of Túnel I) prevented the application of the method of temporal segmentation used by Yacobaccio and Guraieb (1994) at the Pinturas river, who carried out 39 dates for five sites.

For the first two TS, arbitrary periods of 3000 years were taken, which was what the available radiocarbon dates allowed. TS III spans only half that time (1500 years). This segmentation arose as a compromise solution to be able to compare the samples. To have done it otherwise would have made the older sites seem under-represented (i.e. by being in a single, longer TS) or the more recent, over-represented (for being distributed in several shorter TSs, while many of the older segments of the same duration would have no sites). This is why it was decided to modify the time span of TS III.

	Sites and layers	**Radiocarbon dates**	**Laboratories**	**N**
Time Segment I TS I (7500-4500 AP)	-layer F inferior and E from Tul (*) -layer D of Tul (*) -layer Dz, Xy and E from LP	6980 ±110 6070 ± 70 5630 ±120 6140 ±130 4215 ± 305 4900 ± 70	Beta 2517 CSIC 310 AC 683 Beta 2819 MC 1068 CSIC 307	166
Time Segment II TS II (4500 -1500 AP)	-BCI - layer C from Tul	2730 ± 90 1527 ± 58 4300 ± 80 3530 ± 90	 Beta 4385 AC 702	35
Time Segment III TS III (1500 AP -now)	-RS1 -SHI -layers D, A, B and C from LP -layer Beta from TU I -TU VII -SP4 -PM2 -BVS1	970 ± 90 (**) 1220 ±10 1080 ± 100 280 ± 85 450 ± 60 100 ± 48 1750-1950 300 ± 100	 MC 1065 CSIC 1064 Beta 4388 INGEIS AC 43 Relative dating	221
Time Segment IV TSIV (Museo de La Plata collection)				60

(*) Taken from Orquera y Piana (1986-1987 cuadro I: 214).
(**) Unpublished radiocarbon dating obtained by Junius Bird from a wood fragment. Taken from his field notebook stored at the American Museum of Natural History.

Tabe 7.4 – Time segments composition

From the point of view of the quantity of sites it encompasses, as much as its geographical variety and size, the sample belonging to TS III is excellent. This is the only time segment in which differences caused by the two phytogeographical regions inhabited by prehistoric human populations on the island can be evaluated (Punta María 2 and San Pablo 4 are in the Fueguian Park district, whereas the remaining sites are in the Subantarctic forest).

TS IV overlaps with TS III, but owing to its very limited time span (19th century and the beginning of the 20th) and because it would be representing a biased situation due to the moment of contact with the Europeans (see above) it was kept apart.

The distribution of frequencies resulting from each MGT per time segment figures in Table 7.5.

As steps to check the concordance of these data with the proposed model, the following will be analyzed:

1) differences in the use of different bone raw materials: in this case these differences will be evaluated simply by considering the percentage of raw materials per time segment;

2) distribution of the groups per time segment and their diversity. The quantity and MGT present will be evaluated in each time segment in percentage terms. To evaluate the richness, both the quantity of classes per TS and the Shannon-Weaver index will be used. Although the use of this index has been criticized (v. Bobrowsky & Ball 1989), its wide employment in archaeology will permit comparisons. The index, besides, can be used provided the necessary precautions are taken as regards the size of the sample;

3) the absence of standardization or variation of the metric variables by analyzing a certain MGT per time segment. It is to be expected that the segment with most variability in terms of raw materials and richness of morphological groups, will also present morphological groups with less standardization or greater variability in the metric variables, since we would be dealing with a moment of experimentation in which the morphological groups are still being explored. Therefore this expectation of greater metric variability in the segment of greater material and morphological variability will also be put to the test. This variability will be measured in terms that it is expected that the metric variables of the tools belonging to a time segment considered to be a moment of experimentation should show greater amplitude around the mean than that same variable considered in the same morphological group but in the other time segments representing an exploitation moment.

One of the problems that had to be solved was how to evaluate statistically that lack of standardization. Initially the proposal was the possibility of considering the analysis of variance (ANOVA) for the diverse metric variables.

	BPCAM	PCAM	SBCAM	MBCAM	ODB CAM	BCAM	BT CAM	P CAN	PCET	PCET TANG	SB	SB MICRO	MB	VS	ODB	BCET	PBIRD	BPIN	PPIN	TOTAL POR ST
I	4					5			5		16	3	8	6		6	113			166
II									1		2		2	1		7	21	1		35
III	22	18	6			9	16	1	19	22	15	7	8			19	53	3	3	221
IV	3		2	3	3						23		18		8					60
TOT	29	18	8	3	3	14	16	1	25	22	56	10	36	7	8	32	187	4	3	482

Table 7.5 – MGT Frequencies by time segment

But this analysis supposes a normal distribution, which cannot be held *a priori* in the case of a population of archaeological artifacts. In addition, in such a case the size of the sample would also influence the results. The possibility was also considered of analyzing directly the values obtained in each variable by the standard deviation but, as this statistic is obtained by means of variance, it has the same drawbacks as ANOVA. Finally, thanks to a suggestion by Dr. Hugo Yacobaccio, it was concluded that box-plot graphs could solve the problem. These graphs are based on the comparison and analysis of percentiles. Thus they have the advantage of not being determined by the particular values of the series but by the number and order of the terms, and are not affected by extreme values (Toranzos 1971). Box plot allows clear observation of the dispersion of the values of the variables in percentile terms. The five horizontal lines of the box represent the 10th, 25th, 50th, 75th, and 90th percentile. Values below the 10th percentile and above the 90th are represented as dots. The 50th percentile coincides with the mean. Thus it was considered that a variable could be defined as standardized if the dispersion around the mean is limited. If the dispersion is wide then we are facing variability, which can be related with an experimental moment, as established in the model. At the same time and with the necessary precautions— since they depend on the size of the sample and normal distribution— the standard deviation and arithmetical mean of these variables will be analyzed.

Before the results of this analysis, the mechanical determinations found for the bone raw materials used in Tierra del Fuego will be presented.

CHAPTER 8

DETERMINATION OF THE MECHANICAL PROPERTIES OF BONES USED AS RAW MATERIALS IN TIERRA DEL FUEGO

Introduction

As was stated in Chapter 3, though there are a number of bone characteristics that are constant in different animal species— such as the histological pattern (defined between woven and lamellar bone) and the chemical nature of the matrix (altered only by the high or low calcification of specialized bones) c.f. Ferretti Ms.— the variability in the process of bone modelling and remodelling brings about significant differences between the different bones of different species or even the same bone but belonging to different species. These differences are related to the degree of porousness, the transformation of compact into cancellous bone, the disposition of trabecular tissue, the thickness of bone walls, the area and moment of inertia of the diaphysary sections of bones, and the general morphology, among other factors (Ferretti Ms.) When, as happens in this work, bone raw materials are considered, differences among the diverse types of bone and animal species are relevant.

One of the axis of this work rests on the determination of the properties of bone raw materials exploited in Tierra del Fuego. These determinations were deemed essential since they allowed:

a) the evaluation of differences between bone raw materials utilized in Tierra del Fuego in quantitative and qualitative terms;

b) the generation of expectations with respect to the functional aptitude of each tool in tems of its raw material. Thus, in adding this knowledge to that of the tool's morphology and data available from the ethnographic record, one can evaluate whether the employment of certain raw materials for the manufacture of certain artifacts obeyed criteria related to the efficiency of the material or other criteria

Since no bibliography existed that offered these determinations for the moment I wrote these work (the one and only reference to the animal species of Patagonia being that of *Aptenodyptes* sp. in Currey 1987), it was necessary to carry out specific mechanical tests. This involved entering the territory of bone biomechanics. The use of the techniques and methods of bone biomechanics for the solution of archeological questions has few precedents (Albrecht 1977, and Mac Gregor & Currey 1983). Given the theoretical and technical difficulties this new field of research presented, this work required a joint undertaking with other specialists. In the first place, there was a collaborative effort with engineers of the Comisión Nacional de Energía Atómica (CNEA, the National Atomic Energy Commission), specialized in the Sciences of Materials. The results of this first approach were presented in Herbst *et al.* (1994). However, as the specialists were not aware of the specific problems of bone, the continuation of the work was carried out in collaboration with a specialist in that field, Dr. José Luís Ferretti (Centro de Metabolismo Fosfocálcico - Universidad Nacional de Rosario and the Instituto de Investigaciones Metabólicas —IDIM— Buenos Aires city/ Phosphorus/ Calcium Metabolism Centre - Rosario National University and the Institute of Metabolical Research in Buenos Aires). The results of the work were published in Scheinsohn *et al.* (1991), Ferretti *et al.* (1991 and 1992), Scheinsohn & Ferretti (1994 a and b), and Ferretti & Scheinsohn (1997). A more conclusive work is Scheinsohn & Ferretti (1995). In this chapter a summary of the determinations derived from all these works will be presented.

Species Exploited in Tierra del Fuego and Tool Functionality

Whereas in continental Patagonia only certain guanaco (*Lama guanicoe*) and bird bones were exploited, in Tierra del Fuego those of the guanaco, pinnipeds (*Arctocephalus australis* and/ or *Otaria flavescens*), cetacea (e.g. the sperm whale *Phiseter catodon*) canidae and different birds (mainly *Phalacrocorax* sp., Procellarians, and Anatids, see Scheinsohn *et al.* 1992) were exploited.

In the Isla Grande sample, a high recurrence in the use of certain bones as blanks for certain tools was observed, (e.g. cormorant humeri to fashion bird bone points or awls). Then, we have assumed that the choice of those specific bones implied the choice of their mechanical properties, and that these have an intimate relationship with tool's functionality (Scheinsohn & Ferretti 1995).

The assignation of functionality of an archaeological tool can be inferred by a variety of ways. The more accurate is the so-called functional analysis or microwear analysis. This requires the implementation of an experimental program, involving a great deal of time (cf. Le Moine 1990 for bone tools). Although in this work a few limited experimental series were carried out (v. Scheinsohn & Massi 1996, Nami & Scheinsohn 1997, and Scheinsohn 1997), a complete research would require more time than the available. Another line of research is the attribution of functionality hypothesis from the ethnographical record by seeking the diverse functions recorded for each artifact. In this case there can be inexactitudes in the sources, or missing data.

Given the problems posed by these methods, tool morphology and the properties of its raw materials allow a series of expectations to be made with regards to their functional fitness, at least on a general level.

Thus, once functional analysis was discarded, a combination of data collated from the ethnographical record and a morphological analysis of the tool and the mechanical properties of its raw material were considered. The functional hypotheses— elaborated from the ethnographical record— will be presented in terms of modes of action. The hypotheses will be compared with the expectations deriving from the properties of the raw materials involved and the morphology of the tool in question. If there is agreement between these lines of analysis it is possible, on the one hand, to support these hypotheses with argumentations generated in other ways and, on the other, to evaluate whether the raw materials for tools were selected on the basis of the relation between their mechanical properties and their function.

Methods and Materials

For mechanical testing, three-point bending was chosen, as it was the one that offered least practical difficulties to carry out (see Figure 3.5, Chapter 3). Given the diversity in size of the different bones involved (see Table 8.1), it was necessary to standardize the way of testing them, as those variations in size would have influenced the results. For this reason it was decided samples consisting in rectangular prismatic pieces should be made, to be extracted from the cortical region of the anterior mesial face of the diaphysis of the different bones (see Table 8.1). The pieces measured 1.5 to 2.5 mm in width, and 4 cm in length, and were regularized by abrasion.

The test pieces were placed between two supports with a separation of 13 mm, constant for all the tests, and loaded at their centre at a growing rate of 1 N/min until they fractured (see similar tests in Evans 1973, Baker & Haugh 1979, Currey 1984 and 1987, Ferretti *et al* 1992).

The following geometrical properties of the mean section of the whole bones were determined with a caliper:

—External and internal height (H,h) and width (B,b) (see Figure 3.7)

—Area of the bone (in mm^2)

—Moment of inertia relative to the horizontal axis (Ix, in mm4): in the case of ellipse-shaped sections (pinniped bones) the moment of inertia was calculated as

$$Ix = 3.14\ (H3B - h3b)\ /\ 64 \qquad (1)$$

In the case of sections with more complex contours— such as those of guanaco bones— it was calculated by means of a special computer program.

Testing pieces, being of the same shape and size, allowed us to obtain results that can be considered independent of the geometry of the bone. In this case, in order to carry out the calculations related to the material properties— which were to be on the basis of the test pieces and not the whole bones— the following properties were taken into account:

—vertical (H) and horizontal (B) cross section, in mm

—moment of inertia relative to the horizontal axis, in mm4

$$Ix = H3.B/4 \qquad (2)$$

For each test piece a typical Load (W)/Deflection (d) curves was obtained. From these curves it was possible to determine the following structural properties:

— Load-bearing capacity (Ultimate load or ultimate strength) Wf, in N

— Stiffness or load-to-deformation ratio, in N/mm

$$Wy/dy \qquad (3)$$

— Elastic energy absorption (EAC), in N.mm

$$Eabs = Wy.dy/2 \qquad (4)$$

All the bones were tested in a dry state, which can bring about a shortening of the plastic portion and a change in the slope of the elastic part of the curve W/d (cf. Scheinsohn & Ferretti 1995). However, if it is borne in mind that bone tools must possibly be in similar conditions, at least at the time of use (since very fresh bones would not be usable as tools because the fat attached to them would prevent a firm grasp), and that all of them were in the same situation, the results are pertinent.

Regarding the material properties of the bone, Young's elastic modulus (in MPa) was calculated as follows:

$$E = Wy\ L3\ /\ 48\ dy\ Ix \qquad (5)$$

The way to determine material properties by this procedure is indirect: it is done starting out from certain structural and geometrical properties ascertained directly with some error, from the load/ deformation curves, and presupposing a mechanical and geometric isotropy, which is just an approximation. Therefore the results have a relative or comparative value, but not a descriptive one in a strict sense (Ascenzi & Bell 1972).

Expectations

Based on the morphology of archaeologically known bone tools and the data obtained from the ethnographical record, each of the former were assigned a mode of action and expectations relative to the mechanical properties expected of the raw materials with which the tools were made (see Table 8.2).

In this way the following modes of action were defined (Scheinsohn & Ferretti 1995):

Taxa	Bone Blank	Bone Blank Size (lenght mean in mm.)	Procedence	Testings
Cetacean (*Physeter catodon*)	Clavicle	950	Ea. Viamonte Tierra del Fuego	7
Guanaco (*Lama guanicoe*)	Metapod	217,5	Bahía Valentín Tierra del Fuego	16
Pinniped (*Arctocephalus australis*)	Radii	110,33	Cabo Polonio R.O. del Uruguay	9
Pinniped (*Arctocephalus australis*)	Cúbitus	145	Cabo Polonio R.O. del Uruguay	6
Cormorant (*Phalacrocorax* sp.)	Humeri	122	Canal Beagle Tierra del Fuego	6

Table 8.1 – Bone samples characteristics

(1) Penetration: tools used in this way should be made of a material with a high elastic modulus (E) so as to resist the forces they are subjected to without breaking.

(2) Leverage: tools used for this mode of action, given the elongated modulus of the pieces, should possess good geometric and structural properties, specially their moment of inertia (Ix) and stiffness (Wy/dy). The longer a tool, the greater must the Ix of its section be to afford it reasonable resistance.

(3) Pressure: in this case the Ix of the piece is also important. Yet the bone blank must have a significant E so as not to give way to the material that is going to be worked.

(4) Impact Penetration: in this case two types have been differentiated. In one (4a) it is a penetration through impact in which the mass of a projectile is the critical factor, as an harpoon head; while in the other (4b) tools are used as intermediaries between a striking tool and a material to be worked, which generally have a beveled end (see Gusinde 1986: 479, Spegazzini 1882: 162, Cooper 1967: 218 among others).

			Structural properties			Geometrical properties	Material properties
Tool	Mode of action	Bone	Wf (*) X S	Wy/dy (**) X S	Eabs (***) X S	Ix (+) (****) X S	E (*****) X S
Awl	1.Penetration	Cormo-rant Humerus	0,42 0,14	73,4 26	4,49 2,88	77 24	13458 2637
Decorti-cator	2.Leverage	Guanaco Metapod	0,88 0,29	154,2 76,0	4,5 3,5	7643 3858	4823 1751
Flaker	3.Pressure	Guanaco Metapod	"	"	"	"	"
Fixed harpoon heads	4ai. Impact Penetration	Guanaco Metapod Ceta-cean clavícle	" 2,7 0,86	" 95,2 13,9	" 17,58 10,75	(+) (+)	" 822 244
Detachable harpoon heads	4aii. Impact Penetration	Ceta-cean clavícle	2,7 0,86	95,2 13,9	17,58 10,75	(+)	822 244
Point	5.Undetermined	Ceta-cean clavícle	"	"	"	(+)	"
Chisel	4b. Impact Penetration	Pinniped Radus	1,5 0,76	150,1 60,6	8,11 5,43	1426 446	4664 2418
Chisel	4b. Impact Penetration	Pinniped Cubitus	0,93 0,7	201,4 34,3	17,24 9,34	1007 367	2417 947

References:
X: mean S: Standard deviation
(*) in N (****) in mm⁴
(**) in N/mm (*****) in MPa
(***) N.mm
(+) This column refers to bone blank moment of inertia. Its value is noted only when bone blank and tool moment of inertia is the same

Table 8.2 – Tools, modes of action and mechanical properties of bone blanks

Tools used as projectile heads, in turn, can be classified in two groups:

(4ai) Fixed harpoon heads: when the head is firmly tied to the shaft. In this case an inverse relation can be expected between E and Ix. If the E material is low, the Ix, whether the bone's or that obtainable by the tool design, must be high, and vice-versa.

(4aii). Detachable harpoon heads: the head is loosely tied to the shaft. Thus, when a harpoon strikes a prey, the head comes loose from the shaft and remains tied to it by a longer or shorter thong. The handle acts as a float, showing where the prey is and preventing it from sinking. This harpoon was used to hunt sea mammals (v. Bridges 1978 [1879]:93; Hyades & Deniker 1891:353; Gusinde 1986:498-500; Hyades 1885:536-537 among others). In this case deformability would be more important than resistance since the fracture of the head would mean losing the prey and, in these conditions, an excessively rigid material would tend to break. It must show a lower E and Wy/dy than in the previous instance. They must also have a considerable energy absorption capacity (Eabs) to resist impact without breaking.

Tools used as intermediaries (4b) should manifest high values in Wf and Eabs, so as to accumulate large amounts of energy in elastic conditions without suffering microfractures.

Results

The data in Tables 8.2 and 8.3 link the expectations with the results obtained in the tests.

Thus Table 8.3 shows that:

—In the case of the mode of action 1 (penetration) cormorant humeri and the long bones of the guanaco were used for tool making. Both have a high E expectation. The difference resides in that guanaco bones have high stiffness whereas in cormorant it is low. In this case it must be remembered that tools made with cormorant humeri are of a smaller size (see Table 8.1). The size of guanaco bones is advantageous for the production of long tools made of high quality material without a great increase in deformability (relatively high Wy/dy values) though with a slight sacrifice of the elastic module. This makes them suitable for, with the same morphology and mode of action, working different materials in accordance with a given tool size. This presumption is corroborated

			Structural properties			Geometrical properties	Material properties
Mode of action	Expected Mechanical Properties	Bone	Wf (1)	Wy/dy (2)	Eabs (3)	IX (4)	E (5)
1. Penetration	<E	Cormorant Humerus	*	*	*	*	***
		Guanaco Metapod	*	***	*	***	**
2.Leverage	< Wy/dy < Ix	Guanaco Metapod	*	***	*	***	**
3.Pressure	< Ix	Guanaco Metapod	*	***	*	***	**
4ai. Impact Penetration	<E y >Ix or <Ix y >E	Guanaco Metapod	*	***	*	(+)	**
		Cetáceo clavicle	***	*	***	(+)	*
4aii. Impact Penetration	>E >Wy/dy <Eabs	Cetacean clavicle	***	*	***	(+)	*
4b. Impact Penetration	<Wf <Eabs	Cetacean clavicle	***	*	***	(+)	*
		Pinníped Radius	**	**	**	*	*
		Pinníped cubitus	**	***	***	*	*

>: minor <: major

(1): * between 0,42 and 1,00, ** between 1,00 and 1,6 *** over 1,6 on cf. Table 8.2

(2): * between 70 and 110, ** between 111 and 150 *** over 151on cf. Table 8.2

(3): * between 4 and 7, ** between 7,1 and 11 *** over 11,1 on cf. Table 8.2

(4): * between 70 and 2570, ** between 2571 and 5070 *** over 5070 on cf. Table 8.2

(5): * between 800 and 4800, ** between 4801 and 8800, *** over 8801 on cf. Table 8.2

(+) This column refers to bone blank moment of inertia. Its value is noted only when bone blank and tool moment of inertia is the same

Table 8.3 – Expectations and results on bone mechanical properties

by the ethnographical record which reports the use of guanaco bones as awls for leatherwork, whilst cormorant awls would be used for basket-making (Gusinde 1986:478, Cooper 1946:89, Skottsberg 1913:602 among others).

—As regards mode of action 2 (leverage) only guanaco bones were used, which coincide with the high Ix and stiffness required (Wy/dy). However it were, as regards material properties, a bone with a relatively high E is being used.

—In the case of mode of action 3 (pressure) the use of guanaco bones was recorded. To the extent that they were fashioned making use of much of the bone's original morphology, they agree with the expectation of a high Ix.

—For mode of action 4ai (penetration by impact by a fixed harpoon head) the use of two bones was observed: cetacean and those of the guanaco. The latter fulfills the expectation of high E, unlike the former. In the case of cetacean bone, harpoon heads were designed with a larger Ix than that of guanaco bone, in which this was unnecessary owing to the high E.

—As for mode of action 4aii (impact penetration by detachable harpoon head) the tools were made of cetacean bone, which agrees with the expectations of low E and stiffness (Wy/dy). Cetacean bone is the one that show the greatest Eabs, which also agrees with expectations.

—As for mode of action 4b (penetration by impact via an intermediary) cetacean and pinniped bones were used. The latter, used by maintaining the original shape of the bone, will have had a notable resistance to fracture. In the case of cetacean bone, stiffness was provided by the design of robust tools, which is allowed by the great size of the bones used as blank. Both have a great capacity of energy-absorption, which agrees with the expectations.

Conclusion

If the modes of action have been correctly assigned, the chosen raw materials offer mechanical properties suitable to answer the requirements of the tool. In all cases it has been possible to corroborate the functional hypothesis derived from the ethnographical record by an independent pathway, such as the determination of the mechanical properties of bone raw materials.

Guanaco bone, given its material and geometrical properties, offers a wide range of possibilities. Still, the availability of a larger variety of raw materials— as is the case in Tierra del Fuego— enables mechanical properties to be increased.

Many tools retain the geometrical properties of the bones they are made of, but others (specially those made of cetacean bone) acquire different properties via the design of the tool.

These results will be collated with the ones deriving from the metric and morphological analysis of the tools.

CHAPTER 9

RESULTS OF THE MORPHOLOGICAL ANALYSIS OF BONE TOOLS

This chapter will present the results of the metrical and morphological analysis of the bone tool samples, segmented as established in Chapter 7.

Differences in the usage of bone raw materials

Global analysis of the samples. As one can appreciate from Figure 9.1, in the whole of the sample, comprising all the temporal segments, cetacean bones predominate, (40%) together with bird bone (38%), followed by guanaco bone (18%) and pinniped bone (4%). Canid bone, which is frankly marginal (0,2%), does not figure in the graph.

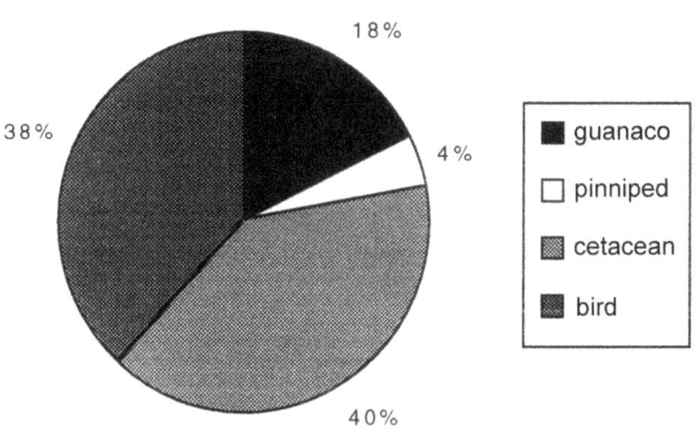

Figure 9.1 – Taxa utilized as bone raw materials

Leaving aside the sample of Time Segment IV (of ethnographic origin), the characteristics of which were defined previously, percentages show only slight variation (see Figure 9.2): there is slightly more bird bone presence (44%) and a decrease in cetacean (34%), but both continue to predominate. The comparison of the two samples can be seen in Figure 9.3. Hence it results that the ethnographic sample causes an increase in tools fashioned from cetacean bone and, to a smaller degree, from guanaco bone, while the rest remain the same.

According to these results, the most widely used bone raw materials in the whole sequence are those of cetaceans and birds. However, the abundance of bird bone would seem to be magnified by the Túnel I site sample, with a total of 121 PBIRD, which makes up 61% of the total tool sample. If this sample is left aside, bird bone points would attain a percentage similar to that of guanaco bone (17%). In addition, as will be seen further on, the dominance of these raw materials has not been uniform along the sequence.

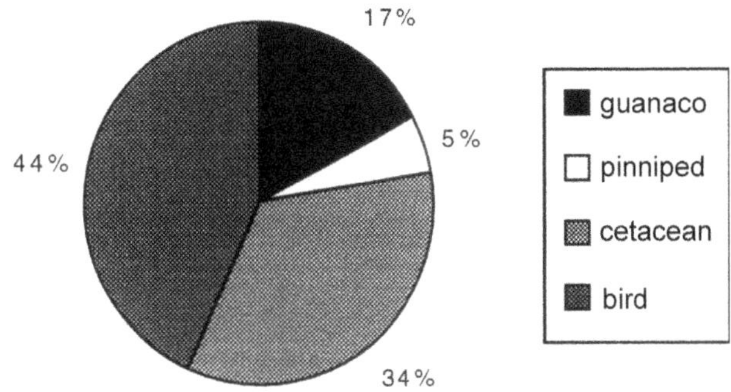

Figure 9.2 – Taxa utilized as bone raw materials excluding ethnographical sample (TS IV)

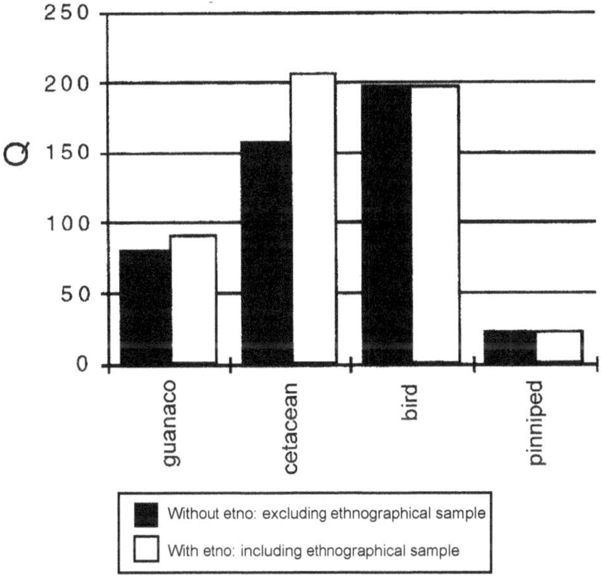

Figure 9.3 – Bone raw materials: taxa utilized with and without ethnographical sample (TS IV)

Raw materials in the different time segments

Segment I (7500-4500 AP)

For this moment four employed raw materials have been detected (Figure 9.4): bird (predominating at 65%), cetacean (22%), pinniped (8%), and guanaco (5%). It can be thus stated that the beginning of the sequence starts out with a fairly high diversity of raw materials. At this time guanaco bone is less important than that of pinnipeds. In fact, this is the time segment in which pinniped bones acquire greatest importance in tool production. The predominance of bird bones, as mentioned, must be related to the high representation of Site Tu I in this sample. If one leaves aside Tu I, the time segment is dominated by cetacean (53%), followed by pinniped (20%), bird (15%), and guanaco (12%). All the same, Tu I is part of the sample even if it does increase the amount of bird bone, and must be taken into account.

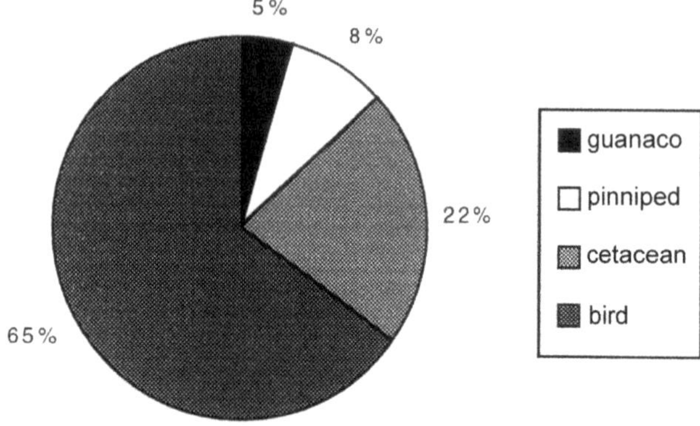

Figure 9.4 – Taxa utilized as bone raw materials in TS I.

Segment II (4500-1500 AP)

As is seen in Figure 9.5, and in relation to the previous period (Figure 9.4), use of cetacean bone increases (37%), that of birds (60%) and pinnipeds (3%) decreases, and there is no record of guanaco bone. This absence could be owed to a problem of sample size, since this segment has a reduced N. Besides, it was to be expected that the BC I sample should contain no guanaco bones as at this site, located on the Isla de los Estados, there exists no evidence of those mammals.

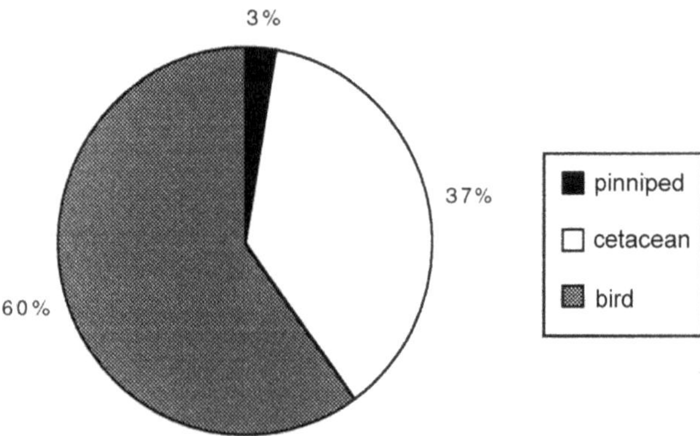

Figure 9.5 – Taxa utilized as bone raw materials in TS II.

Segment III (1500- AP the present)

In Figure 9.6 can be observed an increase in the use of cetacean bone (44%) and a reduction in that of bird bone (23%), while that of pinnipeds remains constant (3%). Guanaco bone makes its reappearance at a higher percentage than in TS I (30%). There is only one case of a canid bone tool. This segment is the one that shows the greatest diversity of raw materials.

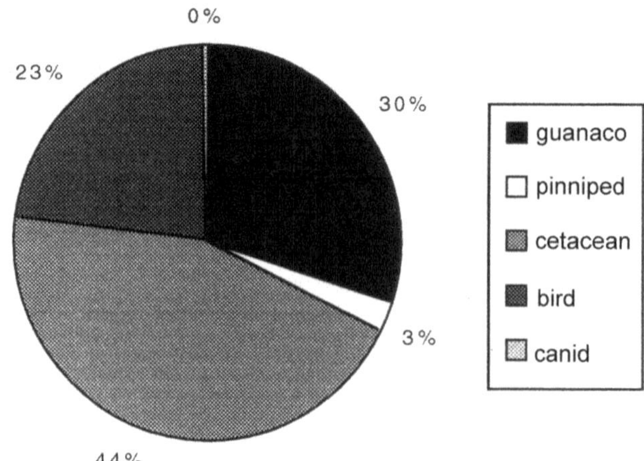

Figure 9.6 – Taxa utilized as bone raw materials in TS III.

Segment IV

Only guanaco (20%) and cetacean (80% v. Figure 9.7) are present. Still, owing to what was said about this sample in the foregoing chapter, this might be simply indicating the preference of ethnographers for certain tools.

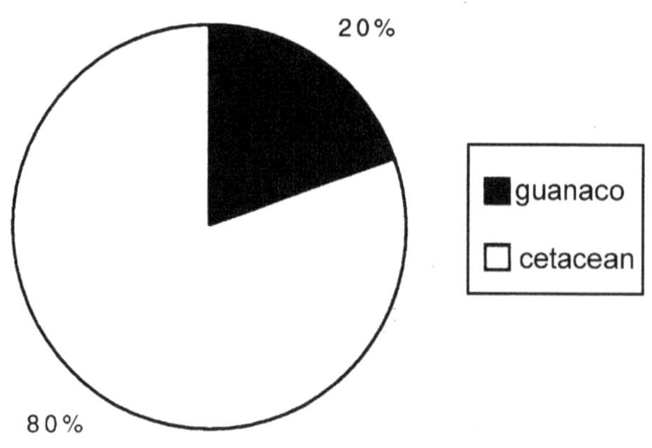

Figure 9.7 – Taxa utilized as bone raw materials in TS IV.

In Figure 9.8 can be seen a comparison of the diverse raw materials in the different time segments. Two characteristics become immediately apparent: on the one hand, cetacean bone, as from its apparition, tends to increase its representation. In contrast, bird bone tends to diminish. Pinniped bone remains fairly stable, though with a slight downward tendency. The case of guanaco is more complex: it exists in TS I, disappears in II, and reappears in III with a considerable percentage. In IV it shows a slight decline, even though it is known that the characteristics of this sample render it unreliable in terms of the archaeological situation.

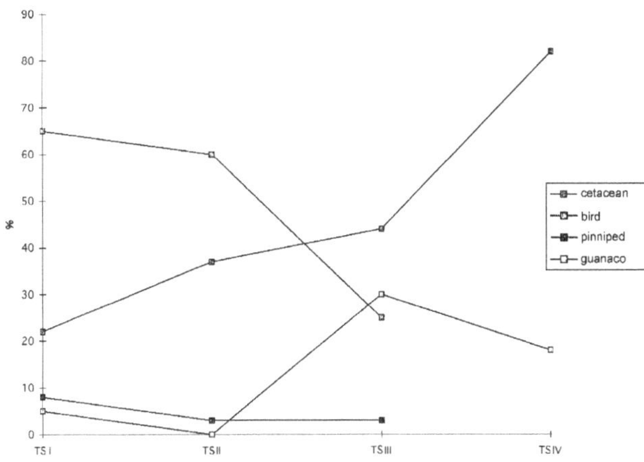

Figure 9.8 – Taxa utilized as bone raw materials by TS.

Distribution and Diversity of the Morphological Groups according to Time Segment

Global Analysis

Figure 9.9 represents the whole of the 19 morphological groups studied in the sample, showing their presence in the diverse time segments (the black line indicates presence alone, without specifying the number of specimens or percentages).

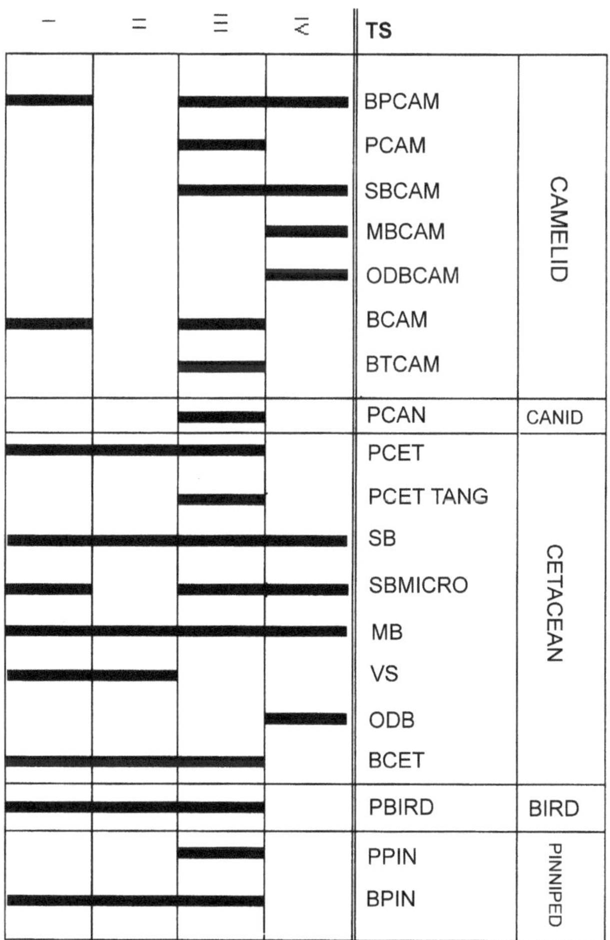

Figure 9.9 – Morphological groups of tools by time segment.

Although, as stated previously, cetacean bone is the prime raw material, the number of classes of morphological groups it presents (8) is almost the same as that of the guanaco (7), whereas pinniped bone presents 2 groups, and bird bone, 1.

There is a notable relationship between the number of specimens per class and class diversity (Figure 9.10). Cetacean bone can be placed at one end (which shows a high number of specimens and variety of MGT) and, at the other, bird bone (with a large number of specimens and no MGT variety.)

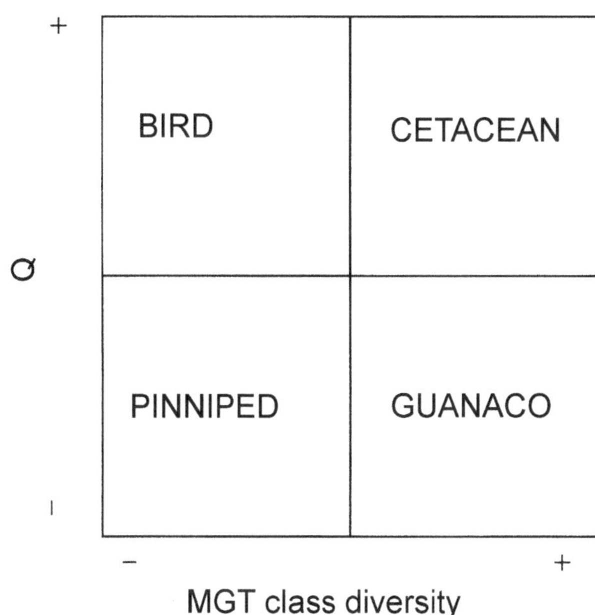

Figure 9.10 – Quantity and class diversity of morphological groups of tools.

Analysis by time segments

Figure 9.11 shows the percentages of each MGT per time segment. We see high percentages of PBIRD in TS I, II, and III, though with a drastic reduction in the last case (22,5%). In TS IV, SB predominates. Nevertheless, given the characteristics of this sample, this would indicate the barbed harpoon head (SB with almost 40%, MB with 30%, and ODB with 15%) bias of the collectors.

Thus it is arguable whether, as was pointed out, the predominance of PBIRD is owed only to the bias implied from Tu I Site, since in TS III— in which the influence of this site in the sample size is lesser (only 4 pieces apported to the sample)— this group also predominates. Figure 9.12 which exclude PBIRD of Tu I throw up the same results.

In this way it is seen that SB and BPIN predominate in TS I, with percentages close to 20%. PBIRD is also important (15%) whilst all the remaining groups have percentages below 10%. In TS II BCET predominates (35%), closely followed by PBIRD (30%). All other groups would show percentages equal to or below 10%. In TS III, PBIRD is still in the lead (with approximately 20%, followed by

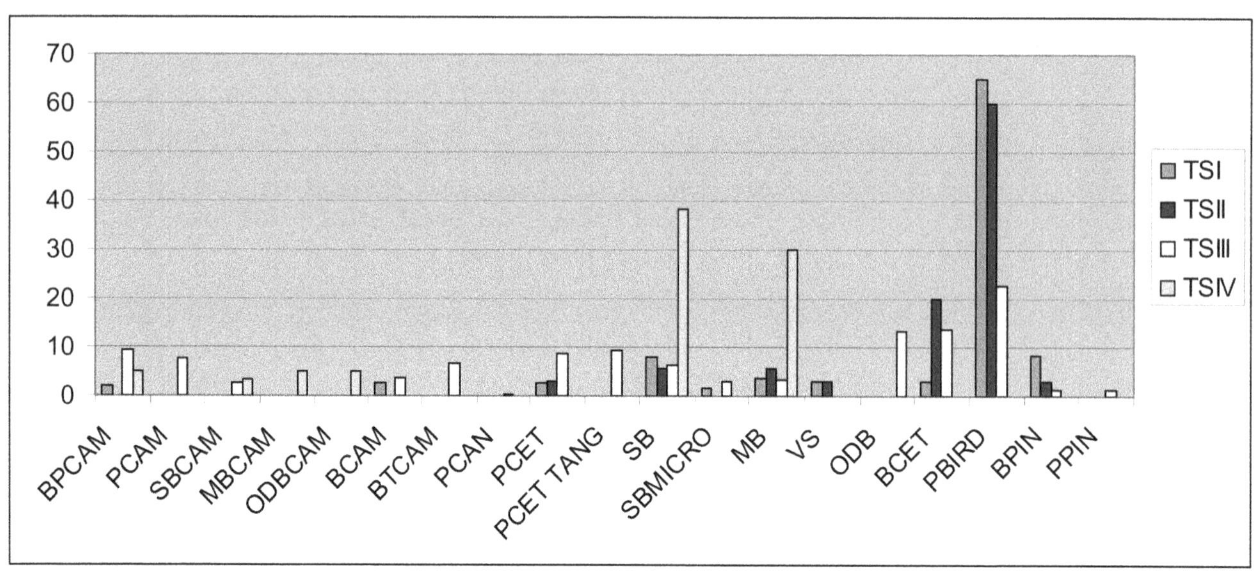

Figure 9.11 – Morphological groups of tools percentages by time segment.

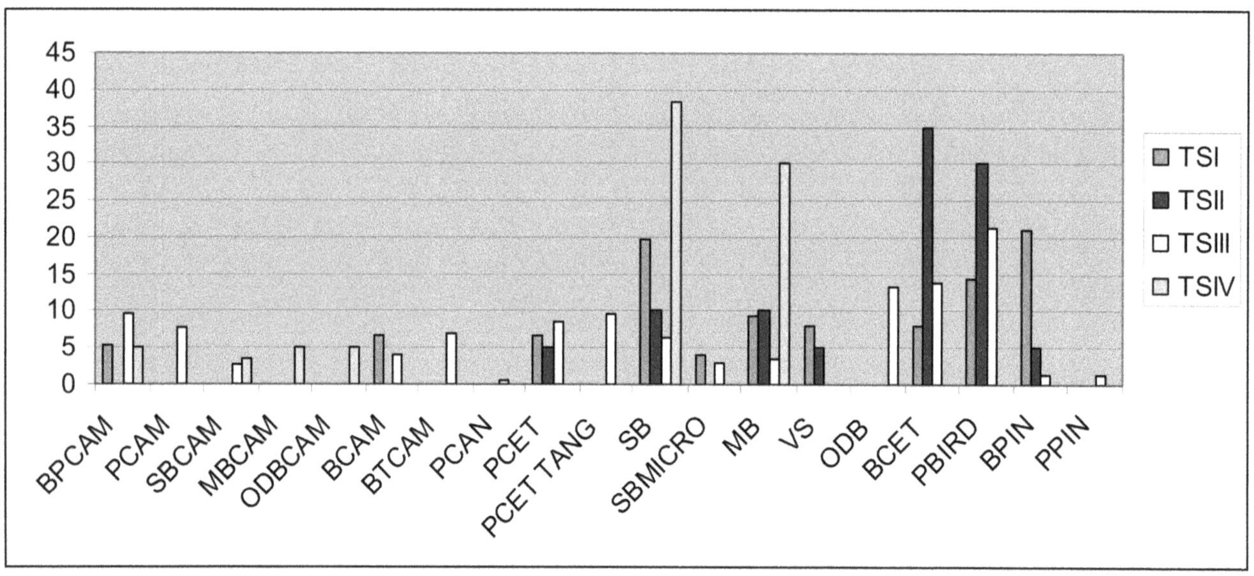

Figure 9.12 – Morphological groups of tools percentages by time segment excluding PBIRD of Tu I.

BCET (slightly under 15%), whereas all remaining groups show percentages below 10%. In TS IV— from which subsample Tu I is absent— there are no variations with regard to the first case. Thus it can be said that, though not with the same values, the presence of PBIRD is still important in the diverse TS and important in TS III.

In general terms it may be stated that:

1) beyond the Tu I sample, which magnifies the number of specimens in TS I and II, the presence of PBIRD is significant in every TS;

2) bevels predominate in TS I (BPIN), II, and III (BCET);

3) in TS IV, as the reflection of a contact situation, barbed heads predominate (possibly for being preferred by collectors);

4) apart from these MGT, the presence of the others is low (under 10%).

Class richness or the number of MGT per raw material and time segment can be seen in Figure 9.13.

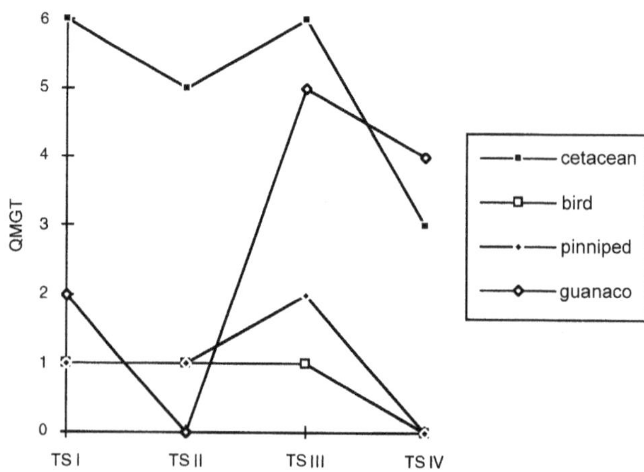

Figure 9.13 – Morphological groups of tools frequencies by time segment.

Let us now look at the situation per time segment.

Segment I (7500-4500 AP)

Bird and pinniped are represented by one class or MGT each, whereas cetacean are represented by 6 MGT and camelids by 2 (see Figure 9.13). Of these 10 morphological groups, SB, PCET, BCET, PBIRD, BPIN and MB show a significant continuity in time, as they will remain throughout the record (v. Figure 9.9). BPCAM, BCAM and SBMICRO only appear in this TS, but will be taken up once again in TS III (BCAM), TS III and IV (BPCAM), or TS IV (SBMICRO). Possibly the case of BCAM and BPCAM must be related to the general absence of camelid bone in TS II. VS is the only MGT that, save its continuity in TS II, will not be resumed later in the sequence.

It is noteworthy that the four main raw materials of the five used in the whole sequence already make their appearance here.

Segment II (4500 -1500 AP)

No new MGT appears at this time. Those known in TS I are simply continued, but some of these disappear. Of the 10 MGT known in TS I, 7 are retained. Guanaco bone disappears, which accounts for the absence of two MGT. Bird and pinniped remain stable with one MGT each (see Figure 9.9 and Figure 9.13).

Segment III (1500 AP-present)

Six new MGT arise (PCAM, SBCAM, BTCAM, the sole case of PCAN, PCET TANG and PPIN). Of these, 2 are proper to PM2 site (PCAN— represented by a single tool— and BTCAM) and they are not found, before or since, at any of the other sites (Figure 9.9). Possibly the PM2 site BTCAM were hafts, rather than tools themselves. However, this has to be confirmed by microwear patterns study of these pieces.

In this TS each raw material reaches its peak of richness (see Figure 9.13). BTCAM and BCAM are present once more, and VS disappears. This is the period of greatest diversity of MGT, with a total of 15.

Segment IV

Of 7 MGT detected at this time, 3 are new (MBCAM, ODBCAM, and ODB). These incorporations, rather than new designs, represent changes in raw materials and/or basic forms. MBCAM and ODBCAM, are in fact multibarbed or bi-barbed heads similar to those fashioned with cetacean bone, but morphologically adapted to the characteristics of camelid bone. In addition, ODB and ODBCAM are reported in the available ethnographic record as harpoon heads present in the Alkaluf area. As in the ethnographic collections no mention was made of the place of origin, it is possible that they come from that area and, so, are foreign to the Isla Grande.

Contrastation of the Model

So as to evaluate the richness of bone tools in the diverse time segments in a statistically valid manner, the calculation of indices were performed. Although these calculations pose certain problems (cf. Chapter 7), their results are reliable. Here we shall use them as a means to confirm or reject the results obtained by the simple quantification of morphological classes.

The Shannon-Weaver richness index, and that of homogeneity were chosen as they are the most widely used in archaeology (Lanata 1996). We have not taken heterogeneity indices into account since, according to Brobowsky and Ball (1989:7), they are unsuitable for archaeological research: they may mask results rather than clarify them (see also Lanata 1996). The results obtained can be seen in Table 9.1.

Sample	Shannon-Weaver	Evenness	Q Classes
TSI	0,5922	0,5922	10
TSII	0,5473	0,6476	7
TSIII	1,0358	0,8808	15
TSIV	0,6892	0,8155	7

Table 9.1 – Shannon-Weaver and Evenness by time segment. Indices calculated with MultiVariate Statistical Package (MVSP), Warren L. Kovach, 1986.

According to the Shannon-Weaver indices, in TS I an initial medium diversity with a medium homogeneity can be observed (Low values are here considered as those between 0 and 0.45; medium, those between 0.46 and 0.70; and the high ones are those above 0.71). For TS II the Shannon-Weaver indices show no significant changes with respect to the previous period, remaining at medium values. Homogeneity is also average. In TS III diversity and homogeneity are high. In TS IV there occurs a significant descent in the Shannon-Weaver, taking up a middle position once more. Homogeneity is high.

If TS III turns out to be the segment that offers greatest variability so far in terms of the raw materials employed and the richness of morphological groups, it may thus be identified with a moment of experimentation. In this sense it is also to be expected that the morphological groups belonging to this time segment should present less standardization or greater diversity in the metrical variables. In forthcoming paragraphs we will attempt to verify this expectation of greater metrical variability in the morphological groups of TS III. In order to verify this expectation the metrical variables of each morphological group in the different time segments will be compared. It is expected that the tools belonging to TS III will show greater variation with respect to the mean than the same variables as they appear in other TS.

Morphological Groups of Tools in the Different Time Segments

In terms of the outlined expectation, the changes that take place within each MGT in the diverse time segments will be evaluated. The MGT occurring within only one time segment will merely be described, pointing out their salient characteristics, and they will be compared with other MGT that, due to their morphology or metrical characteristics, could be thought to have analogous functions.

Barbed Harpoon Heads

This major group takes shape from the moment a key innovation is incorporated, common to different MGT: the setting of one or several barbs in the active end of the piece. From that basic structural plan (bauplan) was developed the morphological diversity that subsequently existed. We will briefly peruse the results obtained for each MGT:

The following morphological groups of barbed tools can be recognized:

Cetacean bone:

1)SB: Present from TS I through TS IV, covering the entire sequence;

2)VS: Contemporary to the previous, it is present in TS I and II;

3)MB: Present from TS I to TS IV, covering the whole sequence;

4)SBMICRO: It appears in TSI, TSIII, and TSIV;

5)ODB: only in TS IV. Travellers refer to this morphology as coming from the Alcaluf area.

Camelid Bone:

6) ODBCAM: Present only in TS IV

7) SBCAM: Present in TS III and IV.

8) MBCAM: Present only in TSIV

1) Single-barbed harpoon heads (SB): This group is found in all the time segments. Nevertheless, it is necessary to discriminate two designs, one ancient (A), the other (B) more recent (see Figure 9.14).

Design A consists in a single-barbed head with a cruciform base (*sensu* Orquera *et al.* 1977:148), that is, presenting

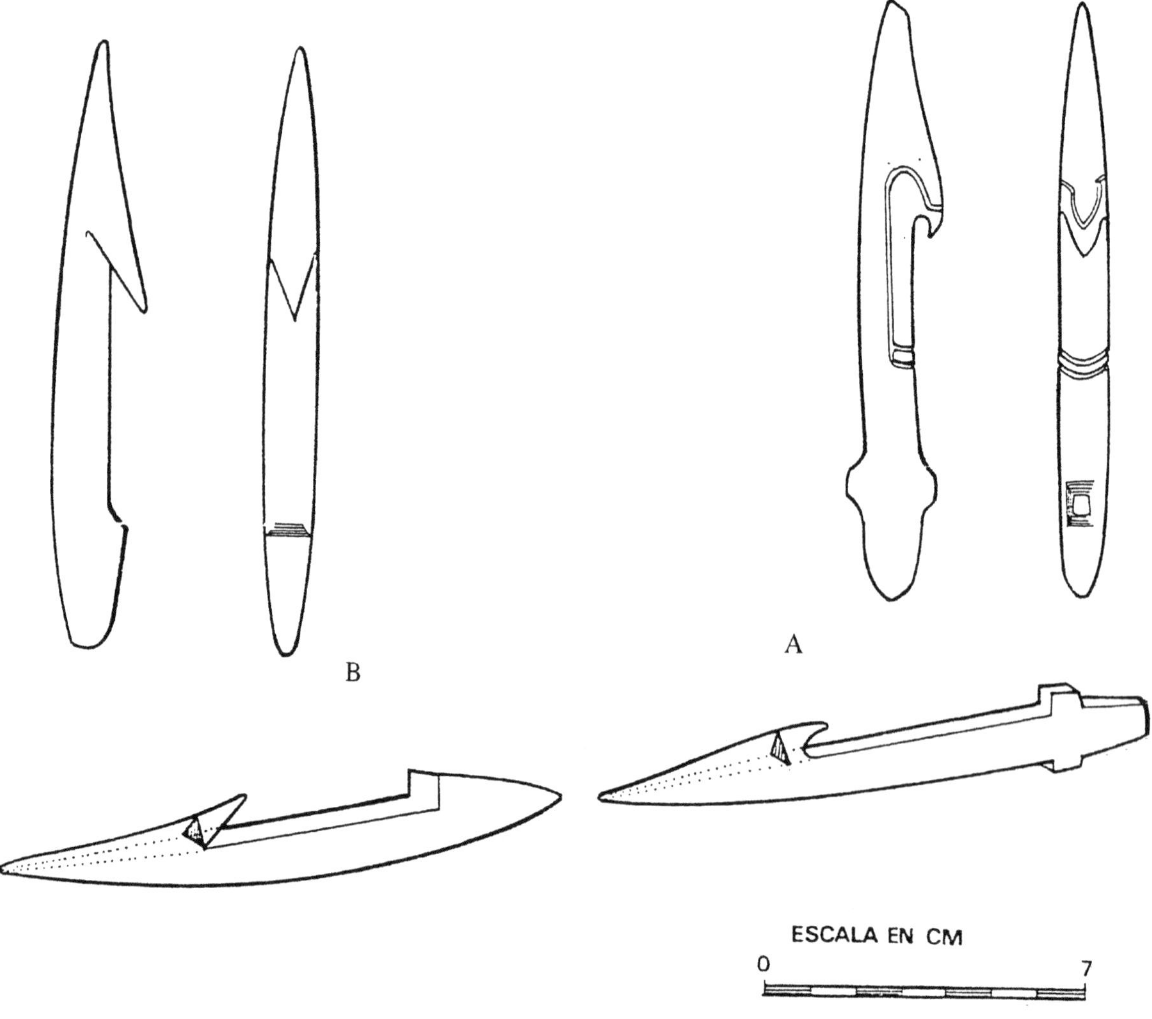

Figure 9.14 – Pattern A and B of Single Barbed points. Drawing by Diana Alonso.

two protuberances issuing from opposite sides, in the form of a cross (see Figure 9.14). If it is looked at from its base, it can be seen that the barb is fashioned by thinning down the sides of the head, which meet in a sort of bevel. The section of the barb is triangular (Figure 9.14), whereas the section of the shaft is lenticular or oval. It must be mentioned that the cruciform base is also a characteristic of double-barbed harpoon heads (VS), named "vulpicephalic" by Piana (1984:54 see Figure 14). This design is contemporary of design A of the single-barbed ones.

Instead, design B, has a tang at its base. As for the barb, viewed from a basal angle it does not have bevelled sides, but the base was fashioned by making a cut at an acute angle to the major axis of the piece. The shaft also has a different section, called "shield-like".

It must be pointed out that the fracture pattern presented by these harpoon heads is different: in the case of design A, it is common to find fractures near the middle of the shaft, whereas in case B the most frequent fracture is at the base of the barb. Design A is only found in TS I, whereas design B is to be found from TS II onwards. An analysis of the implications of this change in design can be read in Herbst & Scheinsohn (1991). Here both designs were analysed jointly.

In Table 9.2 can be seen the summary of the diverse metrical variables for SB according to different TS.

The expected greater variability for TS III holds good for the majority of variables, as observed by the standard deviation of those variables in Table 9.2 (in general greater in TS III, except in the variables specified below) and the box plots of the for variable ANG — Figure 9.15—, FOR— Figure 9.16—, RES— Figure 9.17—, in which, leaving aside outliers, dispersal is always greater in TS III. This can also be seen in the variables BARB ANG, SL, ST and FLAT not graphed here in sake of brevity.

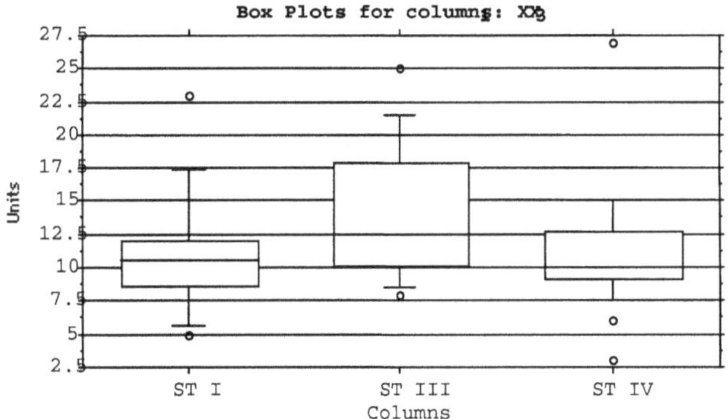

Figure 9.15 – Box Plot for ANG variable (in degrees) for the different TS of single-barbed harpoon heads. TSII is not graphed given its small simple size.

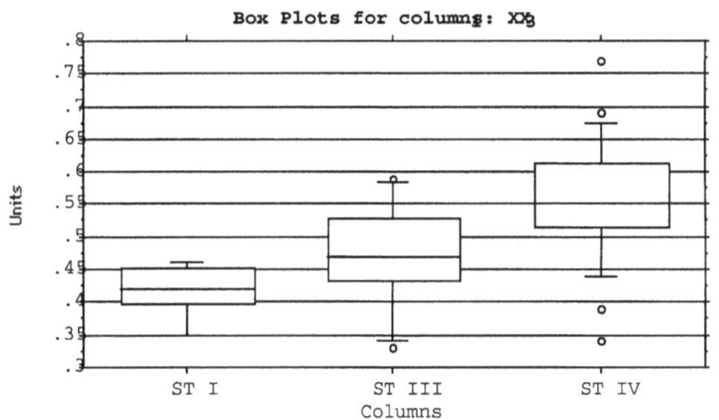

Figure 9.16 – Box Plot for FOR variable (index) for the different TS of single-barbed harpoon heads. TSII is not graphed given its small simple size.

	ANG	BARB ANG	ML	SL	SW	TS	AL	W	FOR	RES	ELONG	FLAT	RES MOD
TSI-X	10,92	35,38	162,8	57,71	14,6	10,25	89,5	21,06	0,42	0,83	9,44	1,42	62,25
S	4,5	9,75	22,73	13,21	4,55	1,79	23,7	10,95	0,04	0,3	3,98	0,35	36,65
TSII- X	11	46	148,5	49,5	12	10	68,5	22,5	0,45	0,84	8,21	1,23	64,69
S (*)													
TSIII-X	13,8	46,83	169,3	64	13	8,17	72,7	35,9	0,4	0,8	8,32	1,66	30,51
S	5,02	13,62	31,14	24,5	3,95	3,6	14,8	31,94	0,18	0,45	2,88	0,52	44,36
TSIV-X	11	39,45	278,2	78,22	15,5	12,29	161	69,86	0,56	0,74	10,63	1,27	209,96
S	4,35	5,88	101,1	20,64	3,16	3,06	86,1	38,32	0,09	0,21	2,62	0,15	126,73

(*) Not calculated due to small simple size (N=2)

Table 9.2 – Single-barbed harpoon heads (SB) mean (X) and standard deviation (S) of different metric variables. See variables abbreviation in chapter 7.

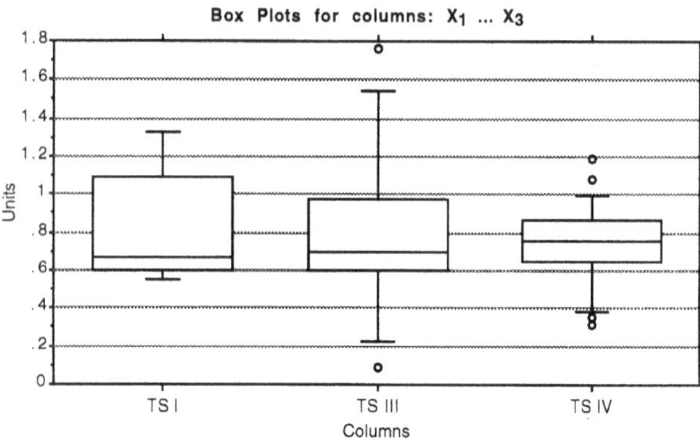

Figure 9.17 – Box Plot for RES variable (index) for the different TS of single-barbed harpoon heads. TSII is not graphed given its small sample size.

Certain variables (ML, AL, W, and RES MOD) show greater dispersal in TS IV. In Figure 9.18 can be seen one of these cases, that of the ML variable.

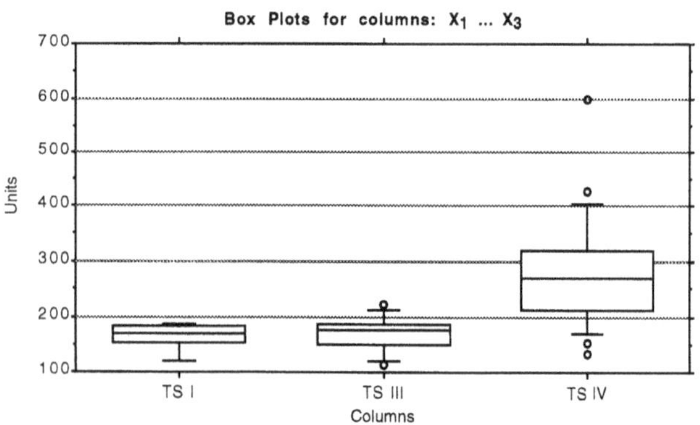

Figure 9.18 – Box Plot for ML variable (in mm) for the different TS of single-barbed harpoon heads. TSII is not graphed given its small sample size.

This time segment also shows higher absolute values. The graph allows the supposition that two populations lived together in this TS: one that encompasses the range of sizes present in other TS, in coherence with designs A and B which, in consequence, will have served for the mode of action assigned to the group (penetration by impact), and another population of too great a size to have been able to function according to that mode of action, since its length would make it very fragile. In fact, many of these pieces show recent fractures, as a result of being moved around in the boxes in which they were deposited.

If the resistance index variable (RES)— Figure 9.17— is analysed it will be appreciated that TS I and III samples have greater values than those of TS IV, which is to say that TS IV pieces are less resistant. In a previous work it was suggested that these large-sized pieces were not made to hunt with, but to exchange with Europeans (see further details in Scheinsohn 1990-1992). Thus, since this is a special case of a sample of ethnographic origin, in which the variables connected with length appear magnified, it is to be expected that the expectations for the model should not be fulfilled.

There are another two variables that do not fulfil expectations: SW (Figure 9.19) and FLAT, for which a greater dispersal occurs in TS I. As SW is used to calculate FLAT, what happens in one must necessarily be so in the other. In any case, the range is wide in the three TS we have considered (the TS II sample is very small). This may be related to design A (present in TS I) not being fully standardized at that time. Let us remember that fractures in this design appear in the middle part of the shaft, which would be related to the SW variable.

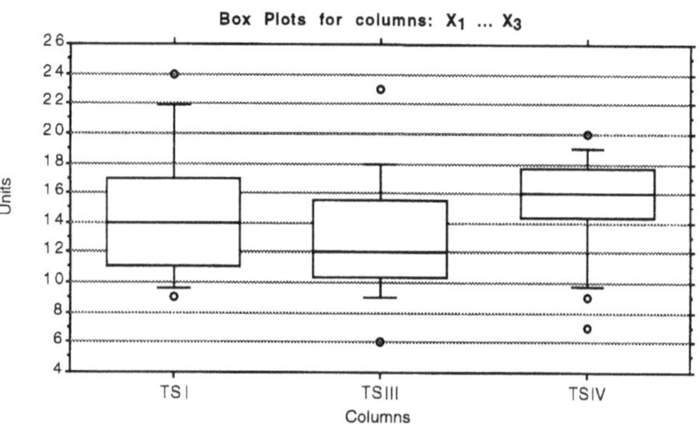

Figure 9.19 – Box Plot for SW variable (in mm) for the different TS of single-barbed harpoon heads. TSII is not graphed given its small sample size.

2) V-shaped harpoon heads (VS): This MGT is found only in TS I. There is only one more recent example (TS II), but it is fractured for which reason it has not been taken into account in this work. In this way this group can only be described and compared with the other barbed harpoon heads.

As a general characteristic it can be stated that size variables, do not show values different from SB (save, of course, the sample from TS IV), the average values and standard deviations being similar although these are more limited in VS than SB— except in ANG and BARB ANG— (v. Table 9.3). For this reason one may imagine a greater standardization in VS. The high average of SL and RES must be stressed in comparison with the SB sample, nonetheless. It can be seen that the range of VS overlaps the rest, though with a notable dispersal, similar to that of SB in TS III.

In Figure 9.21 one can discern the dispersal around the mean for RES MOD variable in VS and SB (TS I, II, III, and IV). VS and SB dispersal is similar to that of SB in TS I, two groups that are contemporary, whose values are also similar, although SB in TS I tends towards higher values. In other words, despite the different morphology of the barb, RES MOD (the variable that measures the

	ANG	BARB ANG	ML	SL	SW	TS	AL	W	FOR	RES	ELONG	FLAT	RES MOD
TS I - X	12,4	42	165,50	70,33	13,80	11,60	66,60	22,17	0,35	1,19	5,73	1,21	44,23
S	4,27	13,21	9,50	9,18	1,17	1,85	39,70	8,17	0,03	0,15	1,01	0,14	35,37

Table 9.3 – V-shaped barb harpoon head (VS) mean (X) and standard deviation of different metric variables. See variables abbreviation in chapter 7. N=6.

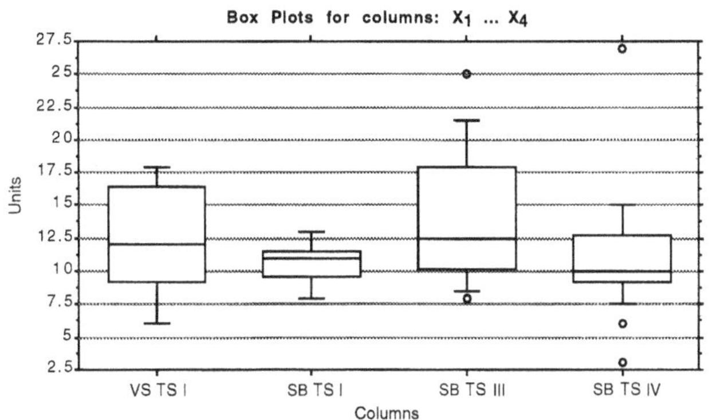

Figure 9.20 – Box Plot for ANG variable for TSI of VS and TS I,II and III of SB harpoon heads.

resistance of the barb) attains similar values in both cases. The wide dispersal of TS IV is owed to the existence of two populations, as was explained above.

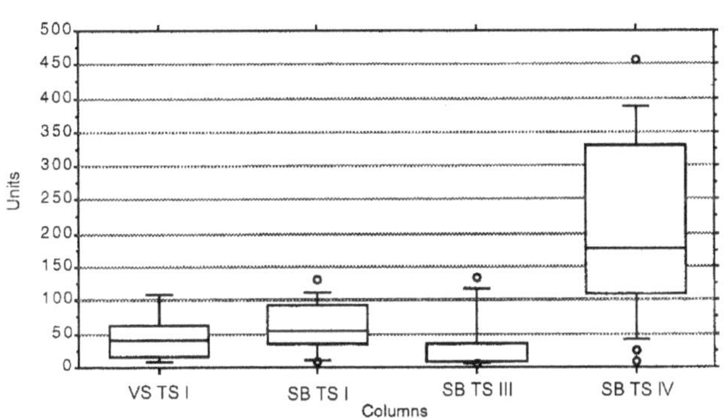

Figure 9.21 – Box Plot for RES MOD variable for the different TS of SB and VS harpoon heads.

3) Multi-barbed heads (MB): Multi-barbed heads appear as from TS I and carry through to TS IV. All heads possessing more than one barb placed in a line on one of the sides is considered to belong to MB group. There is a fair heterogeneity in the morphology of the diverse pieces that compose this MGT but they are not related to a particular TS. These differences have to do with the outline of the barb (straight or curved), the degree of elaboration of the barbs (highly elaborated or barely hinted at), the kind of hafting (a simple spike, protuberances, grooves), etc. The number of barbs present on these harpoon heads is variable (see Table 9.4).

In this case we are not dealing with detachable harpoons heads, as in the anterior case but fixed harpoons heads used for fishing that would function as a pike. This same functionality, according to the ethnographic record, is attributed to the single-barbed camelid bone heads of the Atlantic coast (SBCAM).

In this MGT, too— as was suggested with regard to SB— there is an increment in the size of the pieces in the TS IV sample. Still, the length of these pieces was already considerable in the case of TS I, in which they also show a notable standard deviation (v. Table 9.4 and Figure 9.22).

The largest standard deviations also occur in TS IV for the variables ANG, ML, SL, AL, W, FOR, and FLAT, which can be related to the reasons put forward for the case of SB. The mean values of certain variables seem fairly stable in the different TSs (SW. ST, FOR, ELONG, RES, FLAT), while others (ANG, ML, SL, AL) are more heterogeneous, but with a tendency towards higher values for TS IV and lower ones for TS III.

	ANG	ML	SL	SW	TS	AL	W	FOR	RES	ELONG	FLAT	BARBS (*)
TSI - X	11,86	226,6	75,6	14,88	8,63	51,5	28,6	0,21	0,74	12,48	1,72	4,6
S	4,12	73,6	40,42	3,41	2,39	23,12	11,56	0,1	0,38	7,04	0,23	
TSII- X	8	116	63	10	5,5	12	8	0,68	0,34	9,67	1,8	3,5
S (**)												
TSIII- X	8,67	157,33	60,33	14,5	7,38	38,71	14,01	0,2	0,6	11,41	1,95	5,2
S	1,25	28,45	16,82	4,21	1,87	26,26	3,8	0,07	0,08	1,07	0,21	
TSIV- X	15,94	253,38	132,18	16,06	8,38	39	29,53	0,19	0,58	15,12	1,93	9,41
S	4,78	101,49	88,66	3,06	1,87	32,49	16,66	0,14	0,18	5,45	0,36	

(*) Only in case of complete pieces.
(**) Not calculated given the small sample N=2.

Table 9.4 – Multi-barb harpoon head (MB) mean (X) and standard deviation (S) of different metric variables. See variables abbreviation in chapter 7.

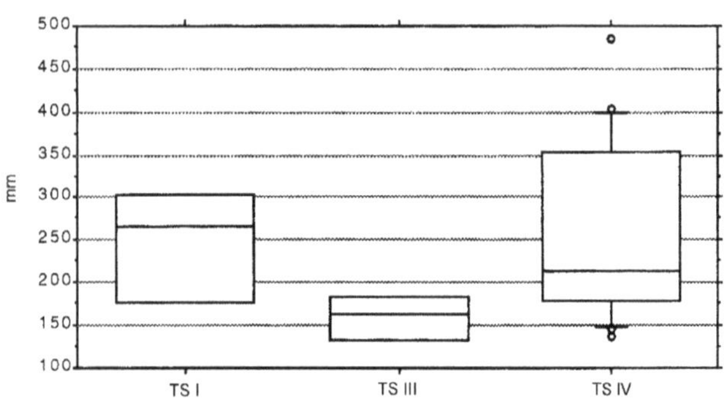

Figure 9.22 – Box Plot for ML variable for the different TS of MB harpoon heads.

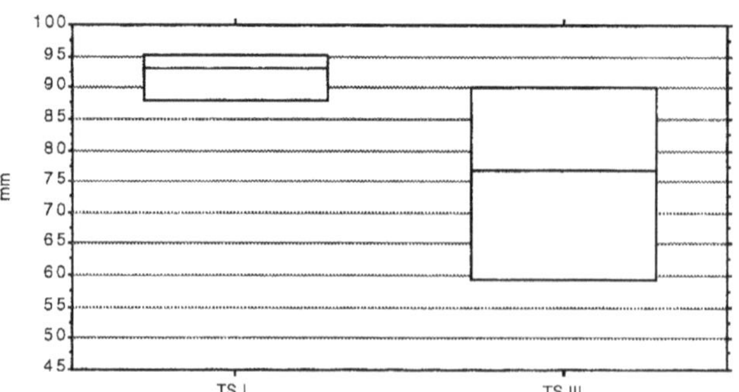

Figure 9.23 – Box Plot for ML variable for SBMICRO harpoon heads in STI y III.

In relation to SB, the average ANG and SW remain within the same range, whereas for the remaining variables the values are higher in TS IV in both cases (SB and MB).

The expectation of variability, measured in terms of standard deviations and dispersal round the mean value, is fulfilled only in the case of SW. Actually, for MB, TS III seems to be a moment of reduction in variability (see Table 9.4 and Figure 9.22).

4) Small single-barbed heads (SBMICRO): This is present in TSs I, III, and IV. In the case of TS I they show protuberances for which reason they mimic SB design A, whereas those of TS III correspond to design B in possessing a tang. The mean values of the variables of both TSs are similar (v. Table 9.5). The variability expectation for TS III is fulfilled as it always shows a greater standard deviation than TS I (see Figure 9.23 for the case of ML), with the exception of variables FOR and RES MOD (see Table 9.5). Nevertheless one must take into account that this may be due to the TS I sample (N=3) being small. The TS IV cases were not analysed, as these harpoon heads were found in association with the so-called "canoe models," which contained whole tiny harpoons with shaft, so that it was not possible to measure the heads on their own.

5) Double-barbed harpoon heads with opposed barbs in cetacean bone (ODB) and 6) double-barbed harpoon heads with opposed barbs in camelid bone (ODBCAM).

Both MGT are found only in TS IV. As was mentioned, this would be a design restricted to the Alcaluf area, at least in ethnographic times. In one case the blank is cetacean bone (ODB) and in the other, camelid (ODBCAM). The latter consists of a small sample (N=3) which makes its analysis difficult. A descriptive summary of these two MGT can be seen in Table 9.6.

In Figure 9.24 can be seen the dispersal around the mean

	ANG	BARB ANG	ML	SL	SW	TS	AL	W	FOR	RES	ELONG	FLAT	RES MOD
TSI -X	7,33	45	91,67	35	6,33	5,67	36,33	3,33	0,39	0,39	9,6	1,12	3,06
S (*)	3,09	0	4,19	5,35	0,47	0,47	8,5	0,47	0,08	0,04	0,94	0,09	3,19
TSIII - X	11,71	41	80,33	31,17	6,71	4,07	36,14	1,73	0,41	0,36	9,23	1,72	0,98
S (**)	5,15	10,23	19,21	10,03	1,38	1,43	11,48	0,81	0,07	0,26	2,58	0,31	0,98

(*) Protuberances at the base
(**) Tang Base

Table 9.5 – Micro Single-barbed harpoon head (SB MICRO) mean (X) and standard deviation (S) of different metric variables. See variables abbreviation in chapter 7.

	ANG PUN	ANG DIEN	ML	SL	SW	TS	AL	W	FOR	RES	ELONG	FLAT	RES MOD
CET X	12,86	29,87	220,5	42,8	12,25	12	139,75	45,67	0,64	0,72	7,93	1	118,07
S	3,68	8,89	61,05	19,4	1,85	1,07	35,89	14,40	0,03	0,15	1,48	0,17	96,66
CAM X	17,33	29,5	161,3	28	12,67	11	96,67	24	0,6	1,21	6,68	1,18	31,21
S	11,02	21,92	60,47	1	2,08	0	63,52	1,41	0,13	0,7	3,08	0,25	15,27

Table 9.6 – Double-barbed harpoon heads with opposed barbs in cetacean bone (ODB) and double-barbed harpoon heads with opposed barbs in camelid bone (ODBCAM). Mean (X) and standard deviation (S) of different metric variables. See variables abbreviation in chapter 7.

value of variable ML for ODB, ODBCAM, and SB. The range of this variable is similar for ODB and ODBCAM, although the latter acquires smaller values due to the limitations of the blank bone (see CET and CAM in Figure 9.25). The values of this variable in both MGT overlap those of SB I and III, though the dispersal is greater. In contrast SB IV has higher values and greater dispersal than either MGT.

In Figure 9.26 can be seen the comparison between ODB

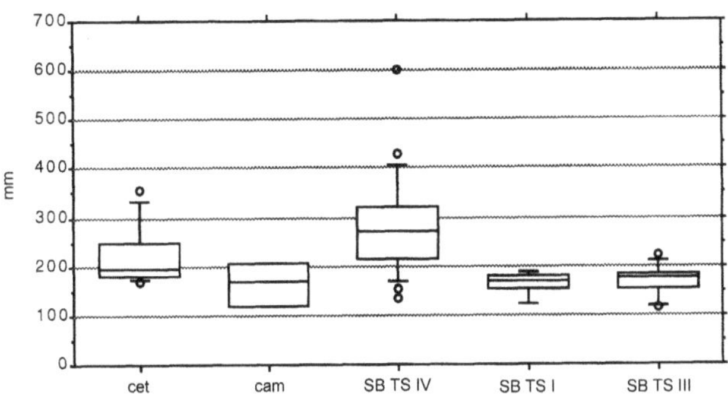

Figure 9.24 – Box Plot for ML variable for ODB, ODBCAM and different TS of SB harpoon heads.

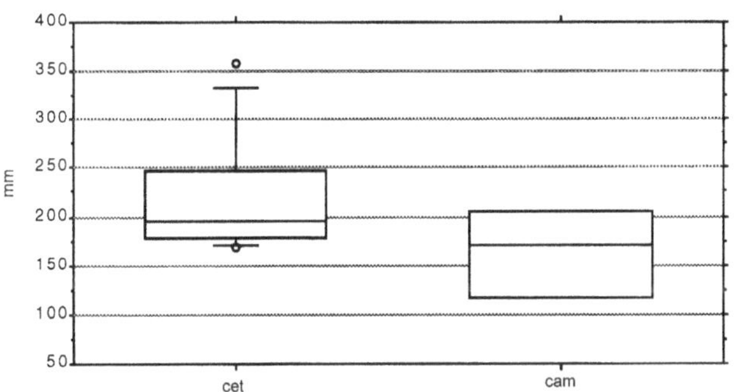

Figure 9.25 – Box Plot for ML variable for ODB and ODBCAM.

and ODBCAM for the ANG variable. A greater dispersal is noticeable for ODBCAM but one must bear in mind that the sample is smaller.

ODBCAM sigmas for the variables ANG, BARB ANG, and AL are large in comparison with those of ODB, and even when compared with those of SB (see Table 9.6), which would indicate we are in the presence of a less standardized MGT. At the same time, as the bone blank is a long camelid bone, the variables related to size must be more limited than in the case of ODB.

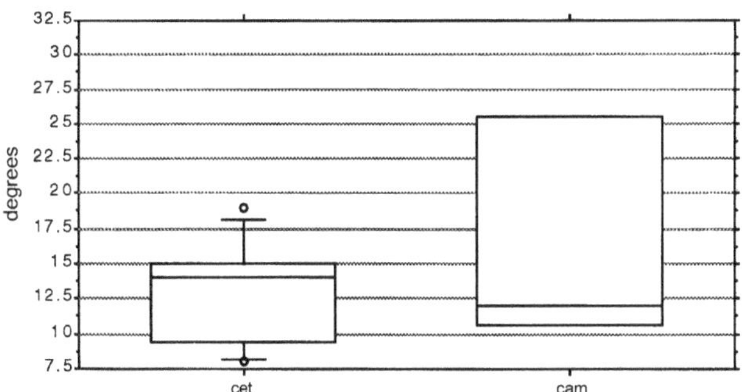

Figure 9.26 – Box Plot for ANG variable for ODB and ODBCAM

7) Single-barbed camelid bone harpoon heads (SBCAM): this MGT is related to SB design, though fashioned in camelid bone. It occurs in TS III and TS IV. In the case of TS III the sample is mostly from PM2 site, on the Atlantic coast of the island, although there is one case from BVS1 (Mitre Peninsula). In PM2 the design among them is similar, different from SB design B (v. Figure 7.5) with no tang. This design allows the extraction of base-forms suitable for the production of these harpoon heads in guanaco bone, which presents serious constraints as to size. The TS IV sample is too small to establish any comparison, but the range of distribution of the variables is included within that of TS III.

SBCAM III shows high values for standard deviation, which agrees with expectations. Its ML range partially overlaps that of SB I and III, though it is wider and shows lower values, possibly due to the conditions imposed by the raw material (Figure 9.27). Indeed the average is lower than SB I and III with a higher sigma (c.f. Table 9.2 and Table 9.7).

Variables SL, BARB ANG, SW, RES, W, and ELONG show similar mean values in SB TS I, III, and SBCAM. Instead ANG, SL, and FLAT show larger values than SB TS I and III. Without doubt this is related to the limitations imposed by the raw material. TS, AL, and FOR cast up smaller values than in SB TS I and III, doubtlessly for the selfsame reason.

The most notable difference with regards to SB arises from ML and MOD RES. In the latter case the low values of MOD RES might be compensated by the high quality of the raw material, or because this MGT has a different function in which a very resistant barb is not needed (as in the case of the fixed head, cf. next chapter). In the first case it is evident these heads are shorter due to the limitations of guanaco bone.

	ANG	BARB ANG	ML	SL	SW	TS	AL	W	FOR	RES	ELONG	FLAT	RES MOD
x	18,60	37	141,75	70	13,5	7,25	44,4	18,76	0,31	0,74	9,44	1,91	1,85
S	6,92	7,58	44,01	24,22	2,57	1,87	12,29	10,68	0,04	0,16	1,66	0,32	0,32

Table 9.7 – SBCAM mean (X) and standard deviation (S) of different metric variables for TS III. See variables abbreviation in chapter 7..

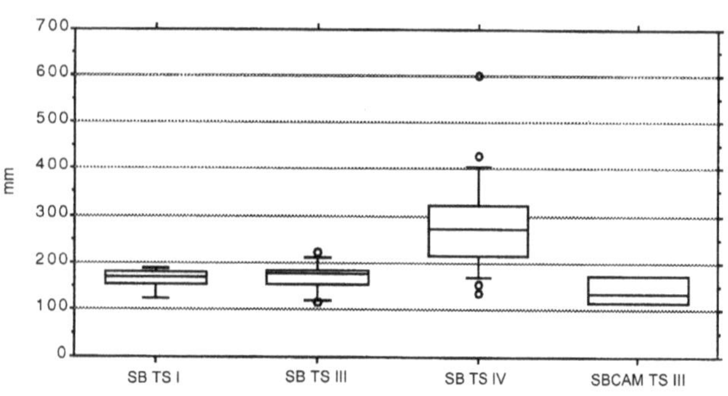

Figure 9.27 – Box Plot for ML variable in SBCAM TS III and SB TS I, III and IV.

8) Multi-barbed heads of camelid bone (MBCAM): this case, due to being a very small sample (N=3) will not be analysed. More to the point, as some of the pieces are fractured, for certain key variables the sample is limited to a single specimen.

POINTS

These are MGT that posses a pointed active end. Most of them are awls but there is projectiles (PCET TANG) and possibly harpoon head preforms (some members of PCET). Within this morphology the following MGTs are found:

-Bird Bone

1) PBIRD: This is one of the MGT most abundant in the record. It carries through from TS I to III.

-Cetacean Bone

2) PCET: It appears in the record as from TS II, and carries through to TS IV

3) PCET TANG: only in TS III

-Camelid Bone

4) PCAM: only in TS III

-Pinniped Bone

5) PPIN: only in TS III

-Canid Bone

6) PCAN: only in TS III, and besides, consisting of a single instance.

1) Bird bone point (PBIRD): for the production of these points the following bones and taxa were utilized:

- Anatid Tibiatarsi (ANAT)

- *Phalacrocorax* sp. humeri (PHALA)

- Procellarian humeri (PROCE)

- Humeri or ulnae of large sea-birds (BIG) such as *Macronectes giganteus* (Giant Petrel) or *Diomedea exulans* (Wandering Albatros). These have been studied as a single class since, from humeri or ulnae it is impossible to differentiate them.

Less frequently the record shows:

- *Eudyptes* sp. tibiatarsi (EUDYP) penguin

- *Spheniscus* sp. tibiatarsi (SPHEN) penguin

- Strigid radii (STRIGIDO)

In Figure 9.28 can be seen the distribution of the different taxa for all the TSs (see references above).

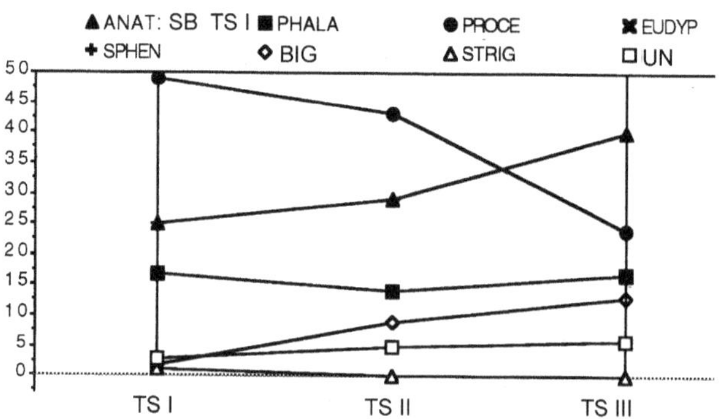

Figure 9.28 – Bird taxa percentage for each TS. References: ANAT= Anatid, PHALA= *Phalacrocorax* sp., PROCE=Procellarian, EUDYP= *Euydptes* sp., SPHEN= *Spheniscus* sp., BIG= Big birds STRIG= Strigid y UN= Undetermined

The moment of greatest variation as regards to bone blanks is TS I, with 6 taxa, though the percentage of Eudyptes (EUDYP), Strigids (STRIGIDO), and Spheniscus (SPHEN) is low (Figure 9.28). In TS II procellarians predominate (PROCE) and, to a lesser extent, anatides (ANAT), followed thereafter by phalacrocoracidae (PHALA) and the large birds (BIG), the two last with low frequencies. In TS III the same taxa persist, but anatides (ANAT) predominate and the percentage of procellarians (PROCE) sinks steeply. It might be possible to point out a temporal trend of declining use of procellarians and a rise in that of anatides. Phalacrocoracidae remain fairly constant, while the use of large birds increases slightly. The decrease in variety of bone raw materials, seen in the passage from TS I to II, is referred to raw materials that showed very low percentages but which, even so, might be interpreted as experiments. Besides, it is necessary to understand the notorious difference in size of the small TS II sample.

The analysis of metrical variables (Table 9.8) shows an increase in the average length of this MGT in TS III, which is seen in ML, SL, and ELONG. This could be related to a rise in the presence of large birds in that sample (N=7 versus N= 2 in TS I and II). As longer blanks exist (due to the ulnae of the large birds), this can result in an increase of the average ML. There is also an increase in the angle of the pieces. AL is larger in TS I, but values remain constant for TS II and III. Save what has been pointed out, the pieces present no great differences in the remaining variables, having similar values.

In Table 9.8 it is seen that the variables SW and ELONG show bigger sigmas for TS I whereas AL and FOR have larger sigmas in TS II. The rest show higher sigmas for TS III, which agrees with expectations.

Looking at Figure 9.29— which represents the box plot of variable ML— it can be seen that TS II shows a limited dispersal, while it is greater in TS I and TS III but with many isolated high and low values. In the case of Figure 9.30— with a graph of the RES variable— the three samples are alike. Finally Figure 9.31, showing the ANG variable, shows a resemblance between TS III y II, whereas TS I present a more restricted dispersal though similar to the other two.

	ANG	ML	AL	SL	SW	ST	FOR	RES	ELONG	FLAT	TAXA
TSI -X	10,37	90,52	39,35	29,88	8,54	5,82	0,43	0,54	5,71	1,5	ANAT=29
S	3,83	19,11	11,64	19,04	2,44	1,35	0,11	0,25	3,59	0,4	PHALA=20
											PROCE=56
											SPHEN=1
											BIG=2
											UN=4
											STRIGIDO= 1
											EUDYP=1
TS II -X	10,92	85,8	29,67	33,63	8,05	5,6	0,45	0,47	5,58	1,44	ANAT=6
S	4,53	12,58	15,24	10,32	2,27	1,46	0,22	0,23	1,91	0,23	PHALA=3
											PROCE=9
											BIG=2
											UN=1
TS III -X	13,67	96,92	28,5	46,88	8,14	5,76	0,3	0,5	6,79	1,45	ANAT=21
S	6,77	19,25	9,53	19,77	2,16	1,76	0,11	0,25	3,2	0,49	BIG=7
											UN=3
											PHALA=9
											PROCE=13

Table 9.8 – PBIRD mean (X) and standard deviation (S) of different metric variables and taxa for different TS. See variables abbreviation in chapter 7

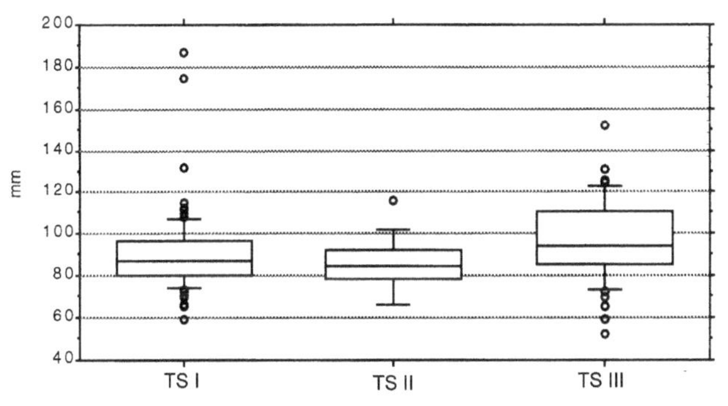

Figure 9.29 – Box Plot for ML variable in PBIRD.

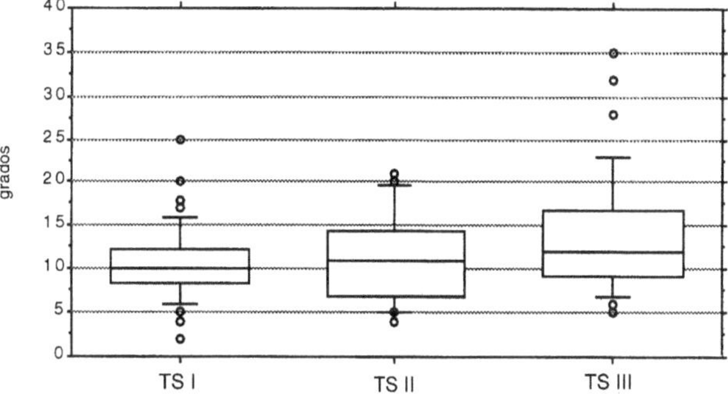

Figure 9.30 – Box Plot for RES variable in PBIRD.

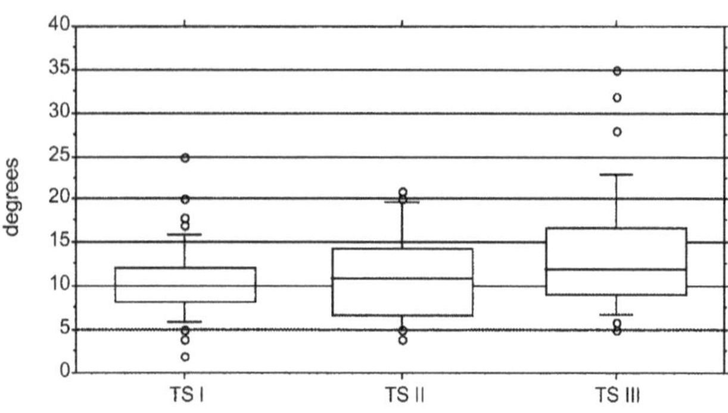

Figure 9.31 – Box Plot for ANG variable in PBIRD.

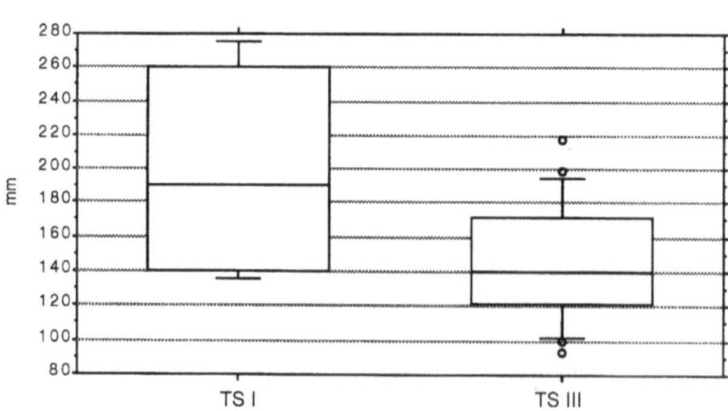

Figure 9.32 – Box Plot for ML variable in PCET.

2) Cetacean Bone Points (PCET): In Table 9.9 the results obtained for the principal metrical variables are presented. The range and average of variables ST and W is quite similar. This is remarkable since in this case the raw material does not limit the size of the piece, for which reason greater variation was to be expected in this sense.

	ANG	ML	LF	SW	ST	AL	W	FOR	RES	ELONG	FLAT
TS I -X	10,2	199,4	133	13,4	9	25,6	26	0,12	0,62	14,32	1,52
S	4,87	57,61	46,58	2,65	2,1	14,87	11,58	0,05	0,17	4,2	0,24
TSII - X	8	292		13	9		35		0,4	22,46	1,44
S											
TS III - X	15,21	144,05	77,83	17,47	10,68	48,68	25,8	0,35	1,37	8,07	1,78
S	3,85	34,35	26,31	3,56	3,66	10,5	11,9	0,08	0,7	2,81	0,54

Table 9.9 – PCET mean (X) and standard deviation (S) of different metric variables for different TS.

Sigmas of the ANG, ML, LF, AL ELONG variables are greater for TS I. In these variables, with the exception of ANG and AL, the averages of TS I are also greater. In the case of SW, FOR, RES, and FLAT, the sigmas are greater for TS III as are also the mean values. These results would indicate that in TS I the aim was to produce longer pieces, while in TS III, it was to obtain more robust ones.

In Figure 9.32 can be seen the dispersal round the mean of variable ML. In this case a greater dispersal is found in TS I. In Figure 9.33 we can appreciate dispersal as regards the mean value of the variable FLAT in which TS III shows greater dispersal. In Figure 9.34 we see the box-plot corresponding to the ELONG variable in which TS I is the most dispersed.

In other words, in this case the variables related to length show greater dispersal in TS I whereas those related to width and thickness are more dispersed in TS III (cf. Table 9.9).

3) Cetacean Bone Points with a tang (PCET TANG): this group appears as a special case of TS III at the Bahía Valentín site, though there exists a corresponding instance in Tu VII. These are single-barbed points that, whether by accident or intentionally, have lost their barb. In every case they retain the tang and all remaining SB morphological features.

In Table 9.10 are presented the results of the different variables.

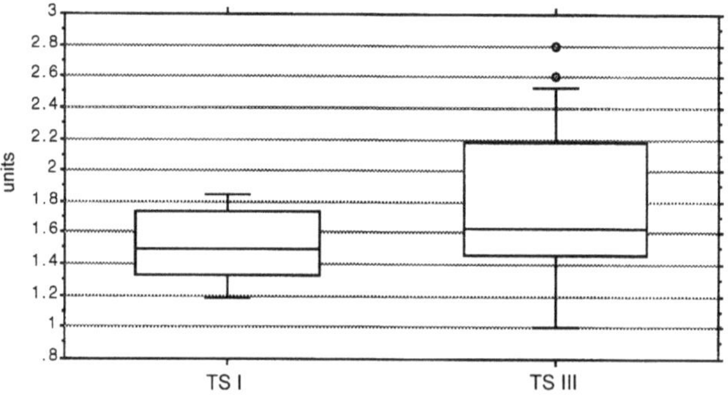

Figure 9.33 – Box Plot for FLAT variable in PCET.

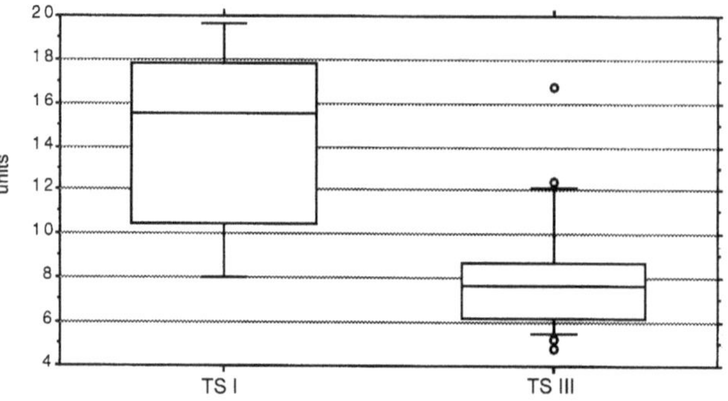

Figure 9.34 – Box Plot for ELONG variable in PCET.

	ML	LF	SW	ST	AL	W	FOR	RES	AL	ACH
X	138,64	64,58	13,6	10,41	42,05	21,08	0,30	1,07	6,43	1,34
S	18,78	16,97	2,71	2,48	15,12	7,87	0,08	0,43	2,22	0,25

Table 9.10. PCET TANG mean (X) and standard deviation (S) of different metric variables for TS III.

Compared with the SB sample (cf. Table 9.2) it is clear that they are shorter (cf. ML, AL, FOR, and ELONG), which would be justified by the breakage of the barb. The variables related to the shaft (LF, SW, ST, FLAT) show a similar mean value to the rest. As for variable dispersal, in no case does it exceed the dispersal of SB variables as a whole, being similar or even lesser than these (cf. ML, SW, W, ELONG). In Figure 9.35 we notice that PCET TANG, being in a similar range as the remaining SBs, is more homogeneous. In Figure 9.36 it is plain that PCET TANG has a respectable dispersal, comparable to that of SB, and with higher values.

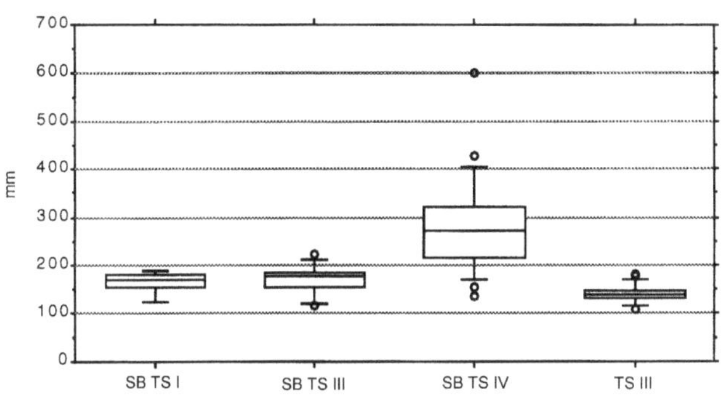

Figure 9.35 – Box Plot for ML variable in PCET TANG TS.

4) Camelid Bone Points (PCAM): This group is composed of camelid bone awls. As a group it appears in several sites, but all of them are on the Beagle Channel: BV, LP, RS1, and Tu VII. Most were fashioned from metapods, with a third of the cases retaining the proximal or distal epiphysis. Keen sharpening predominates, though in many cases the active part appears slightly blunted. In Table 9.11 the variables corresponding to this group are summarized. Funnily, these are encountered only in TS III as, being awls, they should be in other TSs. In order to interpret this, the group will be analysed in comparison with other MGTs that may possibly have been awls.

From comparing PBIRD I, II, and III (see Table 9.8) and PCET TS I, II, and III (Table 9.9) it can be seen that this group is more similar to, on the strength of its mean values and sigmas, PCET TS III (cf. ML, AL, LF, SW, ST, FOR, RES, and ELONG). In general it surpasses PBIRD values in the variables related to length and shaft. This group shows a greater RES than PBIRD but within the PCET range. In Figure 9.37 we notice the resemblance in the PCAM and PCET TS I ranges for the ANG variable. Save the case of PBIRD TS I, all the groups that can be regarded as awls show a wide dispersal from the average, despite the similar mean values of PBIRD TS I and II, and PCAM. Save isolated cases (empty circles), values and ranges are similar.

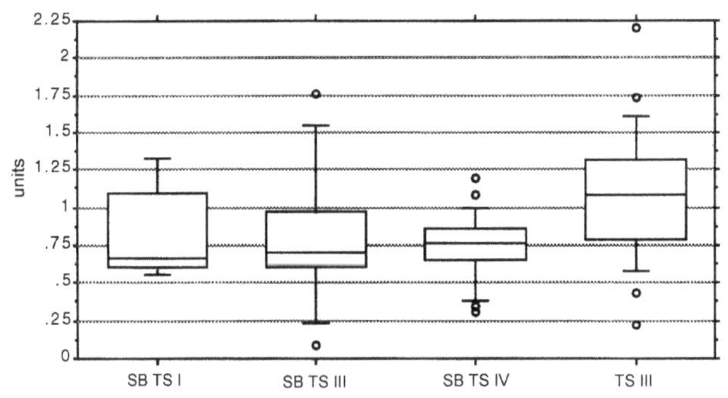

Figure 9.36 – Box Plot for RES variable in PCET TANG TS III and SB TS I, III and IV.

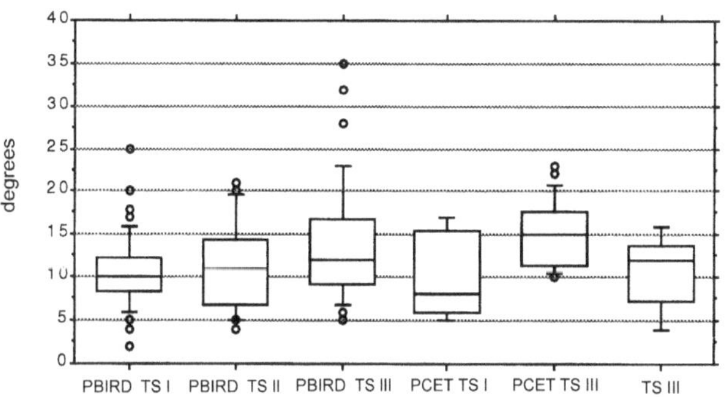

Figure 9.37 – Box Plot for ANG variable in PCAM TS III; PBIRD TS I, II, III; PCET I, III.

	ANG PUN	ML	LF	SW	ST	AL	W	FOR	RES	ELONG	ACH
x	10,80	129,75	65,65	12,53	9	42	18,29	0,32	0,90	7,45	1,48
S	4,26	33,89	27,69	3,64	3,16	12,53	8,84	0,12	0,54	2,47	0,49

Table 9.11 – PCAM mean (X) and standard deviation (S) of different metric variables for TS III.

Figure 9.38 shows homogeneity from PBIRD TS I, II, and III, great variation in PCET TS I, and a similar range in PCET TS III and PCAM TS III.

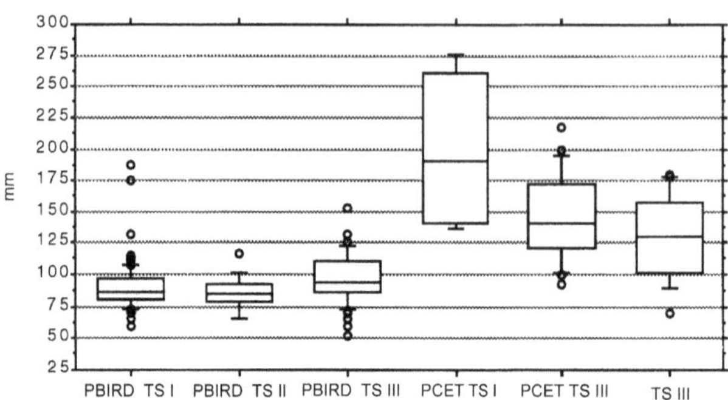

Figure 9.38 – Box Plot for ML variable in PCAM TS III; PBIRD TS I, II, III; PCET I, III.

5) Pinniped bone points (PPIN): found only in TS III. There are three specimens: two made from ribs and one from a fibula. All three are from RS1. The paucity of the sample prevents any analysis of metrical structure.

6) Canid bone points (PCAN). As stated previously, only one specimen exists, from PM2, for which reason it is possible that it is an exceptional case, and not a raw material regularly in use. The scarcity of the sample precludes further analyses.

Blunt points

1) Blunt points in camelid bone (BPCAM): Blunt points are found only in camelid bone. They are found in TS I, not in TS II, they reappear in TS III and go on in TS IV. This is the MGT of greatest geographical dispersal: it is found in every site of the sample barring BCI.

As is seen in Table 9.12, the variables LF, SW, ST, W, FOR, and RES show a greater sigma amplitude in TS III. The largest sigma for ML and its derivation, ELONG belongs to TS IV (although in this case it is similar to TS III), whereas for FLAT and AL it belongs to TS I (in this case also like TS III).

The variables that furnish strength to the piece— as SW, ST, AL, W, FOR, and RES, vital in this kind of tool— have a larger mean value in TS III. They show a similar weight in TS I and III and much less in TS IV. ML, LF and FLAT are greater in TS I.

In Figure 9.39 it can be seen that TS I and IV pieces tend to be longer. TS III shows the greatest dispersal. In Figure 9.40, where the W variable is charted, greater dispersal is seen around the mean of TS III. Additionally this TS shows the highest values for that variable. In Figure 9.41 it can be seen that TS III continues to show a noticeable dispersal around the mean and, besides, shows higher values than in the case of TS I and TS IV. As for the variable ELONG (Figure 9.42) it can be seen that the highest values are those of TS IV. TS I and III show similar values, though with greater dispersal in TS III.

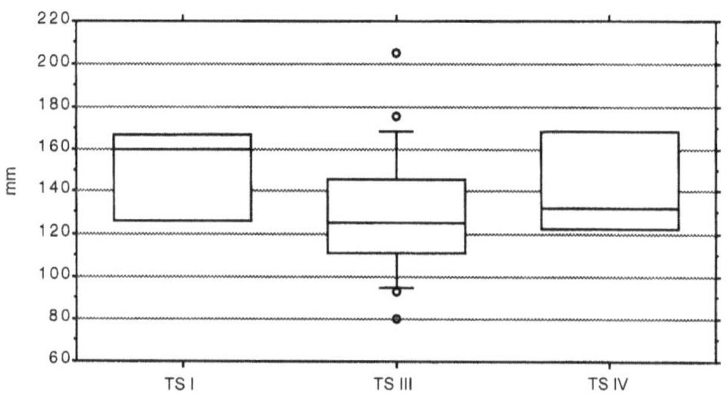

Figure 9.39 – Box Plot for LM variable in BPCAM in different TS.

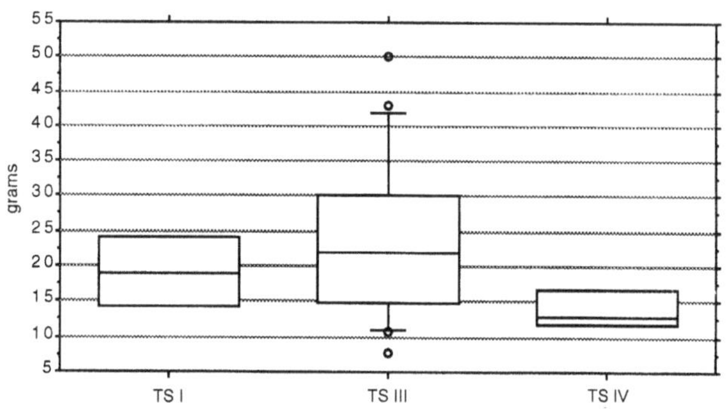

Figure 9.40 – Box Plot for W variable in BPCAM in different TS.

	ML	LF	SW	ST	AL	W	FOR	RES	ELONG	FLAT	EPIF CASOS
TS I -X	164,33	123,67	13,67	8	16	22,17	0,09	0,66	7,57	1,71	2 (PROX)
S	6,13	8,22	3,3	0	12,75	4,55	0,07	0,13	1,09	0,41	
TS III - X	130,1	89,11	15,32	9,79	18,4	23,15	0,15	1,17	7,73	1,56	5(PROX)
S	29,04	21,53	5,1	2,47	12,63	12,63	0,1	0,61	2,15	0,36	1(DIST)
TS IV - X	143,67	111,33	9,33	8	9,33	14	0,06	0,53	12,33	1,17	
S	32,35	3,21	1,15	0	7,51	3,61	0,04	0,08	2,18	0,14	

Table 9.12 – BPCAM mean (X) and standard deviation (S) of different metric variables.

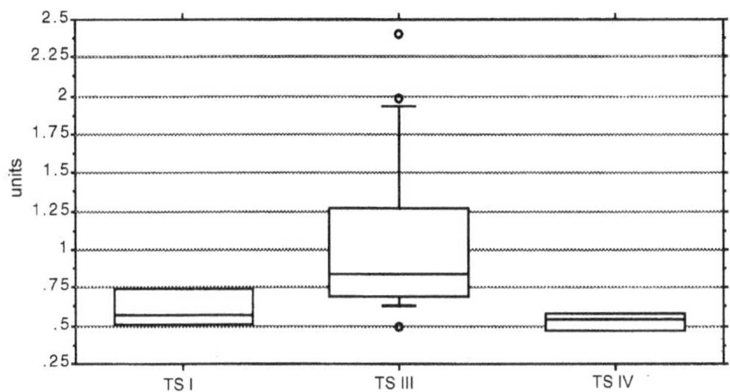

Figure 9.41 – Box Plot for RES variable in BPCAM in different TS.

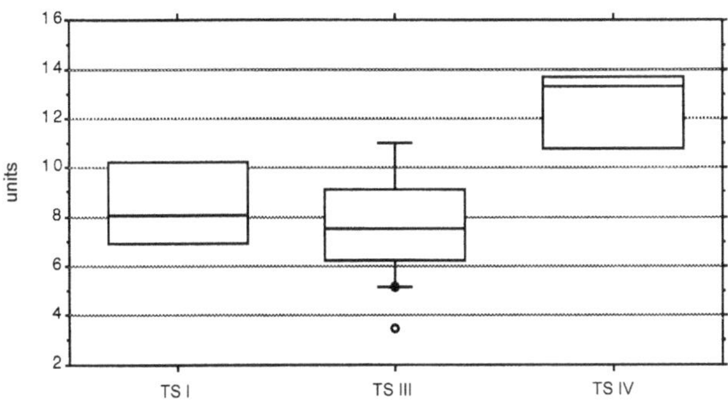

Figure 9.42 – Box Plot for ELONG variable in BPCAM in different TS.

In 8 of the 29 cases given there is a retained epiphysis at the proximal end. In TS I 50% of the sample has the distal epiphysis of the bone, whereas in TS III the percentage is lower (5 proximal epiphyses and 1 distal out of a total of 22). The identified bone blanks are: in TS I, 3 metapods (N=4), in TS III, 11 metapods and 7 tibias (N=22) and in TS IV, 3 metapods (N=3).

Bevels

Within this morphology of the distal end are to be found the following MGT:

1) Cetacean bone bevels (BCET);
2) Pinniped bone bevels (BPIN);
3) Camelid bone bevels (BCAM);
4) Tubular pieces with a chamfered end (BTCAM).

1) Bevels in cetacean bone (BCET): As can be seen in Table 9.13, the largest sigma amplitude belongs to TS III in the variables ML (equal in value to TS II), LF, SW (equal in value to TS II), ELONG, and FLAT whereas it belongs to TS II in the case of AL and RES and to TS I in those of ST and ANG. There exist no noticeable differences in the variables ANG, SW, ST, RES, ELONG, FLAT. In Figure 9.43 greater dispersal can be seen in TS III and IV. In Figure 9.44 there is a greater dispersal in TS I and TS III though ranges are similar in the three cases. In Figure 9.45 it can be seen that the greatest dispersal for SW belongs to TS III. Figure 9.46 shows the greatest dispersal for the variable W in TS III. In the case of the RES variable (Figure 9.47), the greatest dispersal is in TS III. In the same way as in previous cases, on evaluating the variable ELONG (Figure 9.48), the greatest variation is found in TS III. In other words, in this case the dispersal in TS III holds true.

	ANG	ML	AL	LF	SW	ST	RES	ELONG	FLAT
TSI -X	26,75	99,75	23,75	60,5	38,67	19	6,43	2,65	2,11
S	16,05	15,58	5,07	9,18	3,2	4,55	0,95	0,45	0,4
TSII -X	24,8	132	39	60	38,14	21,86	6,69	3,28	1,77
S	5,78	30,57	7,65	20,26	5	2,29	1,94	1,25	0,33
TSIII-X	28,88	117,83	27,79	73,47	33,47	16,05	4,77	3,59	2,11
S	8,25	30,56	5,56	26,25	5,46	2,96	1,47	1,29	0,38

Table 9.13 – BCET mean (X) and standard deviation (S) of different metric variables for different TS.

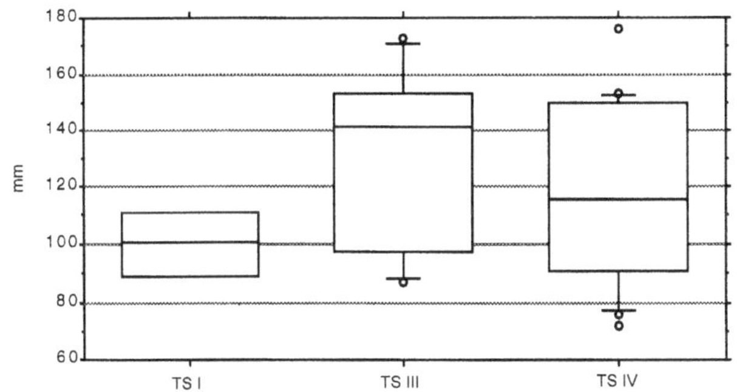

Figure 9.43 – Box Plot for LM variable in BCET in different TS.

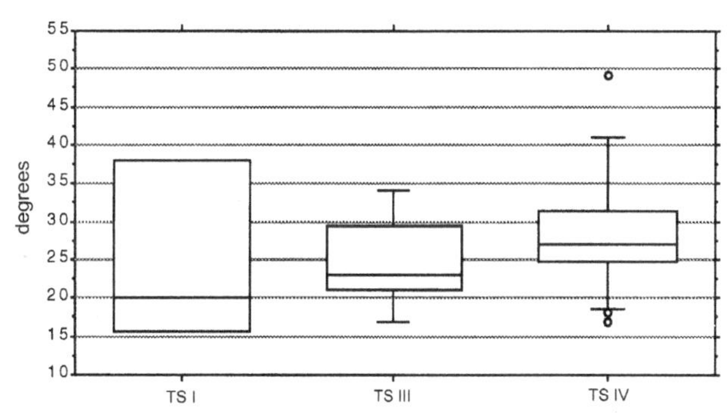

Figure 9.44 – Box Plot for ANG variable in BCET in different TS.

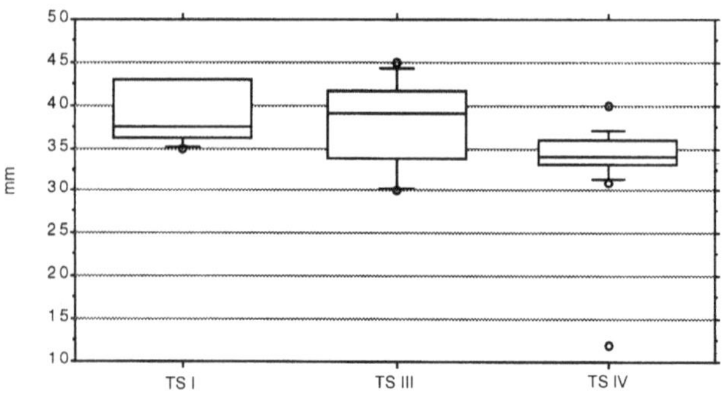

Figure 9.45 – Box Plot for SW variable in BCET in different TS.

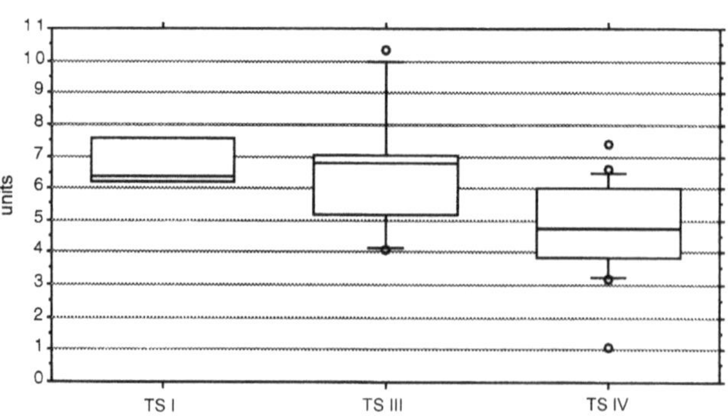

Figure 9.47 – Box Plot for RES variable in BCET in different TS.

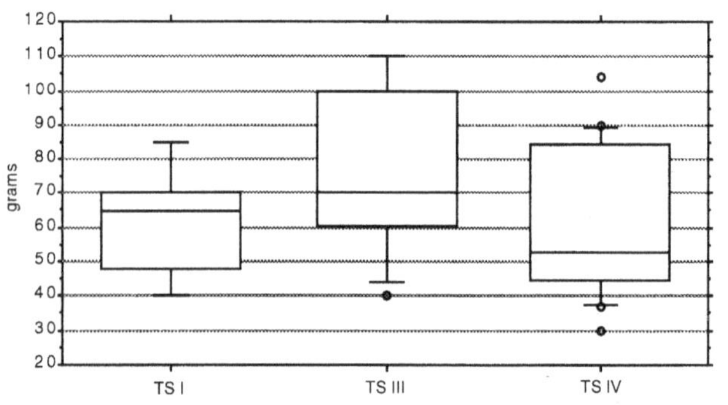

Figure 9.46 – Box Plot for W variable in BCET in different TS.

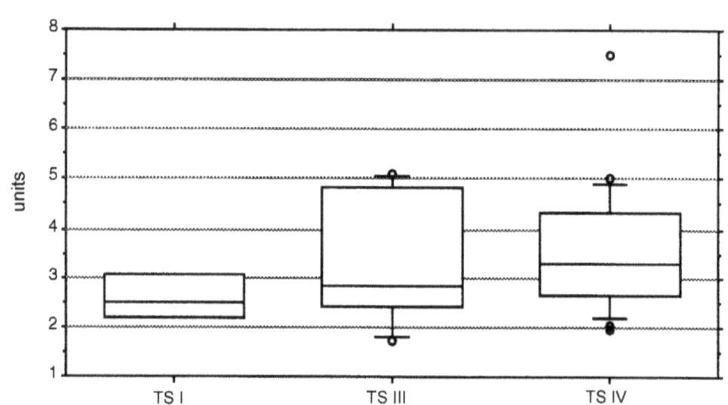

Figure 9.48 – Box Plot for ELONG variable in BCET in different TS.

2) Bevels in pinniped bone (BPIN)

This group begins in TS I and carries on till TS III. The TS II sample is very tiny (N=1) for which reason it will not be considered in this analysis, although it is shown in Table 9.14. This same Table shows a greater sigma amplitude in TS III when the variables refer to the size of the piece (ML, AL, LF, and ELONG). The only case in which the expectation is not fulfilled is in the variable ANG, for which the greatest sigma average and amplitude belong to TS I. The TS I pieces are somewhat sturdier than those of TS III (cf. RES). The TS III ones are correspondingly longer (cf. ELONG).

In Figure 9.49, which charts the variable ANG, it can be seen that TS I has a wider distribution than TS III. In Figure 9.50, where the variable ML is represented, it can be seen that TS III has a wider distribution. Figure 9.51 shows a wider distribution for AL in TS I whereas Figure 9.52 shows the same happening with variable RES.

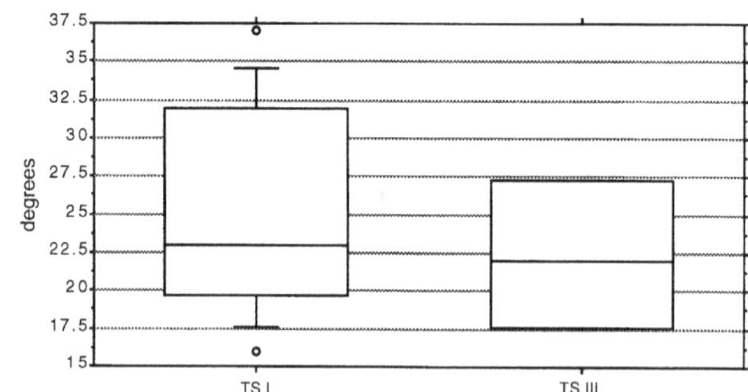

Figure 9.49 – Box Plot for ANG variable in BPIN in different TS.

BPIN	ANG	ML	AL	LF	ST	SW	FOR	RES	ELONG	BONE BLANK
TS I - X	30,33	97,67	55,33	34	14,67	19	0,56	2,87	3,46	ULNAE: 12
S	9,07	7,51	5,51	3	0,58	2,65	0,02	0,52	0,06	RADII: 3
										FIBULA: 1
TSII - X	21	75	24	40	13	30	0,32	5,2	2,14	RADII: 1
TSIII -X	22,33	122,67	31	70,67	11	21,33	0,27	2,46	6,01	RADII:1
S	5,31	50,62	9,9	36,71	0,82	3,09	0,05	1,32	3,74	PHALANX:1
										RIB:1

Table 9.14 – BPIN mean (X) and standard deviation (S) of different metric variables and Bone blank determination for different TS

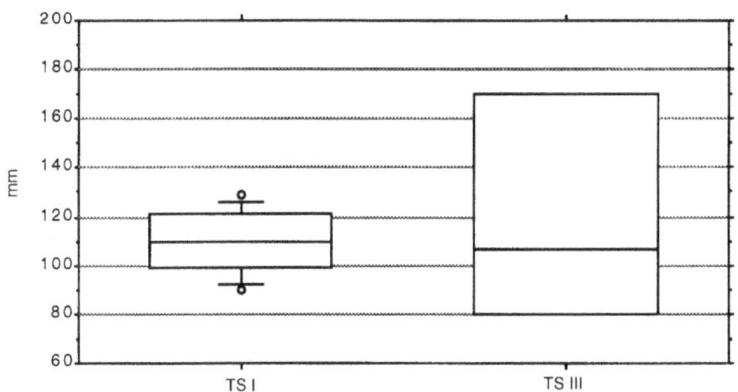

Figure 9.50 – Box Plot for LM variable in BPIN in different TS.

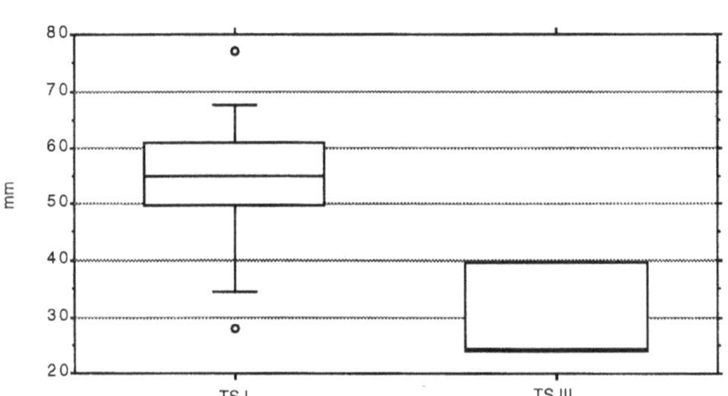

Figure 9.51 – Box Plot for AL variable in BPIN in different TS.

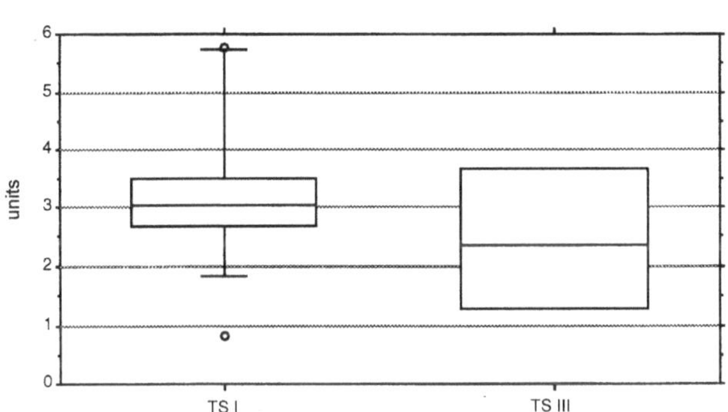

Figure 9.52 – Box Plot for RES variable in BPIN in different TS.

3) Bevels in camelid bone (BCAM): as can be seen in Table 9.15, the greatest sigma amplitude occurs in TS III, with the exception of ANG. In this case the average is greatest for TS I and sigma is slightly greater. As for the variables ML, LF, and RES the mean is greatest in TS III. AL, SW, and ELONG are similar in both TSs.

In the case of the variable ANG (Figure 9.53) dispersal is approximately similar for both TSs, though the higher values belong to TS I. Variable ML (Figure 9.54) shows the greatest dispersal in TS III. The range of values overlaps in both TSs. In the case of variable SW (Figure 9.55) there is a greater dispersal in TS III. The range of values is similar in TS I and III. For variable RES (Figure 9.56) there is greater dispersal in TS III. The range of values is similar in both TSs. Finally, for variable ELONG (Figure 9.57), there is a greater dispersal in TS III. The range of values is similar in both TSs.

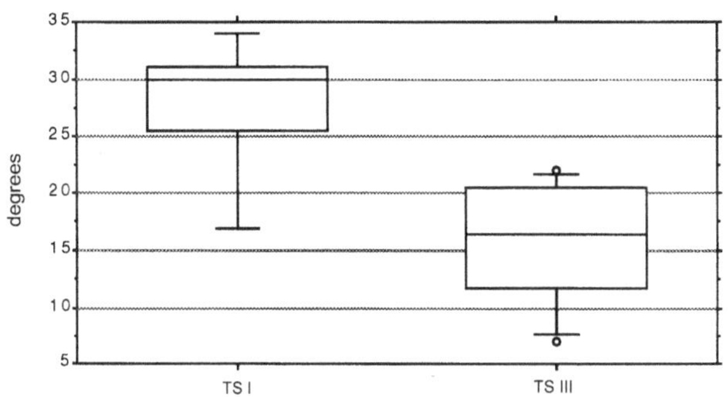

Figure 9.53 – Box Plot for ANG variable in BCAM in different TS.

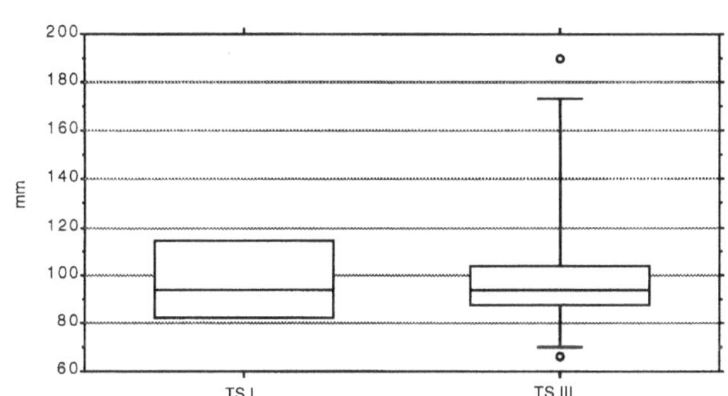

Figure 9.54 – Box Plot for ML variable in BCAM in different TS.

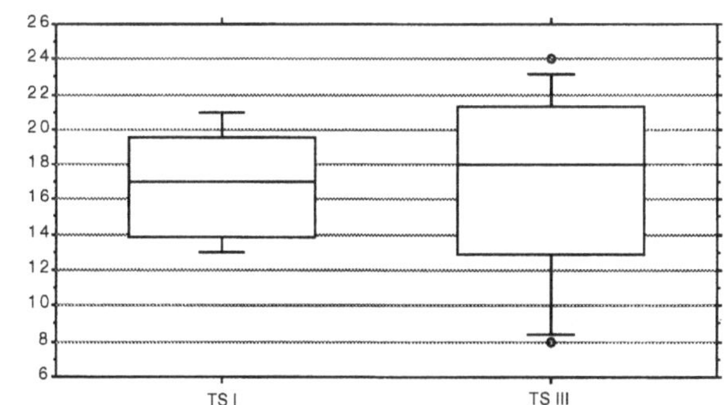

Figure 9.55 – Box Plot for SW variable in BCAM in different TS.

BCAM	ANG	ML	AL	LF	WS	RES	ELONG	FLAT
TSI -X	27,8	97,33	31,4	49	16,8	1,28	6,28	2,38
S	5,74	18,12	7,58	9,8	2,99	0,65	2,12	0,31
TSIII -X	15,75	104,71	27	60,86	16,78	1,5	6,37	1,97
S	5,55	39,66	16,43	35,43	5,59	0,77	2,91	0,51

Table 9.15 – BCAM mean (X) and standard deviation (S) of different metric variables for TS I and III

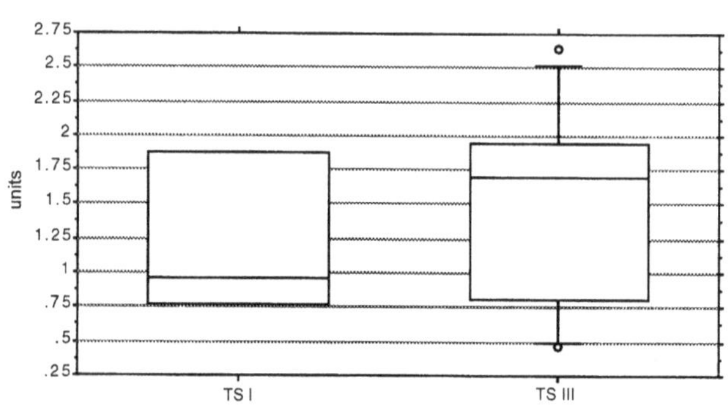

Figure 9.56 – Box Plot for RES variable in BCAM in different TS.

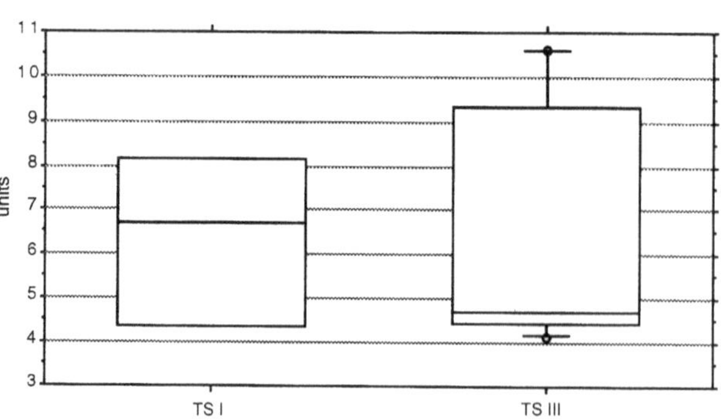

Figure 9.57 – Box Plot for ELONG variable in BCAM in different TS.

4) Tubular pieces with a bevelled end (BTCAM): They are included here for having a bevelled end but, as was previously mentioned, they might well be a haft. They only appear at PM 2 (TS III). Table 9.16 gives a summary of their variables.

	ML	LF	SW	ST	AL	W	FOR	RES	ELONG	FLAT
X	137,93	77,60	25,75	19,97	30,06	55,93	0,24	4,20	5,03	1,40
S	22,22	32,62	4,85	7	16,41	27,51	0,13	2,19	1,61	0,38

Table 9.16 – BTCAM mean (X) and standard deviation (S) of different metric variables for TS III.

CHAPTER 10

DISCUSSION

In this chapter we will begin by discussing each morphological group of tool in each time segment. In this way it will be possible to suggest certain considerations regarding the diverse raw materials employed. We will also attempt to define the differences that may arise between the north and south of the Isla Grande as regards the exploitation of bone raw materials. Finally, through a discussion of the model, an attempt will be made to explain the exploitation of bone raw materials on the Isla Grande de Tierra del Fuego.

Analysis by MGT: Distribution according to Time Segment and Degree of Standardization

In this section we will discuss the results obtained with reference to the morphological analysis of the tools, the properties of the raw material they were made with, and will evaluate whether the expectation of high dispersal of the metrical variables in TS III is fulfilled.

Barbed Heads

Single-barbed heads (SB)

a) Morphology: the first recording of this group is related with A pattern morphology (see chapter 9). In TS II pattern B appears, showing certain changes in the general morphology of the piece (incorporation of a tang instead of the cruciform base and the shield-like morphology of the shaft section), which will displace the former. Pattern A harpoon heads showed fractures at the level of the shaft. Pattern B seems to arise as a correction of this problem, since it shows an increase in the size of the shaft and changes in the section's morphology. Yet B has an additional problem: it shows fractures at barb level, as it was possible to ascertain through the existence of many of these broken barbs in the archaeological record (e.g. Bahía Valentín). Yet, besides what was pointed out, no important changes in size were recorded from one time segment to the next. Instead, the TS IV sample shows two distinct populations: one that was "normal"— insofar as the variables related to size are similar to previous TSs—, and another in which a significant increase in the size of the pieces is evident. This size is too great to imagine an enhancement in the performance of these harpoon heads. In fact, it would seem to affect badly its performance, making impossible to suppose their use as such. It was suggested that they may have served as a means of bartering with the population of European origin (c.f. Chapter 9 and Scheinsohn 1990-1992).

b) Mechanical properties: Given the mode of action assigned to this morphological group, the chosen raw material seems the most suitable. It possesses a high energy absorption capacity, for which reason it is able to resist fracture while the prey struggles to escape from the harpoon.

c) Expectation of variability in TS III: This morphological group fulfils expectations since, in time segment III, in the majority of variables it shows great dispersal around the mean value. Variables related to size show a greater dispersal in TS IV on account of the coexistence of two populations: a utilitarian one, and another that is possibly elaborated for the purpose of interchange and other uses.

V-shaped Barbed Harpoon Heads (VS)

a) Morphology: This group is a contemporary of SB pattern A, for which reason it can be interpreted as a rival design. It appears only in TS I and then disappears. Size-related variables remain fairly similar both in Pattern A and this group. In fact, there is no way of knowing if the fractured proximal parts correspond to VS or to SB pattern A as they are alike. Thus it can not be known if the presence of one or two barbs implied an advantage or disadvantage as regards the fracture pattern. The analysis of whole VS pieces made it possible to ascertain that they had a longer length of shaft (SL) than SB, which allows one to presuppose greater fragility, though also presenting an increase in the resistance index (RES) provided by greater barb breadth or thickness. Actually it can not be known whether, at the shaft level, SB pattern A meant an improvement on VS. Neither is it possible to evaluate whether the presence of one or two barbs minimized the possibilities of fracture at the shaft level. VS did not solve the problems posed by pattern A, and required more work involving the production of two barbs instead of one. SB pattern B is the answer to both problems with less work involved since the production of a barb with the characteristics of this pattern takes less time than those of VS (and also it should be considered the lack of any decorative pattern in this MGT while some VS and SB pattern A pieces present decoration).

b) Mechanical properties: The mode of action assigned to this morphological group would be the same as in the previous case, for which reason this raw material is suitable to resist the mechanical requirements that have been put on the tool.

c) Expectation of variability in TS III: At the time this group appears (TS I), contrary to what would happen in TS III, medium variability and a certain degree of standardization are expected. This can not be evaluated by standard deviation analysis as there are variables in which sigma shows low values (such as ML) and others in which the values are high (e.g. RES MOD and BARB ANG). The fact that this group appears only in TS I precludes further comparisons.

Multi-barbed harpoon heads (MB)

a) Morphology: the group shows high variability as regards the number of barbs and the way the proximal end is prepared for hafting throughout the whole record. There are more barbs in TS IV, which is related to the pieces being longer and so having more room for them. In TS IV the same happens as for SB: two populations coexist. Regarding SB the pieces are lighter (c.f. W) with less formatization of the active end (c.f. FOR), less resistant (c.f. RES) and longer (cf. ELONG).

b) Mechanical properties: In this case, and given the assigned mode of action (Penetration by impact, fixed harpoon-head, 4ai v. Table 8.3), the raw material selected does not seem specifically suited to this purpose for not complying with the expectation of a high elasticity module. Cetacean bone has the lowest elasticity module of the materials analysed. However, this can be compensated— as indicated in Table 8.3— by a high moment of inertia that, in this case, is defined by the design of the piece. I believe the choice here has been on the basis of a raw material that would allow easily the production of several barbs. As it is a harder material (high elasticity module), to fashion several barbs in guanaco bone would be more costly than in cetacean bone. In manufacturing terms, cetacean bone must have been much more economical. Additionally prey, in the case of using a small harpoon head, would have been small, so that a lower quality material can resist just as well;

c) Variability expectation in TS III: In this case the moment of greatest variability, measured in terms of standard deviation and box plots, takes place in TS I and IV. Despite, as stated, two populations of different sizes coexisting in TS IV, the highest averages for certain variables occur in TS I or IV, reaching similar values (e.g. ML, SW, and W). Additionally, save variable SW, the highest sigmas for all variables also correspond to TS I and IV. That is, for this group the greatest variability is recorded in TS I and IV, whereas TS III represents a moment of variability reduction, with standardized pieces. One might understand, then, that the moment of experiment in this MGT would correspond to TS I as the variability of IV is related to the larger size of the pieces.

Small Single-Barbed Heads (SBMICRO)

Morphology: In ethnographic times it was considered this morphological group accompanied canoe models. These consisted of scale reproductions of the canoes used by the Yamanas. Those objects were considerably cherished among 19th century ethnographers. In diverse museums created at that time one can see scale models of canoes. In that context, a letter by Reverend Stirling, the director of the Ushuaia mission during the 19th century (v. Stirling 1868, Ernesto Piana pointed out the existence of this letter to me) suggests he used to order such replicas from the Indians for sale in England, and with that money purchase European products. There are also models at the Magellan Strait which were used for bartering (Borrero pers. com.) But the presence of small single-barbed heads in TS I and III proves that they were preexistent. One may assume they were already part of the bone technology repertoire among the populations of this region. It is improbable they would have had a subsistence function with that size (variable ML of this MGT is below the minimum of that variable in SB, see Figures 9.18 and 9.22). They may have served as toys, though this can only be surmised on the basis of size. But what can be stated is that this morphological group was recovered latter in time by directing it, together with the canoe models, to the obtention of European materials. TS I pieces acquire the greatest average values for all variables save SW, FOR, and ELONG.

b) Mechanical properties: since this morphological group was presumably not related to technical or subsistence activities, the properties of the raw material would not have affected its performance.

c) Variability expectative in TS III: in this case the expectative for TS III is met for all variables save FOR and RES MOD.

Opposed Double-barbed harpoon heads in cetacean (ODB) and camelid bone (ODBCAM)

a) Morphology: They represent the same design carried out in two different raw materials. They appear only in TS IV. Barbs in these morphological groups have on average more acute angles than in SB (see Tables 9.2 and 9.6). On average both are less lengthy than SB. ODBCAM is lighter and shorter than ODB, though this characteristic may possibly be due to limitations imposed by raw material size. Nevertheless the average weight is similar to that of SB (v. Tables 9.2 and 9.6). The values of morphological variables shared by these groups with SB TS I and TS III are similar for which, despite their only appearing in TS IV (which has non-utilitarian populations for MB a much as for SB) it can be supposed that its use is linked to subsistence. It must be borne in mind that the ethnographic information available on this tool group assigns it to the Alcaluf area, so that the tools that make up the sample, belonging to an ethnographic collection, might come from an area of canals outside the region under study here (Isla Grande). RES MOD on average is greater in ODB. This average value is even higher than in SB TS I and TS III. This would suggest that ODB with few changes in the remaining variables related to size allows more resistant barb morphology than that of SB to be generated. The average of variable RES in ODB is less than those of SB and ODBCAM (this latter group surpassing SB).

b) Mechanical properties: This is a joint case of two groups that, with the same morphology, are related to two different raw materials. This would be extremely puzzling if it had to do with a detachable head (penetration by impact, mode of action 4aII) as everything would suggest that in that case cetacean bone would have to be chosen. Instead, the raw material would not be important if it were a fixed head. Nonetheless the ethnographic record refers it as a detachable head (Gusinde 1986:458).

c) The variability expectative in TS III: The sample is

from TS IV alone. In this case one would expect a fairly standardized morphological group. According to the results obtained, ODBCAM is less standardized than ODB. This could indicate that this design began in cetacean and went changing over to camelid for some reason. Anyway, the sample is too small to be able to discuss it with the data obtained.

Single-Barbed Head in Camelid Bone (SBCAM)

a) Morphology: It corresponds to the application of SB design to camelid bone. They are similar to those described by Gusinde (1986:226) as the javelin or dart heads used by the Selk´nam. These were used in fishing, using mode of action 4ai (fixed heads). They are recorded in III and IV time segments. The small size of TS IV sample prevents comparisons. The archaeological cases are found only in the northern sites (PM2), with the exception of one case from Bahía Valentín though of a different design. Compared with SB they show a barb with a more open angle and the frequency distribution of ML indicates that they are shorter. Remaining variables show on average slightly lower values than SB, but the differences are not very notorious, save in the case of RES MOD, which is clearly lower (see Table 9.2. and 9.7). No doubt this design was adopted for allowing that morphology to be extracted from guanaco bone, limited in size. The possibilities of thickness in guanaco bone do not allow a more resistant barb to be fashioned. In any case, this may not have been necessary owing to the mode of action of this tool. Also owing to the same factor, the hafting part of the MGT is different to SB

b) Mechanical properties: in view of the assigned mode of action it is to be expected that the raw material will have a high elasticity module such as guanaco bone possesses. This material does not allow for much variation in design but it is suitable to carry out that function. The high quality raw material allows the RES MOD to be held, which is low in comparison with SB.

c) Variability expectative in TS III: In all cases, save ML, SBCAM sigmas are low, not fitting the expectations for the period. They seem to be a rather standardized morphological group. Nevertheless, it must be borne in mind that it appears mostly in only one site, for which reason it might be reflecting a specific situation.

Multi-Barbed Head in Camelid Bone (MBCAM)

For the reasons put forward in Chapter 9 it is difficult to evaluate this group. It suffices to say that values do not differ from those of MB and specially MB TS IV— the contemporary morphological group— except the case of ML, which is related to the possibilities of size of the raw material.

Points

Points in Bird Bone (PBIRD)

a) Morphology: The antiquity of the use of bird bone is evident from Tres Arroyos site in the Chilean sector of the island. Here, artifacts made of bird bone were found on level V and dated at 10.280 and 11.880 BP (Massone 1988). This author reports having found two fragments of bird epiphyses— as well as another indeterminate bone fragment— showing transversal cuts, and he interprets that beads for necklaces will have been extracted from these bones. We cannot compare these materials directly with the sample presented here since, as has been stated, we are dealing exclusively with tools. However, it is a fact to be taken into account as it means this raw material was used by the most ancient Fueguian populations.

In general it can be said that the pieces belonging to TS III are longer than the remainder on average and have a wider point angle. Usually SW and ST do not vary much in their means and standard deviations, as these variations possibly are due more to the conditions imposed by the diverse bone blanks than to an attempt at formatizing.

b) Mechanical properties: From a mechanical point of view, the assigned mode of action (penetration) implies a high elasticity module expectative, which is borne out in fact. Regarding the taxa used, a temporary trend of a decreasing use of procellarians and an increase in that of anatides must be pointed out. It would be interesting to compare whether there exists a correlation of this tendency in the archaeofaunal record of birds. In most cases it is not possible to carry out this comparison since the only studies on bird fauna are from northern sites (PM2 and SP4) where, though anatides are certainly to be found, they are so in small proportions (specifically *Chloephaga picta*), while procellarians are absent (Lefèvre 1989). In the case of PM2, all PBIRDs are of anatides, but a specific identification was not obtained. Phalacrocoracidae are relatively stable throughout the sequence, while there is a slight increase of large birds towards TS III. No mechanical tests were carried out on the bones of these different taxa as to evaluate their differential properties (only cormorant was tested Scheinsohn and Ferretti 1995). We suppose that on a level of material properties the differences will not have been significant, though they certainly might be with regard to geometrical and structural properties.

c) Variability expectative in TS III: For most variables linked to length, this group shows a greater sigma amplitude in TS III, which can also be seen in the box plots though certain TS I (ELONG) and TS II (AL) variables acquire considerable dispersal. Besides, the greatest variety of taxa used is found in TS I. Nonetheless the differences among the diverse TSs are not significant (see Figures 9.29 to 31). The main changes appearing in the sequence have to do with TS III having more large-sized bone-blanks, which allows pieces with a longer module to be made. The variety of taxa in TS I would seem to indicate a moment of experiment there, although this is not altogether clear.

Cetacean Bone Points (PCET)

a) Morphology: These are cetacean bone artifacts with a point that, given the characteristics of the raw material, is usually blunt. The variability of its middle section (which can be quadrangular, rounded, and lenticular) and the proximal end of the piece (serrated or pointed) do no allow it to be determined whether they were used hafted or not. It is possibly a heterogeneous group with miscellaneous functions. There exists no ethnographic record on these tools, so that no functional hypothesis can be suggested. However it were, it is not a group with a significant representation in the record. The oldest pieces are from a single site (Tu I), whilst the more recent come from two, LP and BV, being very abundant in the latter. Results make it possible to hold that there is a tendency to make sturdier pieces in TS III.

b) Mechanical properties: though a mode of action assignation was not obtained through the ethnographic record, everything would lead to believe the properties of the raw material would rather place them in a situation of penetration by impact. In this case they must have been projectile heads, for which reason they must have had a shaft, though there is no evidence of hafting. This fact is strengthened on considering the contemporary appearance in the same site (BV) of PCET TANG , single-barbed heads from which, either by accident or intention, the barb was removed and the distal end repaired so as to remove the barb remains. PCET TANG may have served as a weapon head, as Hernán Vidal held (pers. comm.) In this sense PCET TANG and PCET could have had the same function. Given the blunted morphology of the proximal end, another possible function of this group may have been that of pressure flakers in stone knapping. All the same, Hugo Nami (pers. comm.) held that cetacean bone is not very efficient for that function, which coincides with the mechanical properties that raw material imply. Their use as awls is also thinkable as the ML range of PCET and, above all, most PCET TS III variables are almost coincident with those of PCAM, but this must be yet proved. Actually these tools are very generalized, so that their functional possibilities are manifold. In this sense, and according with Borrero (1993b), they show conditions for the appearance of cases of exaptation and, thus, of technological innovation. What is more, it might also be considered that certain pieces of PCET were a preform suitable for the fashioning of different morphological groups rather than a morphological group in itself. However it was, the facts we possess so far do not allow any advance on this hypothesis.

c) Variability expectative in TS III: This morphological group fulfils the expectative of greater variability in TS III for variables SW, FOR, RES, and ELONG, although dispersal is also high in TS I of variables ANG, ML, SL, AL, and ELONG.

Cetacean Bone Points with a Tang (PCET TANG)
Morphology: This is a case of single-barbed harpoon head what, intentionally or not, lost a barb and were re-used possibly for a different function (v.s.) This morphological group appears only in two recent sites (Tu VII and BVS1). This is a group related to SB though it is more standardized as sigmas in general are lower than in that group. The question on the loss of the barb remains open. Vidal (pers. comm.) suggested the barbs had been detached on purpose for the opportunistic use of some resource that did not require barbed heads (e.g. penguins, sea-lions on land) or to fight against another human group. In the first case, however, it should be noted that the quantity of tools devoted to the task is not justified by a single event. Also both hypotheses require the presence of the discarded barbs. It is remarkable that there are a number of barbs but it has not been possible to carry out any remontage of harpoon heads and barbs. This may be due to the harpoon heads having been reworked in order to remove remains of the detached barb. On the other hand, in the case of an accidental breakage during a sea-lion hunt, the barbs could also have been recovered if, finally, the prey had been caught in an attempt after the failed one. It is also worth considering the possibility— suggested by Borrero (1993-1994)— on the use of the archaeological materials as a source of raw material. This might well be the case, though there is no way to establish the time between the breakage of the barb on the harpoon head, accidental or intentional, and its later reformatization.

The variables of the shaft lead one to think of a similarity between PCET, PCET TANG, and PCAM. It is an interesting question since, had this morphological group been fashioned from SB, the resemblance could only be explained if PCET and SB had been made from the same preform, as there is no thinning down of the raw material as to set a length, width, and thickness that would make them similar. What has been said reinforces the possibility that PCET is made up of preforms and not finished tools.

b) Mechanical properties: When cetacean bone is used, Vidal's hypotheses are consistent with the mechanical properties of this raw material.

c) Variability expectative in TS III: This can not be evaluated on being present only in TS III.

Camelid Bone Points (PCAM)

a) Morphology: These would be awls (mode of action: penetration). They are longer than the PBIRD group. With regard to metrical variables, they resemble PCET in TS III, so they may have the same function. Yet they have sharper angles, like those of PBIRD. Compared with the other awls, this group appears as quite standardized (little dispersal).

b) Mechanical properties: The properties of the raw material suggest a tool that can be used to transmit force, which agrees with its assigned mode of action.

c) Variability expectative in TS III: They are only present in TS III, for which reason it can not be evaluated.

Canine Bone Points (PCAN) and Pinniped Bone Points (PPIN):
These are exceptional pieces, for which reason no suitable discussion can be carried out.

Blunt Points

Blunt Points in Camelid Bone (BPCAM)

a) Morphology: These are long pieces with a blunted end. They appear in Patagonia and Tierra del Fuego and are probably pressure flakers for stone working. These pieces tend to be shorter and sturdier in TS I and IV. This circumstance could indicate greater reactivation of pieces in this period or a different pressure technique, since a greater or lesser length of the flaker allows a different force to be applied on the stone artifact that is being made (Hugo Nami, pers. comm.)

b) Mechanical properties: Given the assigned mode of action (pressure), a high moment of inertia is to be expected which, in this case, is given by the morphology of the piece independently from that of the bone blank. In many specimens microwear corresponding to this kind of work was positively identified (see Nami & Scheinsohn 1997).

c) Variability expectative in TS III: The expectative if fulfilled as most of the variables show the higher sigmas and a broader distribution around the mean value in TS III.

Tubular Pieces with a Bevelled End (TBCAM)

a) Morphology: This is a group found exclusively in PM2. They could be bone hafts to which a stone tool such as a scraper would be attached.

b) Mechanical properties: It is one of the few groups in which the tubular structure of certain long bones such as tibias is made use of. If, as was supposed, they are bone hafts, they should not have been considered in this work. The hypothesis, however, still remains to be proved. Their good state of preservation makes it possible to speculate that microwear analysis will allow a function to be adjudicated to them.

c) Variability expectative in TS III: It can not be evaluated as they are only found in TS III.

Bevels

Cetacean Bone Bevels (BICET)

a) Morphology: This group is present in the record from the beginning, and remains throughout almost the whole sequence with a high degree of stability.

b) Mechanical properties: The mode of action assigned to this group, according to ethnographic references, is that of an intermediary in woodwork (4b). The tool was placed between the piece of wood to be worked and a hammer stone. Many of them show a flattening of bone fibers in their proximal zone or base, obtained from this type of action. In this case the choice of a raw material is in answer to the need for a tool that will stand pounding and be sturdy. Thus, cetacean bone is the indicated material.

c) Variability expectative in TS III: The variables do not show a definite pattern. Their distribution is quite homogeneous. The pieces are quite standardized since the beginning of the sequence.

Pinniped Bone Bevels (BPIN)

a) Morphology: It is more abundant in ancient times though not including a great quantity of pieces, and it tends to have progressively less throughout the sequence.

b) Mechanical properties: These are tools that would serve as intermediaries (4b, chisels), which fit expectatives given the properties of the raw material.

c) Variability expectative in TS III: It is fulfilled.

Camelid Bone Bevels (BCAM)

a) Morphology: bevelled pieces generally made out of guanaco metapods or some other long bone.

b) Mechanical properties: from the ethnographic record they were assigned mode of action 2 (lever). They would be associated with woodwork and used to extract bark. The bark was scored— possibly with tools like BCET— and then the piece was introduced between the bark and the tree trunk. By levering it was possible to separate the bark from the trunk. The chosen bone blank, which owing to the particularities of its middle section shows a high moment of inertia, is especially suitable for the function.

c) Variability expectative in TS III: It is fulfilled.

Summary of the Expectative of High Variability in TS III. Final Evaluation

Regarding the expectative of high variability in TS III, the analysis of the results allowed three situations to be differentiated:

1) There are morphological groups in which a situation of standardization or variability can not be evaluated because it appears in a single time segment or it represents a single situation: ODB, ODBCAM, SBCAM, VS, MBCAM, PCET TANG, PCAM, TBCAM;

2) there are other morphological groups that show a certain stability throughout the entire sequence such as PBIRD and BCET though some metrical variables seem to indicate a moment of variability in TS I. There are also heterogeneous groups showing great dispersal in TS I such as PCET and MB.

3) finally, there are morphological groups whose variables answer this expectative such as SB, SBMICRO, BPCAM, BCAM, BPIN whereas PCET shows high variability for certain variables in STI and for others in TS III;

In short, of eleven GMT in which the aspect can be evaluated, it is fulfilled in six cases.

Use of the Different Bone Raw Materials

From what has here been posited, we will now discuss questions of a general level on Fueguian bone tools.

Bone is a suitable material when it is a matter of manufacturing tools that, given their functionality, must have a long modulus. Under this general pattern significant differences have been found here as related to different bone raw materials by means of the study of their mechanical properties. These differences can be magnified or minimized in relation to the cost of obtaining them.

Bone raw materials can be obtained in two ways:

1) by using bone blanks of hunted animals (for food);

2) by the specific search for certain bone blanks, as a separate activity from hunting. In this case we can distinguish:

2a. Animals hunted for the use of their bones, fur, etc. (e.g. foxes);

2b. The use of carcasses of dead animals

The differences in raw materials will now be analysed together with the estimate cost of obtaining them.

Bird Bones

Mechanical properties: in general this material does not show good mechanical properties, except a high elasticity module given its size (cf. Chapter 8). As mentioned, as this is a property of the material it is not in relation to the geometry and structure of the bone in question. Thus the fact that it possesses a high elasticity module means the possibility of a relatively resistant material in relation to its size. Though bird bones in general and humerii in particular— which was the object of one of the mechanical tests carried out here— can be fractured easily (owing to its structural properties), they offer, when small, a good resistance to fracture. This resistance, with the same size and morphology, could not be achieved with other raw materials (e.g. wood).

The predominance of this raw material in the sample of archaeological tools analysed for this work can be attributed to their overrepresentation, at Tu I site. This site is also the most represented in TS I and II. Yet the presence of bird bones (sometimes with high percentages) goes further than the subsample from Tu I (v. Figure 9.12) and the fact that it is represented in all the analyzed sites (save BV) allow it to be considered one of the most important bone raw materials for Fueguian populations. Now, this raw material was made use of in the form of a single morphological group, that of points (PBIRD). It is possible that, in view of its abundance, the group fulfilled more functions than ethnography assumes, or its supposed function was more important than archaeological evidence allows one to suppose. Both hypotheses will need to be compared by independent means.

Costs: in order to discuss how bone bordes were obtained it is necessary to analyse the works by Lefèvre (1989) and Savanti (1994). Lefèvre finds that in the Sea of Otway sites cormorant (*Phalacrocorax* sp.) predominates, whereas in the sites on the Atlantic coast (specifically PM2 and SP4) the presence of this taxon is smaller, between 15 and 20%. In these sites the zampullín (*Podiceps major*) and the Dominican gull (*Larus dominicanus*) are important. In turn, Savanti (1994) considers that in the steppe an opportunistic pattern will have existed for bird exploitation, while in the southern forest region this pattern will have been more specialized. Thus, the situation in the Magellanic area, studied in Lefèvre's work, can be assimilated to the south of Isla Grande, as they present the same kind of environment (see Chapter 4). In the case of the Beagle Channel, in a partial study we have carried out for recent periods (Scheinsohn *et al.* 1992), potential bone blanks appearing in bird archaeofaunal record shows that, as is the case of the Sea of Otway, the presence of *Phalacrocorax* sp. is noteworthy. This is due to the possibility of mass hunting that cormorants offer, as was ethnographically recorded (c.f. Gusinde 1986). However, in bone tools, it will be seen that procellarians and anatidae predominate, while phalacrocoracidae remain constant (around 17% c.f. Chapter 9). In fact, in the archaeofaunal record of TuI, SHI and LP, there were many phalacrocoracid bone blanks, available and usable for PBIRD . Possibly this is due to this taxon alaways being available in large quantities, so that it is neither possible nor necessary to use all the potential bone blanks. Instead, at these sites there are few anatid and procellarian bone blanks available (for procellarians, 2,19% in TuI, 11,02% in LP and 9,09% in SHI, see Scheinsohn & al. 1992). In general these bones appear only in the form of tools (except some fragmented cases) which would indicate intensive use of them.

In other words, beyond an available species used thanks to its being mass hunted (e.g. cormorants, case 1 above), the case referred to in No. 2 would also have occurred. It is not economical to suppose that hunting of procellarians and anatides would have been practiced exclusively for the provision of bone raw materials and its presence in the archaeofaunal record it is not predominant. This pattern could be explained by an opportunistic hunt for subsistence purposes (1) or by recollection of bone blanks from carcasses of dead birds (2b).

Cetacean Bones

Mechanical properties: They have low mechanical qualities in general (see Chapter 8), but are noteworthy for their high absorption of energy, deformability, and morphological possibilities as— given their size— a great number of tools can be made, and in a significant variety of designs. In fact this is the raw material that sustains a greater variety of morphological groups and, therefore, the one that shows greatest richness. Its mechanical properties make it specially suitable for cases in which the tool must absorb energy (as in the case of a harpoon head striking a prey) and it must have a certain margin of deformability (that is, it should not be brittle, a typical property of stone materials). Six of the MGT manufactured from this raw material would be projectile points and their variants, one would be an intermediary (BCET), and the last class (PCET) has no known function, although it is probably a heterogeneous set of awls, flakers, weapon heads, or preforms. Its mechanical properties are similar to those of deer antlers (cf. Bouchoud 1974 and Albrecht 1977), a material that during the European Upper Palaeolithic was employed in the manufacture of harpoon or projectile heads. Undoubtedly it is an important raw material for the Fueguian human populations, as it was the one that supplied the tools they made use of to gain their means of subsistence— those used for hunting. Cetacean bone— the use of which grows constantly from TS I on (see Figure 9.8)— is a material clearly different from stone and which competes, as regards to properties, with wood. It also possesses the benefit of greater durability and resistance than the latter (see the experiments of Guthrie 1983, and

Arndt & Newcomer 1986 in the case of projectile heads). In hunting from a canoe, the detachable harpoon head stuck in the flesh of a large-sized prey (sea-lion or even a cetacean) needed to resist at least two opposite forces pulling on it: that of the shaft, pulling towards the surface, and that of the animal wanting to sink. These forces change constantly and dynamically in direction and intensity during the prey's struggle to break loose from the harpoon. A brittle material (guanaco bone or stone) in such conditions would probably fracture. A deformable one such as cetacean bone can resist longer without breaking, allowing the hunter to recover the prey. In addition, cetacean bone is also important in providing tools used for woodwork (e.g. wedges or bevels in cetacean bone), a key material for populations living in forest areas and having a way of life based on canoes (cf. Orquera & Piana 1990).

Costs: This is a material that is usually available, since it can be supposed that the rate of stranded whales was similar to that known nowadays, which is fairly often (cf. Proser Goodall 1978, Goodall & Galeazzi 1986). As the place and time of a strand can not be predicted, in ethnographic times information networks would have been organized among hunting groups so that all of them might take advantage of the animal's meat and fat (see in Purísima Concepción n.d.a and b the description made by the shipwrecked crew-members of the Purísima Concepción of a stranding episode cit. in Vidal 1985). In general it may be supposed that the bones of these animals, large and heavy, were left on the shore and only the soft edible parts were carried away. In consequence, it can be said that the skeletons of these animals were available on beaches at all times, as happens nowadays (cf. Borella & Favier Dubois 1994-1995, for Bahía San Sebastián). And for this reason, too, as Borrero (1985a) points out, it is very difficult to evaluate to what extent cetaceans were part of the hunter-gatherers' diet through the analysis of their bone remains. According to this author, the small number of cetacean bones present in the sites could be linked to tool production (Borrero 1985a: 255). But there is no doubt that it was an important resource, as Borrero proposes this as one of the strategies allowing fat consumption to be increased. In summary, it can be assumed that the costs of obtainment were low, being framed within case 2b.

Pinniped Bones

Mechanical properties: The situation of this material resembles that of whalebone to the extent that it has low mechanical qualities in general, but a good energy-absorbing and deformability capacity. The scanty presence of this raw material, which sinks as that of cetacean bone rises (v. Capítulo 9) and its small size in comparison with that of the latter (being impractical to formatize harpoon heads of a suitable size with these bones) justifies the supposition that perhaps they would be used to replace cetacean bones when the latter was unavailable, for the production of intermediary bevelled tools.

Costs: The fact that pinnipeds are gregarious animals and that they have relatively fixed and/or predictable (seasonal, permanent, or occasional) locations ("loberías") allow them to be located in significant quantities (cf. Lanata & Winograd 1988). These animals can easily be hunted on land, without the need of special hardware. As Lanata and Winograd (1988) point out, on land it would be more a matter of a harvest than a hunt. Sea-lions are available throughout the year. Their remains are abundant in LP, Tu I, PM2 (Lanata & Winograd 1988) and, though there are no specific analyses of SP4, they are abundant at all the sites in that area, often surpassing that of the guanaco. Owing to this, it may be presumed that the use of these animals' bones would depend on hunting since, as they are available as food, their bones could easily be taken advantage of. In recorded cases, the bones used, save occasional exceptions, were those of the fin (ulnae and radius), which had no value as food. In this way, though the occasional case of 2b can not be ruled out according to the record, the use of this animal is placed in case 1.

Guanaco Bone

Mechanical properties: Guanaco bone, as stated, is more brittle. It is the most used bone raw material in continental Patagonia, and its recorded use has a considerable antiquity. In general it appears in the shape of blunt points (BPCAM), known in archaeological literature as pressure flakers, and associated with pressure stone knapping. Still, on the Isla Grande de Tierra del Fuego, this material appears in at least seven morphological groups, of which five arise in TS III. The use of this material as a harpoon head is related to those whose efficiency did not depend on their deformability, as is the case of fixed harpoon heads. In that case the objective of the projectile was to pierce a relatively small prey which, in consequence, was not going to offer much resistance. When the tool in question needs to transmit force (flaker, awl) or resist leverage, this material is especially suitable due to the high elasticity module and moment of inertia that its long bones can possess.

Costs: Guanacos were regularly hunted on the Isla Grande. On the southern coast of the island, Orquera and Piana suggest a progressive reduction in hunting these camelids (cf. Orquera & Piana 1990:23). They also consider that, given the availability of canoes, hunting pinnipeds was less costly than that of guanacos. Still, in SH I guanacos predominate, though there is a marked dependence on marine resources, which can be inferred from the large amount of moluscs found at the site (Orquera & Piana 1990). In the north, contrariwise, the guanaco was the main staple around which the groups were organized. The advantage offered by the guanaco is that it can be found at any time of year anywhere on the island (Borrero 1985a). Its disadvantage is that its meat is lean. This involves creating a series of strategies to acquire other game with a greater fat content (see in Borrero 1985a and 1990).

From the preceding it follows that the guanaco would be placed mainly within case 1. The problem consists in that— at least as Borrero sees it for PM2 (Borrero 1985a)— there is a high rate of bone fracture so as to utilize bone marrow. And for obtaining bone marrow the most suitable bones are also the best for tool-making (i.e. metapod, tibia, and femur). The only way these two objectives can be put in practice without disagreeing is to posit that, in sites such as PM2, it is possible that a standardized fracture technique was developed allowing the obtainment of marrow and preforms for tools at the same time. This expectation can be put to the test by studying fracture patterns. Were it not fulfilled, it could be held that gaining bone marrow was preferred, as this objective was the more critical for the group or simply because guanaco bones are available in sufficient quantities.

Canid Bones

This raw material is limited to a single specimen in the analysed sample. It may be linked to the consumption of a single animal in PM2 (for which exists archaeological evidence, see Borrero 1985a: 255). For some momentary need one of its bones was used, but without doubt this is an opportunistic situation. Actually the consumption of canidae does not appear as a common situation as— with the exceptions of the mentioned case and that recorded at BV (Vidal 1985a)— where, although the canid was found *in situ* and associated to other remains of cultural origin, there are no signs that it was eaten— there is no major archaeological evidence of this on Isla Grande. Its presence in the record may possibly be attributed to a usage corresponding to case 2a (use of its fur).

Summary

Thus, regarding the use of different bone raw materials, it can be said that:

1) two types of bone were used: one of them, brittle, and in this sense similar to stone, but possessing a good elasticity module and good geometrical characteristics; and another that, without being of such high quality, could absorb energy, be deformable, and be of a good size to, in this way, acquire diverse shapes. Within the first case are found bird and guanaco bones, whilst in the second are those of cetacean and pinnipeds;

2) Procurement costs of bones are low, since most are dependent on hunting for food purposes (guanaco and pinniped bones, and within bird bones, those of the cormorant). Instead, cetacean bone and that of other birds (e.g. procellarians) would be obtained by opportunistic scavenging (case 2b). The only raw material that can be placed in case 2a is canine bone;

3) Regarding the diversity of morphological groups per raw material, it can be said that the richness of bird bone is minimal, in being limited to a single MGT throughout the different time segments. This also happens with pinniped bone, the richness of which is only increased in TS III with the appearance of another morphological group, though of small significance (see Chapter 9). Guanaco bone shows a tendency to an increase in richness, as also happens with that of cetacea. The richness of cetacean bone is always the greatest throughout the time range covered by the samples, save in TS IV. It also belongs to the two MGTs of greatest continuity in the sequence (BCET, MB and SB).

Differences in the Use of Raw Materials according to Geographical Distribution

From a spatial viewpoint, in Table 10.1 the distribution of different morphological groups of tools coming from diverse sites in two distinct areas is presented. Two areas were differentiated: North (north of Lake Fagnano) and South (to the south of it). These areas are related to phytogeographical criteria: the Southern area belongs to the District of Deciduous or Evergreen Forest, whereas the Northern zone is part of the Fueguian District, what some authors call Fueguian-Falkland Grasslands and Forests (Natenzon 1989 and Daniele 1991) or Steppe and Fueguian Park (Bondel 1984 v. Chapter 4). This analysis wishes to verify whether, as was claimed in Chapters 4 and 5, the environmental differences related to different human adaptations have brought about differences in the use of bone raw materials. This sort of analysis can only be effected for time segment III as, at that moment, there exist samples from sites located in both regions. In the other cases the samples are only from the southern area.

In Table 10.1 the double vertical line separates the southern sites from the northern ones, whereas the double horizontal line separates the raw materials. All sites are located in forest areas except PM2, which is in the steppe, and SP4, in the ecotone or Fueguian Park.

It must be made clear that, beyond the presence of tools, the sample from the southern area is much larger than that of the north (10% of the former). This situation is a reflection of the fact that there is a greater excavated surface in the south than in the north (320 m2 in the south versus 60 m2 in the north, v. Table 7.1). Yet if everything depended on this factor, the proportions should hold, which does not happen. On this account, it could be maintained that the exploitation of bone raw materials would be greater in the south. This approximation would seem to hold good on counting the quantity of morphological groups represented in the south (14) and in the north (8).

The difference is owed basically to the greater utilization of cetacean bone in the south and the absence of pinniped bone in the north. Camelid bone is employed as much in the north as in the south for the same morphological groups.

The morphological groups found in the greatest number of sites of both north and south are BPCAM (recorded in 8 sites, missing only in BCI), SB and BCET (these two recorded in 7 sites and missing at SHI and PM2).

From the point of view of functionality, tools used for the exploitation of wood are found in both areas (BCAM and BCET).

In other words, though there are fewer morphological groups in the north, those that are used there are also to be found in the south. In the case of cetacean bone, what are missing in the north are barbed harpoon heads. This is justified by the fact that in recent times the main prey in that area would be the guanaco. This animal, according to ethnographers (e.q. Gusinde 1982), was not hunted with harpoon heads but with a bow and arrow. Meanwhile, in the south the main prey was the pinniped, whose aquatic hunting required the development of barbed heads.

TS I and II, which would indicate a situation of stasis, an increase of variability in TS III, and a decrease in TS IV. The data do not allow that an initial moment of experimentation to be sustained for the sequence. Some indications, such as the greater dispersal of certain metrical variables in PCET, MB, and PBIRD and the larger number of taxa used in PBIRD point at a moment of experimentation in TS I, though this can not be clearly established. Still, if we suppose there to have been a moment of experimentation before TS I, TS I and TS II would represent a moment of decrease in diversity and consequent stabilization. This can be defended to the extent that the tools found in TS I appear technically developed, and are of a generalized type, which agrees with a moment of exploitation. What is

	South							North	
MGT	TUI	TU VII	LP	RS1	SHI	BCI (*)	BV	PM2	SP4
BPCAM	X	X	X	X	X		X	X	X
PCAM		X	X	X			X		
SBCAM							X	X	
BCAM	X	X	X	X	X				X
BTCAM								X	
PCAN								X	
PCET	X		X				X		
PCET TANG		X					X		
SB	X	X	X	X		X	X		X
SBMICRO	X			X			X		
MB	X	X		X			X		
VS	X								
BCET	X	X	X	X		X	X		X
PBIRD	X		X	X	X	X		X	
PPIN				X					
BPIN	X	X	X	X		X			

(*) BCI is actually located in Staten Island but in this work we will consider it in the Southern area

Table 10.1 – MGT recorded in archaeological sites located South and North Lake Fagnano

Diversity of Raw Materials and Comparison of the Model

The expectation of high diversity in TS III previously discussed arose from the identification of this time segment with the moment of experimentation predicted by the model. This identification was made taking into account the number of tool classes per TS and the results of the Shannon-Weaver index (Table 9.1). In that way a greater richness of morphological groups was proposed in TS III, while TS I, II, and IV presented lower richness. Yet according to the model proposed in Chapter 6, a high initial variability was to be expected, which should agree with TS I, and a subsequent descent with stability (stasis). Though the data do not back this expectation, the existence of a general pattern, consistent with that model, can be held, although differently from the expected manner. This pattern presents a moment of medium or low variability in

undoubtedly is that TS III is a moment of experimentation, though not initial, that presents changes, while TS IV is a moment of decrease in diversity or stasis, though prudence is recommendable in this, since lower variability can be related to collectors' biases.

These data then allow it to be maintained that, in the samples analysed, at least a moment of stasis appears, followed by one of variability. The initial moment of experimentation, predicted by the model, would not have left net evidences in the samples analysed here. The reasons for this could be that:

a) the initial moment of experimentation has a low visibility expectative;

b) the sample from ancient sites is smaller, thus not suggesting any tendency;

c) the experimental moment took place elsewhere, not included in this sample or located outside Isla Grande.

d) that initial moment never existed, which compromises the model.

The technical development of TS I tools and the geological features of the island reinforce a greater probability of a), b), o c). Of these, c) seems to gain relevance on remembering that bone raw materials were already known previous to the arrival on Isla Grande, as evidenced by bone artifacts at the Los Toldos site in Santa Cruz and those of Tres Arroyos, a place which is on the island, but with radiocarbon dates prior to the rise of the Magellan Strait. To this should be added the few indications that suggest some experimentation in TS I, which would strengthen this latter possibility, that is, that TS I would represent the end of a period of experimentation begun elsewhere.

As for the effects of the size of the sample in evaluating richness, it can be mentioned that the correlation between the size of the sample and the Shannon-Weaver index is, in this case, of a medium value (R2 = 0,459 v. Figure 10.1).

Though the greater diversity is found in the larger sample (TS III), TS I, also a large sample, gives low values (see Figure 10.1). For this reason, then, it can be claimed that the values of the Shannon-Weaver index approximately reflect an archaeological situation, and are not an effect of sample size.

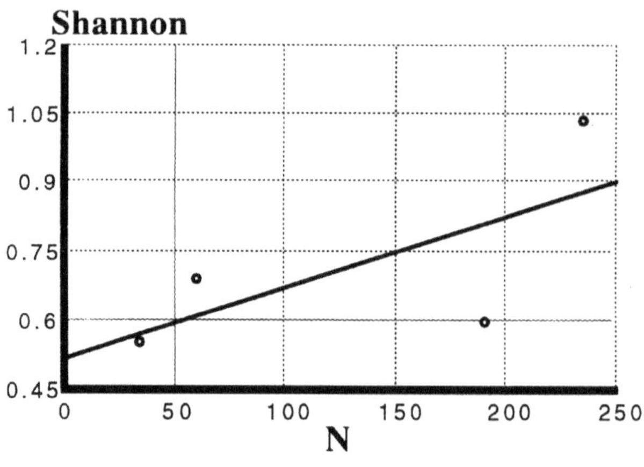

Figure 10.1 – Shannon-Weaver and sample size (N) correlation. P=0,2839.

CHAPTER 11

CONCLUSIONS

The model presented in foregoing chapters— arising from Darwinian evolutionism— as well as the biomechanical determinations of Fueguian bone raw materials, are a new approach— to my knowledge never attempted before— in the study of bone tools.

Apart from the new proposals the process has generated, the contrasting and re-elaboration of the model allows one to suggest the potential of this kind of analysis to apply in other geographical realities, such as those presented by other high latitude islands (for instance, New Zealand), where the environmental variable remains more or less constant. Comparisons at a regional or macroregional level will allow the establishment of whether there is a global answer on the reasons why human populations have exploited bone.

This being said— and limiting ourselves to the objectives of this work in what follows— the conclusions this study has been able to afford in the specific case of Tierra del Fuego will be examined.

Use of Bone Raw Materials in Tierra del Fuego and Their Differential Mechanical Properties

According to what was suggested in the introduction, Tierra del Fuego offers good conditions for bone raw material exploitation to be developed. Though its number of land mammals is limited to ten species, it possesses a significant variety of sea mammals as well as birds (see Chapter 4).

The bone raw materials actually exploited— limited to five taxa— show differentiated characteristics and they cover, on the strength of the potentialities of their mechanical properties, a wide range of possible modes of action. They offer contrasting and attractive options that either precluded or maximized the use of a bone's geometrical properties (Chapter 8).

For some of those modes of action, it was possible to make use of wood— a material able to replace bone thanks to the similarity of certain properties (e.g. anisotropy)— though its use, recorded in dry regions of Patagonia, has not been recorded in the damp Fueguian environment. No evidence of wood was found in the Tierra del Fuego archaeological record, other than charcoal. The question of preservation comes to the fore if it is borne in mind that, according to Gusinde (1986), given the environmental conditions, bark canoes had to be made once a year, every year. At the same time, most Fueguian woods are considered to be soft or half-hard (Chapter 4). Therefore, as bone is a material that offers anisotropic properties like wood, it allows for better preservation and resistance than the latter.

Within the ranges of utilized bone raw materials, cetacean bone is the one that offers the properties most similar to those of wood. It is not as brittle as guanaco bone; it has certain deformability and energy absorption, and its bone blank make possible a wide variety of sizes and designs. This material provided the tools used in the forested region (the ones related to woodworking) and at the coast (those related to hunting marine mammals). Its importance for Fueguian human populations— particularly in the southern area— was considerable. Thus it is to be expected that selective pressures acted on this material.

The samples studied show a constant increase in the use of whale bone, in contrast with a decrease in the use of bird bone, predominant at the beginning of the analysed sequence. This may be an effect of the sample from Tu I, which predominates in the first time segment. However, and going beyond that sample, the presence of bird bone shows considerable importance at that period. In this way, if the ethnographical hypothesis of use is corroborated by microwear— to the effect that those tools would be related to basket-weaving— the abundance of this kind of tool becomes an indirect means to evaluate the importance of basket-making, whereof no evidence exists in the archaeological record. Thus the smaller number of these tools towards the end of the sequence is probably related to a waning importance of that technology.

As regards to procurement costs evaluated in the previous chapter, it can be said that they were low in all cases. Bone raw materials were come by from the hunt for food purposes or by scavenging available carcasses. The case of canid bone— mentioned as marginal in the elaboration of bone tools— perhaps illustrates hunting for non-food purposes (2a, i.e. for fur, etc.), though this is conjectural.

Evaluation of the Model

From the model a methodology was proposed for its evaluation (Chapter 7). The results (Chapter 9) and their discussion (Chapter 10) allowed that model to be contrasted and placed within a context. This procedure made possible the conclusion that there is an agreement between the model and the data, provided the experimental stage is not put on the same level as the initial segment of the archaeological record studied (time segment I).

As argued in the preceding chapter, the existence of an initial experimental stage may be inferred. Possibly due to visibility problems or because it took place out of the Isla Grande there is an insufficient record of it.

If this is so, time segments I and II are equivalent to a period of exploitation in that:

1) there seems to be a lower diversity of basic designs;

2) the four main raw materials appearing throughout the sequence (cetacean, camelid, bird, and pinniped) were exploited;

3) the tool sample belonging to this period reflects a general knowledge of the properties of bone raw materials;

4) standardization (evidenced by the reduced dispersal of metrical variables) is significant in certain groups;

5) no competitive technologies are found.

Instead, time segment III would represent an experimental period in that:

1) it shows a great diversity of morphological groups, many of which are only present in that time segment;

2) certain morphological groups show a high diversity in their metrical structure (v.i.);

3) the greatest diversity of raw materials is found (if canine bone is included as an experimental material or one used opportunistically);

4) apparently new modes of action were incorporated in bone tools since, of the five groups lacking an assigned mode of action, three belong to this time segment and one of them, PCET TANG could be a case of exaptation (v.i.)

In terms of the expectations mentioned, the awaited diversity of techniques is not found. This can be explained if time segment III is considered a non-initial experimental stage. In this case diverse techniques would not have been needed. Experimentation with the materials led to new designs and not the incorporation of previously used techniques. The expectative of greater metrical variability, posited for this last time segment, showed complexity. Leaving out cases that can not be evaluated (due to being present in only one time segment) most morphological groups obey this expectative, but others (e.g. bird-bone points, cetacean-bone bevels) are groups that remain stable beyond what takes place on the general level of bone raw materials. This would seem to indicate the need to suit the scale of analysis to the level of morphological groups. Thus it is possible to interpret that the stables morphological groups — to the extent that adaptation acts as a magnet for stability— are those that, having achieved a certain efficacy in their performance, were not exposed to major pressures.

One case that remains to be discussed is that of small single-barbed harpoon heads. This group fits the expectative of variability, yet can not be considered subject to selective pressure unless their functional assignation had been mistaken.

It can therefore be defended that human populations arriving on Isla Grande already possessed a certain degree of knowledge of bone materials, specially guanaco and bird bones. When Isla Grande was formed, by the creation of the Magellan Strait, marine (cetacean and pinniped) bone materials were incorporated. In this way, at the beginning of the island's record, bone materials show significant technical development, remaining relatively stable until 1500 BP. At this moment an experimental phase arose that should not be associated with their acquisition by a human group. New morphological groups appeared, some of them having modes of action not accounted for in the ethnographical record, coincident with TS IV, for which reason it is thinkable that those modes of action subsequently disappeared.

What factors caused that need to "re-experiment" on bone, an already known raw material? As a hypothesis it may be suggested that Fueguian populations, from 1500 BP to the present, suffered a critical moment of acceleration in changes. The causes are many. In agreement with Borrero's (1989-1990 and 1993-1994) model, it may have been a matter of one of the effects of a stable phase of occupation. Keeping in mind that the places offering possibilities of occupation in the mountain and coastal areas of the island are few, it may be suggested that the space became saturated more quickly than in the north. Were this so, this phase would not be connected only with a rise in population but with the scarcity of spaces that could be occupied (Lanata 1995). Therefore, with the slightest increase in number, the south coast Fueguian populations would have found themselves obliged to occupy non-desirable areas (as the Chilean sites on the Bayly and Herschel islands, in Cape Horn, may suggest, see Museo Chileno de Arte Precolombino 1987). They would also redundantly occupy the more desirable areas, competing for these.

It is noteworthy that time segment III coincides with the period after the dating of the last volcanic tephra (according to Rabassa et al. 1990 Chapter 4), a period that can be interpreted as one of stabilization of the landscape. A greater diversity of bone tools (understood in terms of a larger number of raw materials employed, more morphological groups, greater variability in their metrical structure, and more varied modes of action) would indicate that Fueguian human populations were seeking a new and more competitive way of taking advantage of resources offered by that stabilized landscape. What had been known until then, regarding bone tools, was no longer enough to thrive in that environment.

For more recent periods, Piana (1984) suggested that the indirect presence of Europeans in the region, through the massive, indiscriminate hunting of sea-lions, may have jeopardized the survival of Fueguian populations, particularly those that depended on marine resources.

Still, the analysis of bone instruments allows the inference the the Fueguian populations were already undergoing a process of change, prior to the arrival of Europeans on Isla Grande. Possibly, their intruding in the middle of that critical period provoked greater and more harmful effects. Now, as from 1500 BP an accelleration in the changes in bone tools is observable, which is an indicator of a time of change in Fueguian populations. If this is so, this intensification of change in other raw materials and technologies should also be found. It would be desirable that this hypothesis were put to the test.

The model predicts a moment of abandonment which is not found in the samples analysed. The most recent sample in time, the ethnographical (TS IV), though biased, shows bone tools, that is, those that remained beyond the moment of contact. Still, this sample shows a tendency towards a change of function in bone tools, to the extent that these are limited almost exclusively to barbed harpoon heads. In addition, a significant proportion of them show a large size, which would not be recommendable if the function of these tools were the same as in the past. In this way it can be maintained that these harpoon heads are linked to non-technological uses, since they lack efficiency as hunting weapons. Their use as a means of barter with the European populations has been put forward (Scheinsohn 1990-1992), which confirms that the present relinquishment of this raw material is linked to the autochthonous Fueguian populations' extinction.

Future Possibilities of the Theoretical Framework

Despite its being presented here only as an enunciation, this theoretical framework opens up the possibility of working with morphological groups as the unit of analysis. For this, the indicated pathway is the cladistic analysis of bone tools and the consequent determination of their macroevolutionary patterns.

In biology, cladistics is the methodology that allows the organization of a systematic genealogy outlining groups of ancestral organisms and their descendants, in order to generate the concept of monophyletic taxa. The bases of phylogenetical sytematics or cladistics were laid by Hennig (1966). The central idea of cladistics is that the modifications of phenotypical traits in organisms are inherited by their descendants. Evolutionary novelties, called synapomorphies, are homologous structures shared by the ancestral species, in which it first appears, and all its descendants. Synapomorphies are of use as indicators in recognizing lines of descent. Cladists must find the point at which a particular trait was introduced through the phylogenetic history. When that trait is correctly identified it becomes a synapomorphy that delimitates the group. The pattern of similarities between organisms is expressed in a branched hierarchical diagram called a cladogram. All the organisms that share a primitive feature or synapomorphy are a monphyletic taxon. The study of macroevolutionary patterns is based on those higher taxa.

Eldredge (1989) considers the pattern of diversity between species, the rate of speciation and extinction, and the mode of selection of the species as the factors intervening in macroevolutionary patterns. This characterization allows him to predict behaviours regarding the degree to which the component species are able to tolerate larger or smaller variations in environmental conditions (that is, whether they are respectively euritopical or steneotopical), their geographical distribution, and the presence of apomorphies (novelties) or plesiomorphies (primitive traits). Thus, he describes the four general types of macroevolutionary patterns in the following terms:

1) Trends: the result of the production and differential survival of ever more specialized organisms that appear in lineages of narrow niche organisms. Eldredge (1989) considers two possibilities: either species become "sorted" (extinguished) on account of the organisms differing as regards the traits that make up the trend, or the "trend" is a side-effect of the rates of differential speciation and/or extinction, caused by different traits in the organisms.

2) Adaptive radiations: These are produced by the (generally rapid) proliferation of species making up a monophyletic taxon. The group as a whole stands the radiation though its subcomponents may diversify, remain adaptationally uniform, or develop one or more trends (Eldredge 1989). Therefore there is no single pattern constituting this case. Actually they are complex mosaics of another sort of phylogenetic patterns. They have to do with the limitations in adaptive design. For example, among mammals there are few ways of being an effective carnivore, and those general strategies bespeak a narrow selection of anatomical and behavioural designs. The rates of speciation and extinction are high especially at the outset. Species are relatively stenotypical and synapomorphies (evolutionary novelties) appear at a rapid rate.

3) Arrested evolution: the organisms show no anatomical changes since the creation of their lineage. If the species of a lineage remain generalized, the rate of production of new species will be low and there will be little or no adaptive change. They can show the following traits: a low diversity of species, long-lasting species, and wide geographical distributions. They would be made up of euritopical species that, as a rule, acquire adaptive change slowly.

4) Steady state: the rates of speciation and extinction appear to be balanced.

The work carried out so far allows certain perspectives to be seen in this sense.

Macroevolutionary Patterns and Cladistic Analysis Applied to Bone Tools

To transfer the developments of cladistic analysis to archaeology is no easy task. All the same, tool classes can be analysed by considering them as analogous to monophyletic taxa. The appearance of a structural novelty (synapomorphy in the cladistic context) would define that taxon. If we consider the history of a raw material like bone, the first evolutionary novelty would be the possibility of implementing a elongated modulus in the tools. Derived traits might be the presence of barbs and the morphology of the performing end. The incorporation of a given synapomorphy would inaugurate a *bauplan*, that is, a basic structural plan common to all members of the group considered as a monophyletic taxon. In this way, cladistic analysis would allow to establish which macroevolutionary pattern has been followed by each morphological group of tools.

Considering the four kinds of macroevolutionary patterns listed by Eldredge (see above), their application to archeological tools would imply expecting:

1) Trends: This is a case of morphological groups of specialized tools, with specific functions. A progressive standardization of the group is expected which would show up a decrease in variance, and successive replacements of apomorphies would take place.

2) Adaptive radiations: From a basic *bauplan*, a series of variations on the same theme and a high proliferation of subgroups or variants within the morphological group are expected. Artifacts of a very specific function, with a limited geographical range, with many apomorphies, and little retention of primitive characteristics (plesiomorphies) are expected to be found. These tools must appear in a relatively short time.

3) Arrested evolution: the morphological group or class of tool shows little change from the time it appears in the record. These are artifacts with a generalized function. Their geographical distribution is widespread. Not many internal variants can be detected. They show an extensive duration in the record.

4) Steady state: it describes a typical state of stasis, in which a high diversity of design it is not expected.

Thus the work carried out so far allows proposing as a case of adaptive radiation, that of barbed harpoon heads, since they occupy a wide range, being present in all the studied sites of the island, and each morphological group would have a limited geographical distribution. It may also be proposed that PBID and BICET, which shows great stability in the record, might represent cases of a steady state or arrested evolution, but it should be necessary to generate the criteria that would allow one case to be differentiated from the other.

Finally, Borrero's (1993b) proposal remains to be explored. Some of the key points he has argued have been mentioned here. For instance, starting out from the results obtained, a case of exaptation such as that of PCET TANG can be proposed. Contrary to what Borrero posited, this morphological group it is not expeditive. What is beyond doubt is that that morphological change implies a change in function. This case of exaptation belongs to time segment III, where the acceleration of change takes place as already mentioned.

Final Words

Bone technology is only one aspect among Tierra del Fuego human populations. The conclusions and hypotheses suggested in this work should be reflected in the other technologies employed by these populations. An interesting way would be to transfer the proposed model to the study of lithic material. The spatial distribution of artifacts and even human remains in the area should likewise reflect the stress that a situation such as that described for the period beginning in 1500 BP must have generated.

It is my wish that this work be of use in exploring those other materials with new ideas in mind. In this way an evolutionary explanation of the processes that took place among the ancient populations of Tierra del Fuego may be proposed.

CHAPTER 12

REFERENCES

Acedo de Reinoso, T.; P. Cámera and H. Vidal

1988. Bahía Valentín: Encuentros en la costa. Paper delivered at IX Congreso Nacional de Arqueología Argentina, Buenos Aires.

Adams, W.

1988. Archaeological Classification: Theory versus Practice. *Antiquity* 62: 40-56.

Aguirre, E.

1973. Industries osteiques anciennes: méthode et un essai de typologie. *VII Congrès Internationale de la Societé Préhistorique et Protohistorique* II: 57-68.

1981. Industries osteïques anciennes: méthode et un essai de typologie. UISPP. Congress Acts.

1985. Torralba: debitage d'ossements d'elephants. Approche d'une analyse morphotechnique *Artefacts* 1. *Outillage peu elaboré en os et bois de cervidés:* 33-44.

1986. Format et technique dans la fracturation d'ossements a Torralba (Soria-Espagne). *Artefacts* 3. *Outillage peu elaboré en os et bois de cervidés:*81-89.

Aguirre, E. and M. Hoyos

1977. Observations méthodiques sur outillage osseux du Paléolithique inférieur. *Deuxième Colloque Internationaux sur l'industrie de l'os dans la Prehistoire. Méthodologie Appliqué à l'industrie de l'os préhistorique*, CNRS: 55-61.

Alaux, J.

1971. Points osseuses à extremité striée de l'Abri des Battuts (Tarn). *Bulletin de la Société Préhistorique Française* 6: 175-177.

Albrecht, G.

1972. Taking Quantitative and Qualitative Data: a New Attribute System for Bone Points of Early and Middle Upper Paleolithic Industries. *Symposium on the Early Upper Paleolithic in Europe*, Tübingen.

1977. Testing of Materials as Used for Bone Points of the Upper Paleolithic *Deuxième Colloque Internationaux sur l'industrie de l'os dans la Prehistoire. Méthodologie Appliqué à l'industrie del'os préhistorique*, Editions C.N.R.S.: 119-126.

Albrecht, G., Hahn, J. and W. Torke

1972. Merkmalanalyse von Geschoßspitzen des mittleren Jungpleistozäns in Mittel und Osteuropa *Archaeologica venatoria* 2.

Allain, J.; R. Fritsch; A. Rigaud and F. Trotignon

1974. Le débitage du bois de renne dans les niveaux à raclettes du Badegoulien de l'Abri Fritsch et sa signification. *Premier Colloque Internationaux sur l'industrie de l'os dans la Prehistoire*, Editions Universitaires, Provence: 67-71.

Ameghino, F.

1880. *La Antigüedad del Hombre en el Plata.* París.

Andrew, P. and J. Cook

1985. Natural Modifications to Bones in a Temperate Setting. *Man (N.S.)* 20: 675-691.

Arndt, S.and M. Newcomer

1986. Breakage Patterns on Prehistoric Bone Points: an Experimental Study. In *Studies in the Upper Palaeolithic of Britain and Northwest Europe*, D.A. Roe (ed.), BAR International Series 296:165-173.

Arnal, J.and M.R. Séronie-Vivien

1983. Les armes en os de la France et leur contexte européen du Néolithique à l'Age des Métaux. *Congrés Préhistorique de France,* XXI Session, Vol 2: 3-14.

Ascenzi, A.and G.H. Bell

1972. Bone as mechanical engineering problem. In *The Biochemistry and Physiology of Bone*, G.H. Bourne (ed.) pp. 311-352.Vol I, Academic Press, New York.

Bächler, E.

1907. Die praehistorische kulturstaette in der Wildkirchli-Ebenalphöhle (Säntisggebirge). *Verhandlungen der Schweizerischen Naturforschenden Gesellschaft in St. Gallen*, St. Gall.

Baker, J.L.and C.G. Haugh

1979. Mechanical Properties of bone: a review. *Transactions of American Society of Agronomic Engineering* 22: 678-687.

Barandiarán, I.

1967a. *El paleomesolítico del Pirineo occidental. Bases para una sistematización tipológica del instrumental óseo paleolítico*,Ph D manuscript, Universidad de Zaragoza.

1967b. Sobre la tipología y tecnología del instrumental óseo paleolítico. *Caesaraugusta* 29-30:7-79.

1969-1970. Arudy 1969. Coloquio Internacional de Tipología. *Caesaraugusta* 33-34.

1977. Arpones decorados del Paleolítico de Santander. Algunas Reflexiones. *XL Aniversario del Centro de Estudios Montañeses* III: 413-434.

1978. Industry in Bone and Shell. *El Juyo 1978. A Preliminary Report on a Magdalenian Site in Cantabrian Spain.* I. Barandarián, L. Freeman, J. González Echegaray and R. Klein (eds.). pp. 41-51.

1985. Industrias ósea paleolítica de la cueva del Juyo: excavaciones de 1978 y 1979. *Excavaciones de la Cueva del Juyo.* I. Barandarián, L. Freeman, J. González Echegaray and R. Klein (eds.) pp. 163-194.

1987. Manipulación y uso de restos óseos. *La cueva de Peña Miel, Nivea de Cameros, La Rioja.* Utrilla, P., J. Vilchez, L. Montes, I. Barandarián, J. Altuna, E. Gil and P. López (eds.): 60-78. Excavaciones Arqueológicas en España, Ministerio de Cultura, Madrid.

Barone, R.
1966. *Anatomie comparée des mammifères domestiques* I, Laboratoire d'Anatomie, Ecole Nationale Veterinaire, Lyon.

Behrensmeyer, A.K.and A. P. Hill
1980. *Fossils in the Making.* Univ. of Chicago Press.

Behrensmeyer, A.K.and S.M. Kidwell
1985. Taphonomy's Contributions to Paleobiology. *Paleobiology* 11: 105-119.

Behrensmeyer, A.K., K. Gordon and G. Yanagi
1986. Trampling as a Cause of Bone Surface Damage and Pseudo-Cutmarks. *Nature* 319: 768-771.

Berke, H.
1977a. Le débitage du bois de renne de Gönnersdorf et la comparaison avec des artefacts d'eskimo. *Deuxième Colloque International sur l'Industrie de l'os dans la Préhistoire, Méthodologie appliquée a L'industrie de l'os préhistorique*, CNRS: 347-350.

1977b. Déchets de fabrication de harpons magdaléniens découverts à Gönnersdorf (Neuwied). *Bulletin de la Societé Préhistorique Francaise* 71: 105-109.

Biberson, P. and E. Aguirre
1965. Experiences de taille d'outils préhistoriques dans des os d'elephant. *Quaternaria* VII: 165-183.

Billamboz, A.
1977. L'industrie de bois de cerf en Franche-Comté au Néolithique et au début de l'age du bronze. *Gallia Préhistoire* 20 (1): 91-176.

Binford, L.
1972. *An Archaeological Perspective.* Seminar Press.

1977. *For Theory Building.* Academic Press.

1978. *Nuniamut Etnoarchaeology.* Academic Press.

1981a. *Bones: Ancient Man and Modern Myths.* Academic Press.

1981b. Behavorial Archaeology and the "Pompeii Premise". *Journal of Anthropological Research* 37(3): 195-208.
1988. *En busca del pasado.* Ed. Crítica, Madrid.

Binford, L. and S. Binford
1966. A preliminary analysis of functional variability in the Mousterian of Levallois facies. *American Anthropologist* 68 (2): 238-295.

Binford, L.and J. Sabloff
1983. Paradigms, Systematics and Archaeology. In *Working at Archaeology.* L. Binford (ed.) Academic Press.

Bird, J.
1946. The Archaeology of Patagonia. In *Handbook of South American Indians, Bureau of American Ethnology Bulletin* 143 (1): 17-24.

1969. A Comparison of South Chilean and Ecuadorian "Fishtail" Projectile Points. *Kroeber Anthropological Society Papers* 40: 52-71.

Bleed, P.
1986. The Optimal Design of Hunting Weapons: Maintainability or Realiability. *American Antiquity* 51 (4): 737-747.

Bobrowsky, P. and B. Ball
1989. The theory and mechanics of ecological diversity in archaeology. In *Quantifying diversity in Archaeology*, R. Leonard and G. Jones (eds.), pp. 4-12. Cambridge University Press, Cambridge.

Bondel, S.
1984. *Tierra del Fuego: La organización de su espacio.* Licenciatura thesis, Universidad de Buenos Aires.

1988. *Geografía de Tierra del Fuego. Guía docente para su enseñanza*, Museo Territorial, Ushuaia.

Bonfield, W. and C. Li
1966. Deformation and Fracture of Bone. *Journal of Applied Physics* 37 (2): 869-875.

1967. Anisotropy of Nonelastic Flow in Bone. *Journal of Applied Physics* 38 (6): 2450-2455.

Bonifay, E.
1974. Outil sur os et os utilisés dans le Paléolihique Ancien du Mas des Caves à Lunel-Viel (Hérault). *Premier Colloque Internationaux sur l'industrie de l'os dans la Prehistoire*, Editions Universitaires, Provence: 157-167.

Bonifay, M.F.
1974. Essai de córrelation entre les os cassés intentionellement

et leur origine anatomique au Paléolithique Ancien (Grottes de Lunel-Viel, Hérault). *Premier Colloque Internationaux sur l'industrie de l'os dans la Prehistoire*, Editions Universitaires, Provence: 21-26.

1985. Le materiel osseux fragmenté determinable au Paléolithique Ancien: Mise en evidence. Categories. Histogramme. *Artefacts* 3: 11-45.

Boninsegna, J.; J. Keegan; G. Jacoby; R. D'Arrigo and R. Holmes
1989. Dendrochronological Studies in Tierra del Fuego, Argentina. *Quaternary of South America and Antarctic Peninsula* 7: 305-326.

Bonnichsen, R.
1979. Pleistocene Bone Technology in the Beringian Refugium. *Archeological Survey of Canada. Mercury Series* 50, National Museum of Man.

1989. An Introduction to Taphonomy with an Archaeological Focus. In *Bone Modification*, R. Bonnichsen & M. Sorg (ed.) Peopling of the Americas Publications, Center for the Study of the First Americans, Institute for Quaternary Studies, University of Maine.

Bonnichsen, R. and M. Sorg
1989. *Bone Modification.* Peopling of the Americas Publications, Center for the Study of the First Americans, Institute for Quaternary Studies, University of Maine.

Bonnichsen, R. and R. Will
1980. Cultural Modification of Bone: the Experimental Approach in Faunal Analysis. *Mammalian Osteology,* B. Miles Gilbert (ed.) pp. 7-30, B. Miles Gilbert Publisher.

Bordes, F.
1961. *Typologie du Paléolithique Ancien et Moyen.* Publications de l' Institut de Préhistoire, Bordeaux, mémoire 1, 2 vol.

1974. Percuteur en bois de renne du Solutréen superieur de Laugerie-Haute Ouest. *Premier Colloque Internationaux sur l'industrie de l'os dans la Prehistoire*, Editions Universitaires, Provence: 97-100.

Borella, F. and C. Favier Dubois
1994-1995. Observaciones tafonómicas en la Bahía San Sebastián, Costa Norte de Tierra del Fuego, Argentina. *Palimpsesto* 4: 1-8.

Borrero, Luis A.
1985a. *La economía prehistórica de los habitantes del norte de la Isla Grande de Tierra del Fuego.* Ph D thesis manuscript, Universidad de Buenos Aires.

1985b. Taphonomic Observations in Guanaco Skeletons. *Current Research in the Pleistocene* 2: 65-66.

1988. Tafonomía Regional. In *De procesos, contextos y otros huesos, Seminario de Actualización en Arqueología*: 9-15.

1989-1990. Evolución cultural divergente en la Patagonia Austral. *Anales del Instituto de la Patagonia* 19: 133-140.

1991. *Los Selk'nam. Su evolución cultural.* Editorial Búsqueda. Buenos Aires.

1993a. Site Formation Processes in Patagonia: Depositional Rates and the Properties of the Archaeological Record. In *Explotación de Recursos Faunísticos en Sistemas Adaptativos Americanos.* J.L. Lanata (ed.) *Arqueología Contemporánea* 4: 107-121.

1993b. Artefactos y evolución. *Palimpsesto* 3:15-32.

1994-1995. Arqueología de la Patagonia. *Palimpsesto* 4: 9-69.

Borrero, L.; M. Casiraghi and M. Hernandez Llosas
1981. Arqueología del Norte de Tierra del Fuego. *Publicaciones del Museo Territorial* 1:1-23.

Borrero, L. and J. L. Lanata
1988. Estrategias adaptativas representadas en los sitios de Estancia María Luisa y Cabo San Pablo. *Precirculados de las ponencias científicas presentada a los simposios del IX Congreso Nacional de Arqueología Argentina,* UBA: 166-174.

Borrero, L. and F. Martín
1996. Tafonomía de carnívoros: un enfoque regional. In *Arqueología. Solo Patagonia.* J. Gómez Otero (ed.) pp. 189-198. Centro Nacional Patagónico (CENPAT)- CONICET, Puerto Madryn.

Bouchud, J.
1974a. L'origine anatomique des matériaux osseux utilisés dans les industries préhistoriques. *Premier Colloque Internationaux sur l'industrie de l'os dans la Prehistoire,* Editions Universitaires, Provence: 21-26.

1974b. Les traces de l'activité humaine sur l'os fossil. *Premier Colloque Internationaux sur l'industrie de l'os dans la Prehistoire*, Editions Universitaires, Provence: 27-33.

1977. Les aiguilles en os. Etude comparée des traces laissées par la fabrication et l'usage sur le material préhistorique et les objets expérimentaux. *Deuxième Colloque International sur l'Industrie de l'os dans la Préhistoire, Méthodologie appliquée a L'industrie de l'os préhistorique,* CNRS: 49-55.

Bouge, L.
1950. *Etudes sur le harpon ancien des îles Marquises*, Max Besson, París.

Bouvier, J.
1974. Sagaies du magdalénien supérieur de plusiers gisements de Charente et Périgord. *Premier Colloque Internationaux sur l'industrie de l'os dans la Prehistoire,* Editions Universitaires, Provence: 181-185.

1979. Le mystère des fendeurs de phalanges ou contribution à la connaisance du travail de l'os au Magdalénien IV *Bulletin de la Societé Préhistorique Francaise* 76 (4): 105-109.

Brain, C. K.
1989. The Evidence for Bone Modification by Early Hominids in Southern Africa. In *Bone Modification*, R. Bonnichsen & M. Sorg (ed.) Peopling of the Americas Publications, Center for the Study of the First Americans, Institute for Quaternary Studies, University of Maine, pp. 291-298.

Breuil, H.
1912. Les subdivisions du Paléolithique supérieur et leur signification. *XIV Congrès International d'Anthropologie et d'Archeologie Préhistoriques*: 165-238.

1932. Le feu et le industrie de pierre et d'os dans le gisement du Sinanthropus à Chou-Kou-Tien. *L'Anthropologie* 42: 1-77.

1938. The use of bone implements in the Old Paleolithic period. *Antiquity* 22: 36-57.

Bridges, T.
1892. Datos sobre Tierra del Fuego comunicados por el Reverendo Thomas Bridges. *Revista del Museo de La Plata* 3: 313-320.

1893. La Tierra del Fuego y sus habitantes. *Boletín del Instituto Geográfico Argentino* XV (5-8): 221-241.

Bridges, L.
1978. *El último confín de la tierra*, Marymar, Buenos Aires.

Bridges, R.
1953. Las canoas yaghanes y un pequeño recuerdo al artesano indígena. *Anales del Museo de Nahuel Huapi* III: 33-36.

Bromage, T.
1984. Interpretation of Scanning Electron Microscopic Images of Abraded Forming Bone Surfaces. *American Journal of Physical Anthropology* 64: 161-178.

Brooks, A.; D. Helgren; J. Cramer; A. Franklin, W. Hornyak; J. Keating; R. Klein; W. Rink; H. Schwarcz; J. Leith Smith; K. Stewart; N. Todd; J. Verniers and J. Yellen
1995. Dating and Context of Three Middle Stone Age Sites with Bone Points in the Upper Semliki Valley, Zaire. *Science* 268: 548-553.

Bunn, H.T.
1981. Archaeological Evidence for Meat-eating by Plio-Pleistocene Hominids from Koobi Fora aand Olduvai Gorge. *Nature* 291: 574-77.

1989. Diagnosing Plio-Pleistocene Hominid Activity with Bone Fracture Evidence. In *Bone Modification*, R. Bonnichsen & M. Sorg (ed.), pp. 299-316. Peopling of the Americas Publications, Center for the Study of the First Americans, Institute for Quaternary Studies, University of Maine.

Burr, D.
1980. The Relationships Among Physical, Geometrical and Mechanical Properties of Bone, with a Note on the Properties of Nonhuman Primate Bone. *Yearbook of Physical Anthropology* 23: 109-146.

Cabrera, A. and A.Willink
1973. *Biogeografía de América Latina.* Monografía N°13, Serie de Biología. OEA.

Cabrera, V.
1984. El hueso poco elaborado. *Biblioteca Praehistoria Hispana* XXII: 427-438.

Cabrera Valdés, V.
1985. La industria ósea: Concepto y Método. *Trabajos de Prehistoria*: 157-167.

Cabrera, V. and F. Bernaldo de Quirós
1977. L'os travaillé du Paléolithique au Nord de l'Espagne. Principes de recherche. *Deuxième Colloque International sur l'Industrie de l'os dans la Préhistoire, Méthodologie appliquée a L'industrie de l'os préhistorique*, CNRS: 49-54.

Campana, D.
1980. *An Analysis of the Use-Wear Patterns on Natufian and Protoneolithic Bone Implements.* Ph. D. Dissertation, Columbia. University. University Microfilms International, Ann Arbor.

1987. The Manufacture and Use of Bone Implements in the Zagros and the Levant. *MASCA Journal* 4 (3): 110-123.

1989. *Natufian and Protoneolithic Bone Tools: the Manufacture and Use of Bone Implements in the Zagros and the Levant.* BAR Series 494.

Camps-Fabrer, H.
1966. Matière et art mobilier dans la Préhistoire Nord-Africaine et Saharienne. *Mémoires du Centre de Recherches Anthropologiques, Préhistoriques et Etnographiques (CRAPE)* V, Argelia.

1967. Typologie de l'industrie osseuse en Afrique du Nord et au Sahara. *Congrès Panafricain de Préhistoire*: 279-283.

1968. Industrie osseuse épipaléolithique et néolithique du Maghreb et du Sahara. *Fiches Typologiques Africaines du CRAPE*, Cahiers 6 and 7.

1971. De l'orientation des objets en os. *Bulletin Société Préhistorique Française* 68: 102.

1976a. L'industrie de l'os du gisement du Collet-Redon à La Couronne (Bouches-du-Rhône). *XXe Congrès Préhistorique de France*: 137-165.

1976b. Le travail de l'os. *Préhistoire Française*, Tomo1: Les civilisations paléolithiques et mésolithiques de la France, Deuxieme partie: L'homme et ses activités: 717-722.

Camps-Fabrer, H. (ed.)
1977a. *Deuxième Colloque International sur l'Industrie de l'os dans la Préhistoire, Méthodologie appliquée a L'industrie de l'os préhistorique*, CNRS.

Camps-Fabrer, H.
1977b. Compte rendu des travaux de la Commission de Nomenclature. Próbleme du lexique, des fiches. *Deuxième Colloque International sur l'Industrie de l'os dans la Préhistoire, Méthodologie appliquée a L'industrie de l'os préhistorique*, CNRS: 19-26.

Camps-Fabrer, H. and L. Bourrelly
1972. *Lexique des termes caracteristiques pour l'analyse des objets en os*, Versión N° 1, Laboratoire de Anthropologie et Préhistoire du Pays de la Mediterranée Occidental, Aix-en-Provence.

1974. Prémiers résultats concernant les méthodes d'analyse et le traitement en ordinateur des objets en os de quelques gisements du Midi méditerranéen. *Premier Colloque Internationaux sur l'industrie de l'os dans la Prehistoire*, Editions Universitaires, Provence: 135-141.

Camps-Fabrer, H., L. Bourrelly and N. Nivelle
1974. *Lexique des termes descriptifs de l'industrie de l'os*, Versión N°2, Laboratoire de Anthropologie et Préhistoire du Pays de la Mediterranée Occidental, Aix-en-Provence.

Camps-Fabrer, H. and A. D'Anna
1977. Fabrication expérimentale d'outils à partir de métapodes de mouton et de tibias de lapin. *Deuxième Colloque International sur l'Industrie de l'os dans la Préhistoire, Méthodologie appliquée a L'industrie de l'os préhistorique*, CNRS: 311-326.

Camps-Fabrer, H. and D. Stordeur
1979. Orientation et definition des differentes parties d'un objet en os. *L'industrie de l'os néolithique et de l'Age des metaux. 1er Réunion du Groupe de Travail sur l'industrie de l'os préhistorique*, CNRS.

Capitan, M.
1906. Le débitage de l'os, de la corne et de l'ivoire à l'epoque magdalénienne. *Congrès International d'Anthropologie*, 13° session, Mónaco, pp. 404 - 405.

Cardich, A.
1978. Las culturas pleistocénicas y post-pleistocénicas de Los Toldos y un bosquejo de la prehistoria de Sudamérica. *Obra del Centenario del Museo de La Plata*, Tomo II: 149-172.

Casiraghi, M.
1984a. Esquema de clasificacion de los artefactos óseos. *Arqueología Contemporánea* I (2): 26-31.

1984b. Arpones y cuñas en hueso provenientes de Rancho Donata (Península Mitre, Tierra del Fuego). *Informes del Programa Extremo Oriental del Archipiélago Fueguino* 1: 24-57.

1985. Análisis de los artefactos óseos de la Cueva de Huachichocana III (Pcia. de Jujuy, República Argentina). *Paleoetnologica* 1: 19-35.

1987. Comentarios referentes al estudio de los artefactos óseos. *Primeras Jornadas de Arqueología de la Patagonia*: 65-68. Dirección de Cultura de la Provincia del Chubut.

Clark, J.G.D.
1953. The Groove and Splinter Technique of Working Reinder and Red Deer Antler in Upper Palaeolithic and Early Mesolithic Europe. *Archivos de Prehistoria Levantina* IV: 57-67.

Clark, J.G.D. and M. Thompson
1953. The Groove and Splinter Technique of Working Antler in Upper Palaeolithic and Mesolithic Europe with Special Reference to the Material from Star Carr. *Proceedings of Prehistoric Society* 19: 148-160.

Clark, R.
1986. *Aves de Tierra del Fuego y Cabo de Hornos. Guía de campo.* Ed. L.O.L.A, Buenos Aires.

Clayton Wilson, M.
1982. Cut marks and Early Hominids: Evidence for Skinning. *Nature* 298: 303.

Clement, G. and Ch. Leroy Prost
1977. Essai de classification automatique sur un algorithme de reconnaissance de formes d'une série de pointes à base fendue.*Deuxième Colloque International sur l'industrie de l'os dans la Préhistoire. Méthodologie appliquée á l'industrie de l'os préhistorique*. París, CNRS: 127-142.

Cocilovo, J. and R. Guichón
1985-1986. Propuesta para el estudio de las poblaciones aborígenes del extremo austral de Patagonia. *Anales del Instituto de la Patagonia* 16: 111-123.

Commission de Nomenclature
1977. Définitions (de termes particulièrment épineux). In *Deuxième Colloque International sur l'industrie de l'os dans la Préhistoire. Méthodologie appliquée á l'industrie de l'os préhistorique*: 351-357. París, CNRS. Ms.

Conkey, M.
s.f. *Bone Tool Typology in Hierarchical Form (by class 100.000 -500.000)* 1978.

Cooper, J.
1967. Analytical and Critical bibliography of the tribes of Tierra del Fuego and Adjacent Territory. *Smithsonian Institution, Bureau of American Ethnology*.

Corchón, S.
1980. Industria ósea y huesos utilizados de la cueva de Las Caldas: Inventario tipológico provisional. *Excavaciones Arqueológicas en España* 115: 243-257.

1981. El tensor: un nuevo tipo de hueso utilizado en el Solutrense y Magdaleniense Asturianos. *Zephyrus* XXXII-XXXIII: 75-86.

Corrain, C. and A. Zucchet
1962. La cultura material de los aborígenes de Tierra del Fuego. Datos extraídos de observaciones sobre materiales etnológicos recogidos en algunos museos Salesianos. *Palestra del Clero*, Istituto Padano di Arti Grafiche:15-16. Traducción: Guillermo Hernández.

Corvi, M.E.; C. Daniele; C. Elli and P. Paleka
S.f. *Determinación de las ofertas del medio natural*. Programa de Evaluación Ambiental, Territorio Nacional de Tierra del Fuego. Ms.

Currey, J.D.
1979. Mechanical Properties of Bone Tissues with Greatly Differing Functions. *Journal of Biomechanics* 12: 313-319.

1984. *The Mechanical Adaptations of Bones*. Princeton University Press.

1987. The Evolution fo the Mechanical Properties of Amniote Bone. *Journal of Biomechanics* 20: 1035-1044.

2002. *Bones. Structure and mechanics*. Princeton University Press.

Chapman, A.
1986. *Los selk'nam. La vida de los Onas*. Emecé, Buenos Aires.

Chauvet, G.
1910. Os, ivoires et bois de renne ouvrés de la Charente. Hypotheses Paléthnographiques. *Extrait du Bulletin de la Societé Archaeologique et Historique de la Charente*. Libraire de la Societé Archaeologique et Historique de la Charente, Angoulême.

Christidou, R.
1989. *Perception et restitution d'une technologie préhistorique: procedure multifactorielle. Breve revue de la recherche sur l'outillage osseux egéen*. Mémoire de Mâitrise, Univ. de Paris I.

Daniel, G.
1974. *Historia de la arqueología*. Alianza, Madrid.

1977. *El concepto de prehistoria*. Labor, Madrid.

Daniele, C.
1991. Regiones Naturales de Argentina. In *Diagnóstico del Sistema Nacional de Areas Naturales Protegidas de la República Argentina*, Informe Nacional para UNCED, Administración de Parques Nacionales, Bs. As.

Dart, R.
1957. The Osteodontokeratic Culture of Australopithecus prometeus. *Transvaal Museum* 10.

Dauvois, M.
1974. Industrie osseuse préhistorique et experimentations. *Premier Colloque Internationaux sur l'industrie de l'os dans la Prehistoire*: 73-84. Editions Universitaires, Provence.

Deffarges, R.; P. Laurent and D. Sonneville-Bordes
1974a. Les harpons de l'abri Morin, Pessac-sur-Dordogne (Gironde). *Premier Colloque Internationaux sur l'industrie de l'os dans la Prehistoiree*: 193-218. Editions Universitaires, Provence.

1974b. Ciseau ou lissoirs magdaléniens. *Bulletin de la Société Préhistorique Française* 71(3): 85-96.

1977. Sagaies et ciseaux du Magdalénien Supériuer du Morin, Gironde: Un essai de définition. *Deuxième Colloque International sur l'Industrie de l'os dans la Préhistoire, Méthodologie appliquée a L'industrie de l'os préhistorique*: 99-110. CNRS, Paris.

Delpech, F. and D. Sonneville-Bordes
1977. L' industrie de l'os à Laugerie-Haute, Dordogne (Fouilles F. Bordes): débitage et 'outils de fortune'. *Deuxième Colloque International sur l'Industrie de l'os dans la Préhistoire, Méthodologie appliquée a L'industrie de l'os préhistorique:* 61-67 CNRS, Paris.

Delporte, H.
1958. Notes de Geographie Préhistorique I: les pointes d'Aurignac. *Annales de la Faculté des Lettres de Toulouse, Pallas* VII (4): 11-29.

Delporte, H. and L. Mons
1977. " Etat des travaux sur les pointes en os magdaléniennes" *Deuxième Colloque International sur l'Industrie de l'os dans la Préhistoire, Méthodologie appliquée a L'industrie de l'os préhistorique*: 161-176. CNRS, Paris.

Delporte, H.; Hahn J.; Mons,L.; Pinçon,G. and D. de Sonneville-Bordes
1988. *Sagaies. Fiches Typologiques de l'industrie osseuse préhistorique*, (H. Camps-Fabrer ed.), Cahier I, Publications Université de Provence.

Dennell, R.
1987. *Prehistoria Económica de Europa*. Ed. Crítica, Madrid.

D'Errico, F. and G. Giacobini
1985. Approche méthodologique de l'analyse de l'outillage osseux: un exemple d'étude. *L'Anthropologie* 89 (4):457-472.

D'Errico, F., G. Giacobini and A. M. Moigne
1984a. Un pesudo-bouton en os néolithique de la Grotte d'Unang (Vaucluse). Approche méthodologique et étude interpretative. *Cahiers Ligures de Préhistoire et Protohistoire* 1: 73-83.

D'Errico, F., G. Giacobini and P. Puech
1982-1983. Varnish Replicas: A New Method for the Study of Worked Bone Surfaces. *Ossa* 9-11: 29-51.

D'Errico, F., G. Giacobini and P. Puech
1984b. Les repliques en vernis des surfaces osseuses faconnées: étude expérimentale. *Bulletin de la Societé préhistorique Francaise* 81: 169-170.

D'Errico, F., G. Giacobini and P. Puech
1984c. An experimental study of the technology of bone implement manufacture. *MASCA Journal* 3:71-74.

Desse, J.
1975. Vestiges témoignant d'une activité de pelleterie sur le chantier néolithique récent d'auvernier brise-lames. *Bulletin de la Société Neuchâteloise des Sciences Naturelles* 98: 203-208.

Dewez, M.
1974. Typologie osseuse. Essai de classification Systématique du matériel archéologique osseux. *Premier Colloque Internationaux sur l'industrie de l'os dans la Prehistoire*: 143-146 Editions Universitaires, Provence.

Diez, C.
1985. Hacia un nuevo enfoque en el estudio de huesos utilizados del Paleolítico Inferior. *Cahier Noir* 2: 71-89.

1986. La fragmentation des os d'équidés et bovidés à Lunel-Viel (Hérault, France). *Artefacts* 3: 23-42.

Dobres, M. A.
1995. Gender and Prehistoric Technology: on the Social Agency of Technical Strategies. *World Archaeology* 27 (1): 25-49.

Dobzansky, T.
1951. *Genetics an the Origin of Species*. Columbia University Press, New York.

Dunnell, R.
1980. Evolutionary Theory and Archaeology. *Advances in Archaeological Method and Theory* 3: 35-99. Academic Press, New York.

1989. Aspects of the application of evolutionary theory in archaeology. In *Archaeological Thought in America*, editado por C. Lamberg-Karlovsky (ed.), pp. 35-49. Cambridge University Press, Cambridge.

Efremov. E.
1940. Taphonomy: New Branch of Paleontology. *Pan-American Geologist* 74: 81-93.

Eldredge, N.
1985. *Time Frames*. Simon & Schuster, New York.

1989. *Macroevolutionary Dynamics*. Mc Graw-Hill, New York.

Eldredge, N. and S. J. Gould
1972. Punctuated equilibria: An alternative to phyletic gradualism. In *Models in paleobiology*., T.J.Schopf (ed.) pp. 82-115. Freeman, Cooper & co., San Francisco.

1974. Reply to Hecht. *Evolutionary Biology* 7: 303-308.

Emperaire, J. and A. Laming-Emperaire
1961. Les gisements des îles Englefield et Vivian. *Journal de la Société des Américanistes* 50: 7-77.

Emperaire, J., A. Laming-Emperaire and H. Reichlen
1963. La grotte Fell et autres sites de la région volcánique de la Patagonie chilienne. *Journal de la Société des Américanistes* 52: 169-255.

Ericson, J.
1984. Toward the analysis of lithic production systems. In *Prehistoric Quarries and Lithic Production*, J. Ericson and B. Purdy (eds.) pp. 1-10. Cambridge University Press, Cambridge.

Evans, F. G.
1973. *Mechanical Properties of Bone*. Charles C. Thomas, Springfield.

Fernández, J.
1988-1990. La Cueva de Haichol. Arqueología de los pinares cordilleranos del Neuquén. *Anales de Arqueología and Etnología* (43-45).

Ferretti, J.L.
Ms. *Bone Biomechanics*, Rosario.

Ferretti, J. L. and V. Scheinsohn
1997. Design and Function of Prehistoric Tools of Tierra del Fuego (Argentina) as Related to the Mechanical Properties of Bone Materiales Utilized in their Manufacture. *Proceedings of the 1993 Bone Modification Conference, Hot Springs, South Dakota*. L. Adrien Hannus and R. Peter Winham (ed). Occassional Publications N° 1, Archaeology Laboratory, Augustana College: 65-75.

Ferretti, J. L, V. Scheinsohn; M. Macchi; C.E. Bozzini and J.R. Zanchetta
1991. Determinación biológica del grosor diafisario por la calidad mecánica del material óseo en seis especies de vertebrados. Presentado a la *VIII Reunión Anual de la Asociación Argentina de Osteología y Metabolismo Mineral*.

Ferretti, J. L., Scheinsohn, V., Macchi, M., Zanchetta, J.R.
1992. Biological determination of diaphyseal thickness according to mechanical quality of bone material in several vertebrate species. *Bone & Mineral* 17(S1): 133.

Figuerero Torres, M. J.
1987. Arqueología de la porción sur del Parque Nacional Tierra del Fuego. *Primeras Jornadas de Arqueología de la Patagonia*: 111-114.

Fiorillo, A. R.
1984. An Introdcution to the Identification of Trample Marks. *Current Research* 1: 47-48.

1987. Trample Marks: Caution from the Cretaceous. *Current Research* 4: 73-75.

1989. An Experimental Study of Trampling: Implications for the Fossil Record. In *Bone Modification*, Bonnichsen, R. and M. Sorg (eds.) pp. 61-72, Peopling of the Americas Publications, Center for the Study of the First Americans, Institute for Quaternary Studies, University of Maine.

Franco, N.
1994. Maximización en el Aprovechamiento de los Recursos Líticos. Un caso analizado en el Area Interserrana Boanerense. In J. L. Lanata and L. A. Borrero (eds.) *Arqueología de cazadores-recolectores. Límites, Casos y Aperturas. Arqueología Contemporánea* 5: 75-88.

Freeman, L.
1978. Mousterian Worked Bone from Cueva Morin (Santander, Spain): A Preliminary Description. *Views of the Past*: 29-51.

Fritz, M.
1977. Understanding Variability in Cantabrian Magdalenian Bone Assemblages by Means of Cluster Analysis Techniques. *Deuxième Colloque International sur 'Industrie de l'os dans la Préhistoire, Méthodologie appliquée a L'industrie de l'os préhistorique*: 143-160. CNRS, Paris.

Gallardo, C.R.
1910. *Tierra del Fuego. Los Onas*. Cabaut and Cía., Buenos Aires.

Garrod, A.
1955. Palaeolithic Spear-Throwers. *Proceedings of the Prehistoric Society* 21.

Gifford, D.
1981. Taphonomy and Palaeoecology: A Critical Review of sisters disciplines of Archaeology, *Advances in Archaeological Method and Theory*, 4: 365-438, Academic Press, New York.

González Doña, C.
1984. Industria del hueso poco elaborado: metodología. La cueva de El Castillo (Puente Viesgo, Santander). *Jornadas de Metodología en la Investigación Prehistórica* (Soria): 183-194.

Gould, S. J.
1977. *Ever since Darwin*. Penguin, New York.

1985. *The Flamingo Smile*. Penguin, New York.

Gould, S. J. and E. Vrba.
1982. Exaptation —a missing term in the science of form. *Paleobiology* 8(1): 4-15.

Goodall, R.N.P. and A. Galeazzi
1986. Cetacean Survey in Eastern Tierra del Fuego and Isla de los Estados. *Antarctic Journal* XXI (4): 15-17.

Gusinde, M.
1982. *Los indios de Tierra del Fuego,* tomo primero: Los Selk'nam CAEA-CONICET, Buenos Aires.

1986. *Los indios de Tierra del Fuego,* tomo segundo: Los Yámana, CAEA-CONICET, Buenos Aires.

Guthrie, R.
1983. Osseous Proyectile Point: Biological Considerations Affecting Raw material Selection and Design Among Paleolithic and Paleoindian Peoples. *Animals and Archaeology: 1. Hunters and their Prey*, J. Clutton-Brock and C. Grigson (eds.), BAR International Series 163: 274-294.

Hahn, J.
1974. Analyse des sagaies du Paléolithic Superiéur Ancien en Europe. Méthodes et premiers résultats. *Premier Colloque Internationaux sur l'industrie de l'os dans la Prehistoire*: 119-127. Editions Universitaires, Provence.

Herbst, G. and V. Scheinsohn
1991. Introducción al estudio mecánico de los instrumentos óseos provenientes del Canal Beagle: los dientes de las puntas de arpón. *Shincal* 3 (3): 165-170.

Herbst, G.; T. Palacios and V. Scheinsohn
1994. Primera Aproximación al Estudio de las Propiedades Mecánicas de las Materias Primas Oseas Utilizadas en Tierra del Fuego, Argentina. *Arqueología de cazadores-recolectores. Límites, casos y aperturas*. J. L. Lanata and L. A. Borrero (Comp.) *Arqueología Contemporánea* 5: 121- 128.

Heusser, C.
1989a. Late Quaternary Vegetation and Climate of Southern Tierra del Fuego. *Quaternary Research* 31: 396-406.

1989b. Climate and Chronology of Antarctica and Adjacent South America over the Past 30,000 yr. *Palaeogeogrpahy, Palaeoclimatology, Palaeoecology* 76: 31-37.

Heusser, C. and J. Rabassa
1987. Cold climatic episode of Younger Dryas age in Tierra del Fuego. *Nature* 328: 609-611.

Hill, A.P.
1976. On Carnivore and Weathering Damage of Bone. *Current Anhtropology* 17(2): 335-336.

1989. Bone Modification by Modern Spotted Hyenas. *Bone Modification*, R. Bonnichsen & M. Sorg (ed.) pp. 317-334. Peopling of the Americas Publications, Center for the Study of the First Americans, Institute for Quaternary Studies, University of Maine.

Hill, J. and R. Evans
1972. A Model for Classification and Typology. *Models in Archeology*, D.L.Clarke (ed.) pp. 231-273, Methuen, London.

Horwitz, V. D.
1990. *Maritime settlement patterns in Southeastern Tierra del Fuego (Argentina)*, Ph. D. Dissertation, University of Kentucky.

1993. Maritime Settlement Patterns: the Case from Isla de los Estados (Staten Island). *Explotación de Recursos faunísticos en sistemas adaptativos americanos*. J. L. Lanata (ed.) *Arqueología Contemporánea* 4: 149-162.

Horwitz, V. and V. Scheinsohn
1996. Los instrumentos óseos del sitio Bahía Crossley I (Isla de los Estados).Comparación con otros conjuntos de la Isla Grande de Tierra del Fuego. In *Arqueología. Solo Patagonia*. J. Gómez Otero (ed.) pp. 359-368, Centro Nacional Patagónico (CENPAT)- CONICET, Puerto Madryn.

Howell, F. and L. Freeman
1983. Ivory points from the Earlier Acheulean of the Spanish meseta. *Homenaje al Profesor Martín Almagro Basch* Vol I: 41-61.

Humphrey, P.; D. Bridge; P. Reynolds and R. Peterson
1970. *Birds of Isla Grande (Tierra del Fuego)*. Preliminary Smithsonian Manual, Smithsonian Institution, Washington.

Hyades, M.
1885. La chasse et la pêche chez les fuégiens de l'archipel du Cap Horn. *Revue d'Ethnographie* 4: 514-553.

Hyades, P. and J. Deniker
1891. Anthropologie et Ethnographie. *Mission Scientifique du Cap Horn (1882-1883)*, Ministerio de Marina and de Instrucción Pública, ed. Gauthier Villars et Fils, tomo VII: 338-380.

Jackson, D.
1987. Componente lítico del sitio arqueológico Tres Arroyos. *Anales del Instituto de la Patagonia* 17: 67-72.

Jéquier, J.
1975. Le Mousterien Alpin. *Eburudurum* II.

Johnson, E.
1985. Current Developments in Bone Technology. *Advances in Archaeological Method and Theory* 8: 157-235, Academic Press, New York.

1989. Human-modified Bones from Early Southern Plains Sites. *Bone Modification*, R. Bonnichsen & M. Sorg (ed.), pp. 431-471. Peopling of the Americas Publications, Center for the Study of the First Americans, Institute for Quaternary Studies, University of Maine.

Johnson, E. and P. Shipman
1986. Scanning Electron Microscope studies of Bone Modification. *Current Research in the Pleistocene* 3: 17-18.

Jones, G. and R. Leonard
1989. The Concept of Diversity: an Introduction. In *Quantifying Diversity in Archaeology*, Leonard, R. and G. Jones (eds.) pp. 1-3. Cambridge University Press, Cambridge.

Julien, M.
1977. Harpons unilatéraux et bilatéraux. Evolution morphologique ou adaptation différenciée? *Deuxième Colloque International sur l'Industrie de l'os dans la Préhistoire, Méthodologie appliquée a L'industrie de l'os préhistorique*: 177-189. CNRS, Paris.

1978-1980. La industria ósea de Telarmachay. Período Formativo. *Revista del Museo Nacional* XLIV: 69-93.

1982. *Les Harpons Magdaleniens*. XVII suplément à Gallia Préhistorie, Editions du CNRS, Paris.

1985. El instrumental óseo. In *Telarmachay, chasseurs et pasteurs préhistoriques des Andes I* D. Lavallée (ed.): 215-235. Editions Recherche sur les Civilisations, Paris.

1986. La fonction des outils d'os peu elaborés de Telarmachay (Perou). *Artefacts* 3: 15-22.

Julien, M; P. Vaughan and D. Lavallée
1987. Armes et outils emmanchés à Telarmachay. Présomptions et indices. *La main et l'outil: manches et emmanchements préhistoriques, Travaux de la Maison de l'Orient* 15: 287-295.

Kintigh, K.
1989. Sample Size, Significance and Measures of Diversity. In *Quantifying Diversity in Archaeology*, Leonard, R. and G. Jones (eds.) pp. 25 -36. Cambridge University Press, Cambridge.

Koby, F.E.
1942. Les soi-dissant instruments osseux du paléolithique alpin et le charriage á sec des os d'ours des cavernes. *Verhandlungen Naturforschenden Gessellschaft in Basel* LIV: 59-95.

Kozlowski, J. and S. Kozlowski
1977. Pointes, sagaies et harpons du Paléolithique et du Mésolithique en Europe du Centre-Est. *Deuxième Colloque International sur l'Industrie de l'os dans la Préhistoire, Méthodologie appliquée a L'industrie de l'os préhistorique*: 205-228. CNRS, Paris.

Laming Emperaire, A.; D. Lavallée and R. Humbert
1972. Le site de Marazzi en Terre du Feu. *Objets et Mondes* XII(2): 225-244.

Lanata, J. L.
1985. Sitios arqueológicos en el área de Ea. María Luisa, Tierra del Fuego. *VIII Congreso Nacional de Arqueología Argentina*.

1988. ¿Huesos quemados, huesos contados? Los datos de un experimento. *De procesos, contextos y otros huesos,*

Seminario de Actualización en Arqueología: 75-90. Instituto de Ciencias Antropológicas, UBA.

1991. Según pasan los años: Análisis de los Procesos Naturales de Formación del Registro arqueológico en el sudeste de Tierra del Fuego. Paper delivered at *47° Congreso Internacional de Americanistas*, New Orleans.

1993. Estados alterados: procesos de formación y conjuntos faunísticos en Rancho Donata, Tierra del Fuego. *Explotación de Recursos faunísticos en sistemas adaptativos americanos*. J.L. Lanata (ed.), pp. 163-182. *Arqueología Contemporánea* 4. Edición Especial.

1996. Cambios para evolucionar: las propiedades del registro arqueológico y la evolución de los grupos humanos en Patagonia y Tierra del Fuego. *Arqueología Solo Patagonia*. J. Gómez Otero (ed.) pp. 99-106, Centro Nacional Patagónico (CENPAT)- CONICET, Puerto Madryn.

Lanata, J.L. and A.Winograd
1988. Gritos y susurros: aborígenes y lobos marinos en el litoral de la Tierra del Fuego. In *Arqueología de las Américas. 45 Congreso Internacional de Americanistas*. pp. 227-246. Bogotá.

Lanata, J.L.; Nami, H. and R. Guichón
1988. Península Mitre: Alternativas exploratorias para un problema arqueológico. Paper delivered at *VIII Congreso Nacional de Arqueología Argentina*.

Larsson, L. and U.-K. Larsson
1977. Sur les points en os à tranchants de silex trouvées dans le Sud de la Suède. *XXe Congrès Préhistorique de France*:: 338-342.

Laurent, P.
1974. Observations préliminaires sur la morphologie des harpons du Magdalénien Supérieur. *Premier Colloque Internationaux sur l'industrie de l'os dans la Prehistoire*: 187-191. Editions Universitaires, Provence.

Lefèvre, C.
1989. *L'avifaune de Patagonie Australe et ses relations avec l'homme au cours des six derniers millenaires*. Ph. D Manuscript. Univerisdad de Paris I.

Legoupil, D.
1978. Aperçu préliminaire sur l'industrie osseuse de Patagonie. *Bulletin de la Société Préhistorique Française* 75 (11-12): 543-558.

1980. Quelques armes en os des indiens de patagonie de la période post-colombienne. *Objets en os historiques et actuels*, Travaux de la Maison de l'Orient 1: 75-82.

1988. Ultimas consideraciones sobre las dataciones del sitio del la Isla Englefield. *Anales del Instituto de la Patagonia* 18: 95-98.

1989. *Punta Baja. Ethno-Archéologie dans les archipels de Patagonia: les nomades marines de Punta Baja*. Editions Recherche sur les Civilisations, París.

LeMoine, G.
1989. Use Wear Analysis of Bone Tools. *Archaezoologia* III(1-2): 211-224.

1991. *Experimental Analysis of the Manufacture and Use of Bone and Antler Tools among the Mackenzie Inuit*. Ph. D Manuscript, University of Calgary.

Leonard, R. and G. Jones
1989. *Quantifying Diversity in Archaeology*, Cambridge University Press, Cambridge.

Leroi Gourhan, A.
1943. *L'homme et la matière*. Albin Michel, Paris.

1945. *Milieu et techniques*. Albin Michel, Paris.

1964-1965. *Le geste et la parole*. Albin Michel, Paris.

1983. Une tête de sagaie à armature de lamelles de silex à Pincevent (Seine-et-Marne). *Bulletin de la Société Préhistorique Française* 80 (5): 154-156. (ed.).

1988. *Dictionnaire de la Prehistoire*. PUF, Paris.

Leroi Gourhan, A.; G. Bailloud; J. Chavaillon and A. Laming-Emperaire
1966. *La préhistoire*. PUF, La Nouvelle Clío, Paris.

Leroy-Prost, C.
1971. Premièr note relative à l'orientation des objets en os. *C.R.S.M. de Bulletin Sociéte Préhistorique Française* 2: 46-47.

1974. Les pointes en matière osseuse de l'Aurignacien. Caractéristiques morphologiques et essais de définitions. *Bulletin de la Société Préhistorique Française* 71 (2): 449-458.

1975. L'industries osseuse aurignacienne,essai regional de classification: Poitou, Charentes, Perigord. *Gallia Préhistoire* 18 (1): 65-156.

1978. Les bases fendues d'Isturitz (Pyrénées-Atlantiques): Morphologie et traces d'utilisation. *Bulletin de la Société Préhistorique Française* 75 (4): 116-120.

Lista, R.
1887. *Viaje al País de los Onas*. Establecimiento tipográfico de Alberto Núñez, Buenos Aires.

Lothrop, S.
1928. *The indians of Tierra del Fuego*, Museum of the American Indian Heye Foundation, New York.

Lovisato, D.
1883. *Di alcune armi e utensili del fueghini e degli antichi patagoni*. Roma.

Lyman, R.
1984a. Bone Density and Differential Survivorship of Fossil Classes. *Journal of Anthropological Archaeology* 3: 259-299.

1984b. Broken Bones, Bone Expediency Tools and Bone Pseudotools: lessons from the Blast Zone around Mount St. Helens, Washington. *American Antiquity* 49 (2): 315-333.

1991. Archaeology of Umpqua/Eden (35 DO 83). Bone and Antler Artifacts. *Prehistory of the Oregon Coast (the Effects of Excavation Strategies and Assemblage Size on Archaeological Inquiry)*, R. Lyman, Capítulo 5, pp. 122-263.

Mac Gregor, A.
1985. *Bone, Antler, Ivory & Horn. The Technology of Skeletal Materials Since the Roman Period*, Croonhelm, Barnes & Noble, New York.

Mac Gregor, A. and J. Currey
1983. Mechanical Properties as Conditioning Factors in the Bone and Antler Industry of the 3rd to the 13th Century AD. *Journal of Archaeological Science* 10: 71-77.

Martin, H.
1907a. Ossements utilisés. In *Recherches sur l'evolution du Moustérien dans le gisement de La Quina (Charente),* 1er fasc. pp.1-67. Schleicher Fréres ed., Paris.

1907b. Présentation d'une photographie obtenue par grandissement direct de l'objet préhistorique. *Bulletin de la Société Préhistorique Française*, seance 24/11/1907.

1910. La percussion osseuse et les esquilles qui en dérivent. Experimentation. *Bulletin de la Société Préhistorique Française* VII: 299-304.

1935. Les manches d'outils etaient connus à l'epoque aurignacienne. *Association Française pour l'Avancement des Sciences*, pp. 370-371.

Massone, M.o
1983. 10.400 años de colonización humana en Tierra del Fuego. *Infórmese* 3(14): 24-32.

1987. Los cazadores paleoindios de Tres Arroyos (Tierra del Fuego). *Anales del Instituto de la Patagonia* 17: 47-60.

1988. Artefactos óseos del yacimiento arqueológico de Tres Arroyos (Tierra del Fuego). *Anales del Instituto de la Patagonia* 18: 107-112.

1989-1990. Investigaciones arqueológicas en la laguna Thomas Gould. *Anales del Instituto de la Patagonia* 19: 87-99.

Mayr, E.
1942. *Systematics and the Origin of Species*. Columbia University Press, New York.

Menghin, O.
1952. Fundamentos cronológicos de la prehistoria de Patagonia. *Runa* 5: 23-43.

1956. ¿Existe en Tierra del Fuego la auténtica casa- pozo?. *Runa* 7: 107-112.

1960. Urgeschichte der Kanuindianer des Sudlichsten Amerika. *Steinzeitfragen del Alten und Neuen Welt:* 343-375.

Mengoni Goñalons, G.
1983. Prehistoric utilization of faunal resources in arid Argentina. In *Animals and Archaeology. 1 Hunters and their prey*, J. Clutton-Brock and C. Grigson eds., BAR International Series 1643: 325-335.

1986. Patagonian Prehistory: Early Explotaition of Faunal Resources (13.500-8.500 BP) In *New Evidence for the Pleistocene Peopling of the Americas*, A.L. Bryan ed., Orono: Center for the Study of Early Man, pp. 271-279.

1988a. "El estudio de las huellas en arqueofauna, una vía para reconstruir situaciones interactivas en contextos arqueológicos: aspectos teórico-metodológicos y técnicas de análisis" en *De procesos, contextos y otros huesos, Seminario de Actualización en Arqueología*: 91-96, Instituto de Ciencias Antropológicas, Universidad de Buenos Aires.

1988b. Extinción, colonización y estrategias adaptativas paleoindias en el extremo austral de Fuego-Patagonia. *Precirculados de las ponencias científicas presentada a los simposios del IX Congreso Nacional de Arqueología Argentina*, UBA: 119-129.

Miller, G.
1970. A Study of Cuts, Grooves and Other Marks on Recent Fossil Bone I: Animal Tooth Marks. *Tebiwa* 12(1): 20-26.

1975. A Study of Cuts, Grooves and Other Marks on Recent Fossil Bone II: Weathering Cracks, Fractures, Splinters and Other Similar Natural Phenomena. *Lithic Technology: Making and Using Stone Tools,* E. Swanson (ed.) pp. 211-226.

Miotti, L. and M. Salemme
1988. De fracturas óseas modernas y arqueológicas: una hipótesis alternativa. Revista *CEIDER* 2: 41-48.

Mons, L.
1979. Les harpons aziliens du Mas d'Azil. Etude préliminaire. In *La fin des temps glaciaires en Europe*. CNRS Nº 271: 623-635.

1980. Essai d'analyse et de classification des poinçons des gisements solutréens et magdaléniens du Placard (Charente), de Laugerie-Basse et de la Madelaine (Dordogne). *Bulletin de la Société Préhistorique Française* 77 (10-12): 317-327.

Mons, L. and D. Stordeur
1977. Des objets nommés 'lissoirs' de la Grotte du Placard (Charente). *Antiquités Nationales* 9: 15-25.

Moore, D. M.
1983. *Flora of Tierra del Fuego.* Anthony Nelson, New York.

Morel, P.
Quelques polis naturels d'apparence trompeuse. *Artefacts* 3: 43-45.

Morlan, R.
1984. Toward the definition of Criteria for the Recognition of Artificial Bone Alterations.*Quaternary Research* 22: 160-171.

Mostny, G.
1991. *Prehistoria de Chile.* Editorial Universitaria, Santiago de Chile.

Movius, H.
1973. Quelques commentaires supplementaires sur les sagaies d'Isturitz: données de l'Abri Pataud, Les Eyezies (Dordogne). *Bulletin de la Société Préhistorique Française* 70 (3): 85-89.

Muñoz, S.
1996. Análisis de marcas naturales en arqueofaunas de los sitios Bloque Errático 1 y María Luisa A3, Tierra del Fuego. *Arqueología. Solo Patagonia.* J. Gómez Otero (ed.), pp. 271-278. Centro Nacional Patagónico (CENPAT)- CONICET, Puerto Madryn.

Murray, C.
1979. Les techniques de débitage des métapodes de petits ruminants à Auvernier-Port. *L'industrie de l'os néolithique et de l'Age des metaux. 1er Réunion du Groupe de Travail N°3 sur l'industrie de l'os préhistorique*, CNRS: 27-35.

Nami, H.
1987. Cueva del Medio: perspectivas arqueológicas para la Patagonia austral. *Anales del Instituto de la Patagonia* 17: 73-106.

Nami, H. and V. Scheinsohn
1997. Use-wear patterns on Bone Flakers. *Proceedings of the* 1993. *Bone Modification Conference, Hot Springs, South Dakota.* L. Adrien Hannus and R. Peter Winham (comp.) pp. 256-276. Occassional Publications N° 1, Archaeology Laboratory, Augustana College.

Natenzon, C.
1989. *Marco Biogeográfico para el Sistema Nacional de Areas Naturales Protegidas de la República Argentina*, Administración de Parques Nacionales, FAO-ORPAL PNUD, Bs. As.

Nelson, M.
1991. The study of Technological Organization. *Archaeological Method and Theory* 3: 57-100.

Newcomer, M.
1974a. Study and replication of Bone Tools from Ksar Akil (Lebanon). *World Archeology* 2: 138-153.

1974b. Outils en os du Paléolithique supérieur de Ksar Akil (Liban). *Premier Colloque Internationaux sur l'industrie de l'os dans la Prehistoire*: 59-65. Editions Universitaires, Provence.

1977. Experiments in Upper Paleolithic Bone Work. *Deuxième Colloque International sur l'Industrie de l'os dans la Préhistoire, Méthodologie appliquée a L'industrie de l'os préhistorique*: 293-302. CNRS, Paris.

Ocampo, C. and P. Rivas
1996. Caracterización Arqueológica del Suroeste de Tierra del Fuego. *Anales del Instituto de la Patagonia* 27: 125-151.

Olsen, S.
1979. A Study of Bone Artifacts from Grasshopper Pueblo AZP:14:1. *The Kiva* 44 (4): 341-373.

1980. Bone Artifacts from Kinshba Ruin: their Manufacture and Use. *The Kiva* 46 (1-2): 39-67.

1984. *Analytical Approaches to the Manufacture and Use of Bone Artifacts in Prehistory.* Ph. D. Thesis, Institute of Archaeology, University of London, Ms.

1988. (ed.) Scanning Electron Microscopy in Archaeology. *BAR International Series* 452.

1989. On Distinguishing Natural from Cultural Damage on Archaeological Antler. *Journal of Archaeological Science* 16: 125-135.

Olsen, S. and P. Shipman
1988. Surface Modification on Bone: Trampling versus Butchery *Journal of Archeological Science* 15: 535-553.

Orquera, L.
1984-1985. Tradiciones culturales y evolución en Patagonia. *Relaciones* XVI: 249-267.

1987. Advances in the Archaeology of the Pampas and Patagonia. *Journal of World Archaeology* 1 (4): 333-413.

Orquera, L. and E. Piana
1983. Prehistoric maritime adaptations at the Magellan-fuegian littoral. Paper delivered at *48th Annual Meeting, Society for American Archeology.*

1985. Octava campaña arqueológica en Tierra del Fuego: la localidad Shumakush. Presentado al *VIII Congreso Nacional de Arqueología Argentina*, Concordia.

1986-1987. Composición tipológica y datos tecnomorfológicos y tecnofuncionales de los distintos conjuntos arqueológicos del sitio Túnel I (Tierra del Fuego). *Relaciones de la Sociedad Argentina de Antropología* 17 (1): 201-239.

1987. Human littoral adaptation in the Beagle Channel region: The maximum possible age. *Quaternary of South America and Antarctic Peninsula* 5: 133-162.

1990. Canoeros del extremos austral. *Ciencia Hoy* 1(6): 18-27.

Orquera, Luis; Sala, A.; Piana, E. and Tapia, A.
1977. *Lancha Packewaia. Arqueología de los Canales Fueguinos.* Buenos Aires, Huemul.

Orquera, L., E. Piana and A. Tapia de Bradford
1987a. Evolución adaptativa humana en la región del Canal de Beagle I. Ubicación en la secuencia areal. *Primeras Jornadas de Arqueología de la Patagonia.* pp. 211-218. Gobierno de la Provincia de Chubut, Trelew.

1987b. Evolución adaptativa humana en la región del Canal de Beagle II. Consideraciones en cuanto al ambiente y el aprovechamiento de recursos naturales. *Primeras Jornadas de Arqueología de la Patagonia* pp. 219-226. Gobierno de la Provincia de Chubut, Trelew.

Ortiz Troncoso, O.
1973. Aspectos arqueológicos de la Península de Brunswick (Patagonia austral). *Anales del Instituto de la Patagonia* IV (1-3): 109-129.

Outes, F.
1916. Sobre el hallazgo de un arpón de hueso en la región de Cabo Blanco (Gobernación de Santa Cruz). *Physis* II: 272-276.

Otte, M.
1974a. Caracteristiques inhérentes à l'analyse par attributs de l'outillage osseux. *Premier Colloque Internationaux sur l'industrie de l'os dans la Prehistoire*, pp. 129-133, Editions Universitaires, Provence.

1974b. Observations sur le débitage et le façonnage de l'ivoire dans l'Aurignacien en Belgique. *Premier Colloque Internationaux sur l'industrie de l'os dans la Prehistoire*, pp. 93-9, Editions Universitaires, Provence.

1977. Les sagaies de l'Aurignaco-Perigordien en Belgique. *Deuxième Colloque International sur l'Industrie de l'os dans la Préhistoire, Méthodologie appliquée a L'industrie de l'os préhistorique*, pp. 193-204. CNRS, París.

Pape, W.
1982. Au sujet de quelques pointes de flèches en os. *L'industrie en os et bois de cervidé durant le Néolithique et l'Age des Métaux. Deuxième reunion du Groupe de Travail N° 3 sur l'industrie de l'os préhistorique* pp.135-172.

Patou, M.
1985. La fracturation des os longs de grands mammifères: élaboration d'un lexique et d'une fiche-type. *Artefacts 1: outillage peu élaboré en os et en bois de cervidés*:11-22.

(ed.) 1994. *Taphonomie/Bone Modification. Artefacts* 9.

Pei, W.
1938. La role des animaux et des causes naturelles dans la cassure des os. *Paleontologia Sinica* 7.

Peltier, A.
1986. Etude expérimentale des surfaces osseuses faconées et utilisées. *Bulletin de la Societé Préhistorique Francaise* 83 (1): 5-7.

Peltier, A. and H. Plisson
1989. Microtraceologie fonctionnelle sur l'os. Quelques resultats experimentaux. *Artefacts* 3: 69-79.

Peyrony, D.
1933. Les industries «aurignaciennes» dans le bassin de la Vézére: Aurignacien et Périgordien. *Bulletin de la Societé Préhistorique Francaise* 30: 543-559.

Piana, E.
1984. Arrinconamiento o adaptación en Tierra del Fuego. In *Antropología argentina año 1984*, pp. 15-110. Editorial de Belgrano, Buenos Aires.

Pickering, M.
1980. Bone Tools from Photographs in the Donald F. Thompson Collection, National Museum of Victoria. *The Artifact* 5 (1-2): 93-97.

Piel-Desruisseaux, J.L.
1986. *Outils Préhistoriques. Forme-Fabrication-Utilisation.* Masson, París.

Poplin, F.
1974a. Deux cas particuliers de débitage par usure. *Premier Colloque Internationaux sur l'industrie de l'os dans la Prehistoire* pp. 85-92. Editions Universitaires, Provence.

1974b. Principes de la détermination des matières dures animales. *Premier Colloque Internationaux sur l'industrie de l'os dans la Prehistoire* pp. 15-20. Editions Universitaires, Provence.

Potts, R. and P. Shipman
1981. Cutmarks Made by Stone Tools on Bones from Olduvai Gorge, Tanzania. *Nature* 291: 577-580.

Prieto, A.
1988. Cazadores-Recolectores del Istmo de Brunswick. *Anales del Instituto de la Patagonia* 18: 113-131.

Prosser Goodall, R.N.
1978. Report on the Small Cetaceans Stranded on the Coasts of Tierra del Fuego. *Scientific Reports of the Whales Research Institute* 30: 197-230.

1979. *Tierra del Fuego.* Ediciones Shanamaüm, Ushuaia.

Prost, C.
1972. Seconde note relative à l'orientation des objets en os. *C.R.S.M. Bulletin Sociéte Préhistorique Française* 4: 99.

Purísima Concepción
n.d.a. *Diario del Navegación y acaecimientos del navío nombrado la Purísima Concepción (alias Los Pasages) en*

su viaje desde el Puerto de Cádiz a los Mares del Sur, que dió principio el 12 de Enero de 1764. Fotocopia del original en archivos del Museo Territorial, Ushuaia.

n.d.b. *Noticia Abreviada de la Costa de los Tres Hermanos de la Tierra del Fuego y de los indios que habitan*. Fotocopia del original en Archivos del Museo Territorial, Ushuaia.

Quiroz Larrea, D.
1988. La punta de arpón Knockaert. Un estudio descriptivo y comparativo. *Museos* 3 (Dirección de Bibliotecas, archivos y Museos, Chile): 1-3.

Rabassa, J.; C. Heusser and R. Stuckenrath
1986. New data on Holocene sea transgression in the Beagle Channel: Tierra del Fuego, Argentina. *Quaternary of South America and Antarctic Peninsula* 4: 291- 311.

Rabassa, J.; C. Heusser and N. Rutter
1990. Late-Glacial and Holocene of Argentine, Tierra del Fuego. *Quaternary of South America and Antarctic Peninsula* 8: 327-351.

Ramseyer, D.
1988. Les harpons néolithiques d'Europe occidentale. *Bulletin Sociéte Préhistorique Française* 85 (4): 122-130.

Ratto, N.
1988. Proyectiles en acción. *Precirculados de los Simposisos del IX Congreso Nacional de Arqueología Argentina,* ICA, Fac. de Filosofía y Letras, UBA, pp. 6-19.

1991a. Elección de rocas y diseño de artefactos: propiedades físico-mecánicas de las materias primas líticas del sitio Inca Cueva 4 (Jujuy-Argentina). *Actas del XI Congreso Nacional de Arqueología Chilena*, pp.127-136. Santiago de Chile.

1991b. Análisis funcional de las puntas de proyectil líticas de sitios del sudeste de la Isla Grande de Tierra del Fuego. *Arqueología* 1: 151-178.

1993. What and how did they hunt?: Methodological essay to approach the question of prehistoric hunting techniques. In *Explotación de Recursos Faunísticos en Sistemas Adaptativos Americanos*, J.L.Lanata (ed.) *Arqueología contemporánea* 4: 135-148.

1994. Funcionalidad vs. Adscripción cultural: Cabezales líticos de la Margen Norte del Estrecho de Magallanes. *Arqueología Contemporánea*. 5: 105-120.

Ms. Estudio arqueológico de la eficacia funcional de puntas de proyectil líticas. First Annual Report 1989, U.B.A.

Reixach, J.
1986. Las huellas antrópicas. Metodología, diferenciación y problemática. *Revista de Arqueología* 60: 6-14.

Rigaud, A.
1984. Utilisation du ciseau dans le débitage du bois de renne à la Garenne-Saint-Marcel (Indre). *Gallia Préhistoire* 27: 245-253.

Rincón, A. and E. Aguirre
1974. Analyse comparative et discriminante des assemblages de fragments osseux pour verification d'hypothese d'action culturelle. *Premier Colloque Internationaux sur l'industrie de l'os dans la Prehistoire*, pp.111-117. Editions Universitaires, Provence.

Rindos, D.
1989. Diversity, Variation and Selection. In *Quantifying Diversity in Archaeology*, R. Leonard and G. Jones (eds.), pp. 13-24. University of Cambridge Press, Cambridge.

Rodanés Vicente, J.
1987. La industria ósea prehistórica en el Valle del Ebro. Neolítico – Edad del Bronce. *Colección de Arqueología y Paleontología* 4. Serie arqueología aragonesa, monografías. Diputación General de Aragón.

Rueda i Torres, J.
1983. *Estudi tecnológic de la industria óssia prehistórica a les comarques gironines (Reclau Viver de Serinyà, Bora gran d'en carreres a Serinyà, Encantades de Martis a Esponella),* Tesis de Licenciatura, Univ. Autónoma de Barcelona.

1985. El treball de les matèries dures animals al Paleolitic Superior del Reclau Viver. *Cypsela* V: 7-20.

Ruiz Nieto, E.; Martinez Padilla,C. and F. Torralba Reina
1983. Ensayo Metodológico para el estudio del Materiales Oseos. *Antropología y Paleoecología humana* 3: 129-144.

Runnings, A.; C. Gustafson and D. Bentley
1989. Use-Wear on Bone Tools: A Technique for Study under the Scanning Electron Microscope. In *Bone Modification*, R. Bonnichsen & M. Sorg (ed.) pp. 317-334. Peopling of the Americas Publications, Center for the Study of the First Americans, Institute for Quaternary Studies, University of Maine.

Russen, N.
1983. The Treatment of Bone as a Raw Material: Insights from Yugoeslavia and Pakistán. *L'industrie de l'os néolithique et de l'Age des metaux. Troisieme Réunion du Groupe de Travail N° 3*, pp. 25-32. CNRS, Paris.

Saddek-Koros, H.
1972. Primitive Bone Fracturing: a Method of Research. *American Antiquity* 37 (3): 369-382.

Sánchez Albornoz, N.
1958. Una penetración neolítica en Tierra del Fuego. *Cuadernos del Sur*, Univ. del Sur.

Savanti, F.
1994. *Las aves en la dieta de los cazadores-recolectores terrestres de la costa fueguina.* Temas de arqueología, CONICET-PREP, Buenos Aires.

Scheinsohn, V.

MSa. *Estudio de criterios descriptivos y clasificatorios para el instrumental óseo aplicados a materiales de Tierra del Fuego.* First Report CONICET.1989

MSb. *Estudio de criterios descriptivos y clasificatorios para el instrumental óseo aplicados a materiales de Tierra del Fuego.* Final report, CONICET.1990.

1990-1992. El sistema de producción de los instrumentos óseos y el momento del contacto: un puente sobre aguas turbulentas. *Relaciones de la Sociedad Argentina de Antropología* XVIII: 121-138.

1993. Use of bone as raw material in Isla Grande (Tierra del Fuego, Argentina). Colloque Internationale *Industries sur matières dures animales. Evolution technologique et culturelle durant les temps préhistoriques*, Centre D'Etudes et Documentation Archeologiques (CEDARC), Treignes, Bélgica.

1994. Los instrumentos óseos de la colección Junius Bird. Paper delivered to *XI Congreso Nacional de Arqueología Argentina*, San Rafael.

1994-1995. Hacia un modelo evolutivo del aprovechamiento de las materias primas oseas en la Isla Grande de Tierra del Fuego (Argentina). *Relaciones de la Sociedad Argentina de Antropología* XIX: 307-324.

1997. Use-Wear Patterns on Bark Removers. *Proceedings of the 1993 Bone Modification Conference, Hot Springs, South Dakota.* L. Adrien Hannus and R. Peter Winham (ed.). pp. 265-276. Occassional Publications N° 1, Archaeology Laboratory, Augustana College.

Scheinsohn, V; J. L. Ferretti; M. Macchi and J.R. Zanchetta

1991. Variación del espesor diafisario en función de la calidad del material oseo en varias especies de vertebrados. Paper delivered at *II Congreso de la Sociedad Internacional de Biomecánica Osea y Metabolismo Mineral.*

Scheinsohn, V. and E. Massi

1996. Análisis funcional de instrumentos óseos: un caso de estudio. *Arqueología. Solo Patagonia.* J. Gómez Otero (ed.) pp. 213-222, Centro Nacional Patagónico (CENPAT)-CONICET, Puerto Madryn.

Scheinsohn, V.G.; A. Di Baja; M. Lanza and L. Tramaglino

1992. El aprovechamiento de la avifauna como fuente de materia prima ósea en la Isla Grande de Tierra del Fuego: Lancha Packewaia, Shamakush I y Túnel I. *Arqueología* 2: 135-148.

Scheinsohn, V. and Ferretti, J. L.

1994a. Biomecánica ósea e instrumentos arqueológicos: métodos, técnicas y posibilidades interpretativas. Paper delivered at Simposyum Metodología y Ciencia en Arqueología, *XI Congreso Nacional de Arqueología Argentina*, San Rafael.

1994b. Relación entre el diseño y la funcionalidad de los instrumentos óseos prehistóricos de Tierra del Fuego y las propiedades mecánicas de las materias primas utilizadas para su confección. IX Reunión Anual de la *Asociación Argentina de Osteología y Metabolismo Mineral.*

1995. Mechanical Properties of Bone Materials as Related to Design and Function of Prehistoric Tools from Tierra del Fuego (Argentina). *Journal of Archeological Science* 22: 711-717.

Schiffer, M.

1972. Archaeological Context and Systemic Context. *American Antiquity* 37: 156-165.

Schobinger, J.

1973. *Prehistoria de Suramérica.* Nueva Colección Labor. Madrid.

Schuerholz, G.

s.f. *Informe de consultoría sobre vida silvestre en el Territorio Nacional de Tierra del Fuego.* O.E.A.

Semenov, S.

1981. *Tecnología prehistórica.* Akal Universidad, Madrid.

Shipman, P.

1981. Applications of Scanning Electron Microscopy to Taphonomic Problems. *Annals of the New York Academy of Sciences* 376: 357-386.

1989. Altered Bones from Olduvai Gorge, Tanzania: Techniques, Problems and Implications of their Recognition. *Bone Modification*, R. Bonnichsen & M. Sorg (ed.) pp. 317-334. Peopling of the Americas Publications, Center for the Study of the First Americans, Institute for Quaternary Studies, University of Maine.

Shipman, P. and J. Rose

1984. Cutmark mimics on modern and fossil bovid bones. *Current Anthopology* 25(1): 116-117.

Shipman, P.; D. Fisher and J. Rose

1984. Mastodon Butchery: Microscopic Evidence of Carcass Processing and Bone Tool Use. *Paleobiology* 10 (3): 358-365.

Sidera, I.

1989. Un complément des données sur les sociétés rubanées: l'industrie osseuse à Cuiry-lès-Chaudardés. *BAR International Series* 520.

Skottsberg, C.

1913. Observations on the natives of the Patagonian channel region. *American Anthropologist* XV (4): 578-616.

Sonneville-Bordes, D.

1960. *Le Paleolitique Superieur en Perigord*, Delmas, Paris.

Spegazzini, C.

1882. Costumbres de los habitantes de la Tierra del Fuego.

Anales de la Sociedad Científica Argentina XIV:159-181.

Speth, J.
1972. Mechanical Basis of Percussion Flaking. *American Antiquity* 37 (1): 34-60.

Standford, D; R. Bonnichsen and R. Morlan
1981. The Ginsberg Experiment: Modern and Prehistoric Evidence of a Bone-Flaking Technology. *Science* 212: 418-420.

Stern, C.
1990. Tephrochronology of Southernmost Patagonia. *National Geographic Research* 6:110-126.

Steward, J.
1955. *Theory of culture change. The methodology of multilinear evolution.* University of Illinois Press.

Stirling, W.H.
1868. Letter January 11. Published by. *South American Missionary Magazine,* Londres.

Stordeur, D.
1974. Note sur la proportion des objets d'os taillés sur bloc et des objets taillés sur fragments à Tell Mureybet (Syrie). *Premier Colloque Internationaux sur l'industrie de l'os dans la Prehistoire*, pp. 101-104. Editions Universitaires, Provence.

1977a. La fabrication des aiguilles à chas. Observation et expérimentation. *Deuxième Colloque International sur l'Industrie de l'os dans la Préhistoire, Méthodologie appliquée a L'industrie de l'os préhistorique*, pp. 251-256. CNRS, Paris.

1977b. Classification multiple ou grilles mobiles de classification des objets en os. *Deuxième Colloque International sur l'Industrie de l'os dans la Préhistoire, Méthodologie appliquée a L'industrie de l'os préhistorique*, pp. 235-238. CNRS, Paris.

1978a. Proposition de classement des objets en os selon le degré de transformation imposé à la matière première. *Bulletin Sociéte Préhistorique Française* 75: 20-23.

1978b. L'outillage osseux. *Les outillages lithiques et osseux de Murybet, Syrie*, M.-C. Cauvin and D. Stordeur (ed.) *Cahiers de l'Euphrate* 1: 81-96.

1979. Quelques remarques préliminaires sur l'industrie de l'os du Proche-Orient du Xème au VIème millenaire. *L'industrie de l'os néolithique et de l'Age des metaux. 1er Réunion du Groupe de Travail sur l'industrie de l'os préhistorique*, pp. 37-46. CNRS, Paris.

1980a. Fabriquer des aiguilles à chas comme il y a 10.000 ans. *Les Doissiers de de l'archaeologie* 46: 12-14.

1980b. Typologie et techniques de fabrication des harpons paléoesquimaux de la region d'Igloulik (Cánada). *Bulletin de la Société Préhistorique Française* 77 (8): 239-244.

1980c. *Objets en os historiques et actuels.* Travaux de la Maison de L'Orient N°1. Presses Universitaires de Lyon, Lyon.

1981. La contribution de l'industrie de l'os à la délimitation des aires culturelles: l'exemple du Natufien. *Colloques Internationales du CNRS. Préhistoire du Levant*: pp. 433-437.

1982. L'industrie osseuse de la Damascene du VIIe au VIe millenaire. *L'industrie de l'os néolithique et de l'Age des metaux. Deuxieme Réunion du Groupe de Travail N° 3.* pp. 9-25 CNRS, Paris.

1983. Quelques remarques pour attirer l'attention sur l'interêt d'une recherche commune entre tracéologues du silex et technologues de l'os. *Traces d'utilization sur les outils néolithiques du Proche Orient*, Maison de l'Orient, 1983: 231-240.

1984. L'industrie osseuse de Khirokitia. In *Fouilles récéntes à Khirokitia (Chypre) 1977-1981.* pp. 129-162. Editions Recherche sur les civilisations, Paris.

1985a. Classification multiple des outillages osseux de Khirokitia, Chypre, VIe millenaire. *L'industrie de l'os néolithique et de l'Age des Métaux.*, H. Camps-Fabrer (ed.), pp. 11-24. CNRS, Paris.

1985b. Préhistoire. Industrie de l'os. *Encyclopaedia Universalis* - Supplément: 49-54.

1987. Manches et emmanchements préhistoriques: quelques propositions préliminaires. *La main et l'outil: manches et emmanchements préhistoriques, Travaux de la Maison de l'Orient* 15: 11-34.

1988. L'industrie osseuse de Cafer dans son contexte anatolien et Proche Oriental. Note préliminaire. *Anatolica* XV: 203-213.

Ms. *CODIOPO. Code pour le traitment Informatique d'Outils en os du Proche Orient Préhistorique.*

S.F. *Proposition de classement des objects en os peu elaborés-problemes de terminologie,* MS.

Stordeur-Yedid, D.
1974. Objets dentés en os de Mureybet, (Djézireh, Syrie) des phases IB à III: 8400 à 7600 B.C. *Paléorient* 2(2): 437-442.

1976. Les poinçons d'os à poulie articulaire: observations techniques d'après quelques exemples syriens. *Bulletin de la Société Préhistorique Française* 73 (2): 39-42.

1986. *Harpons paleo-esquimaux de la region d'Iglulik.* Cahier 2, Editions Recherche sur les Civilizations, Paris.

Stordeur, D. and P. Anderson-Gerfaud
1985. Les omoplates encochées néolithiques de Ganj Dareh (Iran). Etude morphologique et fonctionelle. *Cahiers de l'Euphrate* 4: 289-313.

Straus, L.G.
1987. Paradigm Lost: A Personal View of the Current State of Upper Paleolithic Research. *Helinium* 27: 157-171.

Sutcliffe, A.
1973. Similarity of Bones and Antlers Gnawed by Deer to Human Artefacts. *Nature* 246: 428-430.

Thompson, M.
1954. Azilian Harpoons. *Proceedings of Prehistoric Society* 20: 193-211.

Tinto, J.L.
1978. *Aporte del sector forestal a la construcción de viviendas*. Folleto N° 44 IFONA.

1997. *Tecnología de maderas*. Ed. Agro-Veterinaria, Buenos Aires.

Toranzos, F.
1971 *Teoría estadistica y aplicaciones*. Ed. Kapelusz, Buenos Aires.

Tortorelli, L.
1946. *Maderas y bosques argentinos*. Ediciones Acme, Buenos Aires.

Toth, N. and Woods, M.
1989. Molluscan Shell Knives and Experimental Cut-Marks on Bones. *Journal of Field Archaeology* 16: 250-255.

Tromnau, G.
1983. Ein Mammutknochen-Faustkeil aus Rhede, Kreis Borken (Westfalen). *Archäologisches Korrespondenzblatt* 13: 287-289.

Vidal, H.
1987. Primeros lineamientos para una arqueología etnográfica de Península Mitre. *Primeras Jornadas de Arqueología de la Patagonia*. Gobierno de la Provincia de Chubut: 303-310.

1985a. *Los conchales de Bahía Valentín*. Tesis de Licenciatura, Univ. Nac. de Buenos Aires.

1985b. Bahía Valentín: el primer contacto. Paper delivered at *VIII Congreso Nacional de Arqueología Argentina,* 1985.

Vignati, M.
1927. Arqueología y Antropología de los conchales fueguinos. *Revista del Museo de La Plata* 30 (4): 79-143.

1930. Instrumental óseo aborigen procedente de Cabo Blanco (Gob. de Santa Cruz), *Notas del Museo Etnográfico* 2, Facultad de Filosofía y Letras, Universidad de Buenos Aires.

Vincent, A.
Msa. Préliminaires à la mise en evidence d'une utilisation fonctionelle de l'os au Paléolithique Inferieur et Moyen. *Mémoire de Maîtrise*, Univ. de Paris X, Nanterre.

Msb. Vers une demonstration de utilisation fonctionelle de l'os au Paléolithique Inferieur et Moyen. *Plan de Thèse D.E.A.*, 1985.

1985. Preliminaires experimentaux du faconnage de l'os par percussion directe. *Artefacts* 1: 23-32.

1986. Outillage osseux du Paléolihique Moyen à Bois-Roche (Cherves-Richemont, Charente). Etude préliminaire. *IIIe Congrès National des Sociétés Savantes, Pré et Protohistoire*: 27-36.

1988. L'os comme artefact au Páleolithique Moyen: principes d'etude et prémiers resultats. *L'Homme de Néanderthal* 4: 185-196.

1989. Remarques préliminaires concernant l'outillage osseux de la Grotte Vaufrey. In *La Grotte de Vaufrey (Dordogne)*: pp. 529-533. Mémoires de la Société Prehistorique Française, Paris.

Voruz, J.L.
1983-1984. Typologie de l'industrie en matiéres dures animales: Essai d'extension de la typologie analytique. Premiere étape: le langage descriptif. *Dialektike* 1: 32-54.

1984. *Outillage osseux et dynamisme industriel dans le Neolithique Jurassien,* Ph D Manuscript, Université de Toulouse, Toulouse.

Walker, P. and J. Long
1977. An Experimental Study of the Morphological Characteristics of Tool Marks. *American Antiquity* 42: 605-616.

Webster's Encyclopedic Unabridged Dictionary of the English Language
1989. Gramercy Books, New York.

Weniger, G.
1987. Der Kantabrische Harpunentyp. Überlegungen zur morphologie und klassifikation einer Magdalénienzeitlichen widerhakenspitze. *Madrider Mitteilungen* 28: 1-43.

Willey, G. and J. Sabloff
1980. *A History of American Archaeology*. W.Freeman and Company. Segunda Edición, New York.

Yacobaccio, H. and Guraieb, A.
1994. Tendencia temporal de contextos arqueológicos: Area del río Pinturas y zonas vecinas. In *Contribuciones a la Arqueología del Rio Pinturas, Provincia de Santa Cruz*. C. Gradin and A. Aguerre (eds.), Ed. Búsqueda de Ayllu, Buenos Aires.

Yellen, J.; A. Brooks; E. Cornelissen; M. Mehlman and K. Stewart
1995. A Middle Stone Age Worked Bone Industry from Katanda, Upper Semliki Valley, Zaire. *Science* 268: 553-556.

Yesner, D. and R. Bonnichsen
1979. Caribou Metapodial Shaft Splinter Technology. *Journal of Archaeological Science* 6: 303-308.

www.ingramcontent.com/pod-product-compliance
Lightning Source LLC
Chambersburg PA
CBHW061007030426
42334CB00033B/3398
9781407305707